Degrowth in the Suburbs

Samuel Alexander · Brendan Gleeson

Degrowth in the Suburbs

A Radical Urban Imaginary

Samuel Alexander
Melbourne Sustainable Society Institute
University of Melbourne
Parkville, VIC, Australia

Brendan Gleeson
Melbourne Sustainable Society Institute
University of Melbourne
Parkville, VIC, Australia

ISBN 978-981-13-4736-8   ISBN 978-981-13-2131-3   (eBook)
https://doi.org/10.1007/978-981-13-2131-3

This Palgrave Macmillan imprint is published by the registered company Springer Nature Singapore Pte Ltd.
The registered company address is: 152 Beach Road, #21-01/04 Gateway East, Singapore 189721, Singapore

Foreword

Historians charting the trajectory of industrial civilisation will note the remarkable disconnection between the status accorded to 'evidence-based decision-making' in our culture and the relentless pursuit of perpetual growth on a finite planet. While the contradiction has always been clear to the simplest of folks, the publication of the *Limits to Growth* report nearly half a century ago gave us the means to better understand the complex system dynamics that would characterise humanity's overshoot of global limits.

Because these understandings coincided with the oil crises and resultant recessions, in affluent Western countries there was some public discourse, and even early action, to consider the possibility of futures other than ones of continuous growth. On the fringes of society a flourishing counterculture gave birth to lifestyles and concepts (including permaculture) that have been the source of a continuous lineage of creative change. Some of these fringe ideas—such as the internet—have contributed to powerful creative action that has transformed society, whilst others—such as renewable energy and regenerative agriculture—provide pathways promising to manifest transformation now.

But the full potential of these and other creative bottom-up responses to the *Limits to Growth* were stymied for decades by the neoliberal top-down revolution initiated by Thatcher (UK in 1979) and Reagan (USA in 1981) and emulated in Australia by the Hawke/Keating governments from 1983. While many of the aspects of Keynesian economics and politics that were swept away were hopelessly maladapted to the emerging world of limits, the neoliberal solutions only intensified society's disconnect from non-negotiable realities. While the neoliberal agenda may have capitalised on creativity, the growth it orchestrated was mostly driven by new forms of corporate colonialism, widening wealth disparity in long-affluent countries and doubling down on resource depletion and environmental impact.

The late 1980s scientific consensus on climate change, and endless talk and grand plans since, have done little or nothing to slow the trajectory of industrial civilisation into overshoot beyond planetary limits. But the Global Financial Crisis was a turning point when the limits of resources, signified by the global peak of conventional oil production, converged with the limits to the neoliberal revolution's capacity to sustain supercharged global capitalism. Endlessly expanding global debt was exposed as the secret weapon of the neoliberal revolution that since the GFC has massively inflated assets of all kinds, including land that has underpinned the housing crisis. The global economy is a Ponzi scheme of fake wealth that will inevitably follow the trajectory of previous bubbles in the history of capitalism—but this time, the tightening grip of resource depletion and other limits will make this boom cycle the final one for global capitalism. The potential diversity of energy descent futures is manifold but has been little investigated until recent years. When I began to do so in the early 2000s, I found *Mad Max*, a 1970s road rage movie, was the primary intellectual reference point for consideration of energy descent futures!

While heroic efforts to steer the ship of state and capitalism in new directions have consumed the energy of generations of idealists, activists and entrepreneurs, others have chosen to put their energy into living in ways that model the world we need beyond growth. Affluence and the hubris of the dominant ideology has allowed those with the capacity to create their own 'new normal' in the shadows of, and from the surplus wasted wealth created by, the mainstream economy. Inevitably, a lot of that action has been at the geographic fringes in rural localities but in recent years an increasing number of people are pursuing DIY enlightened self-interest in suburbia, where the majority of Australians live.

Over the years since *Limits to Growth*, suburbia has been seen by cultural critics, planners and environmentalist as the epitome of all that is wrong with society. Perhaps this was best encapsulated by American catastrophist James Howard Kunstler when he said: 'America took all its post war wealth and invested it in a way of life that has no future.'

While I agree with Kunstler in principle, I also believe suburbia represents a potential sweet point between the connection with nature and capacity for household self-reliance we associate with the rural, and the density and diversity of social and economic connection that cities make possible. The fact that the current infrastructure, houses and landscapes of suburbia are hopelessly maladapted to the coming world of energy descent is not a cause for inaction or depression. Low-density detached housing with gardens is the ideal place for beginning a bottom-up revolution to recreate the household and community non-monetary economies that our recent forebears took for granted as the basis for an adequate, even comfortable, life.

Athough, as this book makes clear, there are limits to the degree to which this household level can replace all the important functions of a sustainable and just society, the chances for success look a lot better than through further heroic efforts to reform global capitalism from the top down.

In any case, those pioneering a downshift to radically reduce their ecological footprint, regardless of whether society follows suit, are finding they can live a better life now while building resilience to challenging futures. A combination of permaculture-designed productivity and voluntary simplicity is rebuilding the culture and skill base for the transitions demanded by energy descent futures. In the process, these pioneers are finding surprising synergies with migrants, working class battlers and other fringe folks who may not be are not motivated by environmental ethics or even necessarily believers in climate change.

Mutual respect and learning across the widening identity politics divide is one of the by-products of this broadly based household- and community-led movement. This enlightened self-interest has the potential to grow by viral replication. The most fertile ground for its rapid growth is suburbia, especially the open sunlit suburbs of Australia, which is still the lucky country with surplus capacity to sustain such a bottom-up revolution. While the dysfunction and denial in the political, corporate and media elites rivals anywhere else in the world, Australia has many of the seeds and settings for global leadership.

While I have always acknowledged and articulated the non-negotiability of the limits to growth and the need for consciously designed 'degrowth' or 'powerdown', the populist in me has always called for citizens to vote with their feet and increase the 'participation rate' in the non-monetary household and community economies that will sustain us through the necessary transition as we move deeper into crisis. In the process, we have found that we can live well with a small fraction of the resources that are claimed to be normal and necessary for a comfortable life. In projecting this populist message and supporting the pioneers, it is good to have scholars of suburbia and degrowth providing the conceptual framework for why degrowth in suburbia is becoming a self-organising reality.

Brendan Gleeson is one of the minority of Australian scholars and commentators on urban affairs who has defended suburbia and suburbanites. His previous writing has acknowledged the non-negotiable climate, resource and other constraints threatening to deepen the crisis in suburbia created by neoliberal policies over recent decades.

Likewise, Samuel Alexander is one of the very few Australian scholars to explore the potential for degrowth, considering the historical and contemporary expressions of voluntary simplicity as a cultural response to the limits to growth crisis. In many ways, he inherits the mantle of Ted Trainer who for four decades has been an almost lone voice in Australian academia documenting the need for a radical response to the limits to growth.

Degrowth in the Suburbs brings together these important perspectives to challenge the most powerful and persistent cultural, economic and political orthodoxies in Australia and other affluent countries.

Hepburn Springs, Australia   David Holmgren Melliodora
June 2018

Acknowledgements

This book benefited greatly from the close reading and detailed feedback shared by Josh Floyd. His technical understanding of the issues was our primary reason for seeking his critical feedback. His clarity of thought and skill as a writer were added bonuses.

Josh, thank you for your dedicated assistance, including your help creating the graph in Chapter Two. We are much indebted to you and gratefully acknowledge your input and influence.

David Holmgren's influence will also be seen throughout the following pages. Sometimes that influence is explicit; sometimes it is simmering quietly between the sentences. In fact, we wrote this book in part with the intention of it being seen as a 'companion volume' to David's masterful new practical manual, *Retrosuburbia: The Downshifter's Guide to a Resilient Future* (2018: Melliodora Publishing). We trust that readers will find in the following pages much evidential, theoretical, and political support for a similar vision of suburbia, approached from different but complementary angles. We highly recommend David's new book as a deep and inspiring instruction manual for how to create a thriving and resilient suburbia as the energy descent future takes hold.

David, we are grateful for your astute feedback on the penultimate draft of this book. Your comments helped refine various key issues, and we're honoured to have your words open our book.

We would also like to thank Sangeetha Chandra-Shekeran for many very helpful comments on the first three chapters, and two anonymous reviewers who shared excellent feedback on our book proposal.

Finally, we would like to thank Dennis Horton for some last minute editorial advice and assistance.

Contents

1

Reimagining the Suburbs Beyond Growth

Prelude: The Great Resettlement

This book opens, as it must, by acknowledging that the human species stands at the precipice of self-made destruction. At the very hour when modern humanity arrived at the pinnacle of triumph—a global market economy promising riches for all—the skies have been darkened by the terrible spectres of ecological and social threat. Global warming is only one of these storm clouds, but this alone has the potential to lay waste to our species, as well as most others. At the same time, vast oceans of debilitating poverty surround small islands of unfathomable plenty, exposing the violent betrayal of the growth agenda, euphemistically (or just deceptively) known in public discourse as 'sustainable development'. This is a race leading towards an abyss, both enabled and entrenched by a sterility of imagination.

The late German scholar Ulrich Beck spoke of how triumph and crisis simultaneously emerge and remerge in a world pervasively and continuously remade by capitalist modernisation. Beck cast us in an age of unprecedented global risk marked by a threat that seems integral to capitalism itself: the relentless drive to expand productive capacity

© The Author(s) 2019
S. Alexander and B. Gleeson, *Degrowth in the Suburbs*,
https://doi.org/10.1007/978-981-13-2131-3_1

without limit on a finite biosphere, inevitably producing a global society wracked by the agonies of '...self-dissolution, self-endangerment and self-transformation' (Beck 2009: 163). The dual meaning of 'dissolution' presents itself here as a particularly apt signifier for our age, denoting both the ending of something, and on bankrupt terms. As the global economy trembles under the burden of its own excesses, we see the self-declared triumphs of capitalism coming home to roost in the darkening ecology of the Anthropocene.

The modern conversation has fixed progressively on this great contradiction of human development. Narratives collide. Triumph is reread as calamity, and progress retold as regress. There were foretellings. Karl Marx and Friedrich Engels (1985 [1848]: 85–86) scorned the boasts of the industrial bourgeois who 'like the sorcerer… is no longer able to control the powers of the nether world whom he has called up by his spells'. Optimists still abound, including those heralding the dawn of a new urban age. They enthuse for an epochal opening towards the 'green growth' or 'smart growth' of cities and their underlying economies, while others, like philosopher Slavoj Žižek (2012), in his book *Living in the End Times*, hear the siren cry of closure in the mounting testimonies of human and natural default. The spectre of Apocalypse is hardly new, but its horsemen, as Žižek points out, have never been more terrifyingly present.

We write at a moment of terrible change for humanity and all that we impact. As one good book intones, we must reap as we have sown. Herein however, lies hope. If, as Beck insisted, our peril is self-made then we have the power to change it, or at least redirect its course to less terrible ends and hopefully onwards, after the inevitable great acquittal of capitalist modernity, towards a new beginning. We see that new beginning as involving a great resettlement of the human species, based on a new post-capitalist dispensation. To put our idea in its simplest form, this resettlement begins in a profoundly important human heartland: the suburbs of our carbon civilisation.

This book explores what that great resettlement might look like and how it might transpire, offering a radical urban imaginary that seeks to fracture the linear conception of capitalist urban development and expand the contours of future suburban possibility. But as post-development theorist Gustavo Esteva (2010: 3) notes: 'In order for someone to conceive the possibility of escaping from a particular condition, it is necessary first to feel that one has fallen into that condition'. Before looking to the future, then, this substantive introductory chapter begins by establishing an historical sense of how and why the suburban form has arisen as it has. We then sketch the main lines of argument and analysis that will be unpacked throughout this book.

The Suburban Age

This is the urban age, the era in which most of the human species—*homo urbanis*—lives in cities. Or to specify, the epoch of the great suburban dispensation. Cities emerged through our long species history as a great socio-technical accomplishment that liberated us from the grubbing and servitude of early agrarian life. Suburbs appeared much later, initially in Western nations, taking the achievement to a new form of agreeable, spacious living dispensed to an ever-growing share of the populace.

This was both a triumph of, and a solution to, the industrialism that swept outwards from Western Europe in the late eighteenth century, initially through its new colonies, especially in North America and Australasia, and later via globalisation to the world. Indeed, the lure of suburbia was taken up with greatest fervour in the Anglophone 'new worlds' where land was plentiful, spirits were high and technological take up was swift. Of course, this land was taken, usually violently, from indigenous peoples—urbanisation went hand in hand with dispossession. The historian, Graeme Davison (1995) describes Australia—from where we write this book—as 'the world's first suburban nation'. Urbanisation was the great wave that carried capitalism through the twentieth century to the shores of global preponderance, freighted with the models and machinery for mass consumption and the lifestyles that enacted it. Its principal model-machine was the suburb.

Suburbanisation was at first the escape route of Victorian middle classes from hellfire industrialism. It was opened out through the twentieth century, offering a giant blotter that absorbed working class aspiration. Eventually it was the principal physical means for sating a broadening desire for material improvement. Most other dimensions of human realisation—certainly cultural and aesthetic expression—were subordinated in a century of escape from the ravages of the industrial city. Other human possibilities were reserved to the 'exclusive garden' of formal culture that was cultivated by elites.

The suburban epoch was marked by the rise of its anaemic social expression, mass culture: a great dispensing of material and aesthetic improvement to the many. The end to which all means were deployed was the 'suburban lifestyle', centred around a patriarchal nuclear family. In the process, many lives and identities were circumscribed, not to say brutalised, through rigid role assignment. And yet, imperfect as we may now see it, liberation it was. Species response tells us much. In Europe and its new worlds, fecundity had been withheld, much by women, in the harsh and insecure years of Depression (from 1929) and War (1939–45). With the ending of such extreme deprivation, rationing and violence, it was restored. This unleashed a demographic wave that lifted the work of economic accumulation, and, for a time, a form of social prosperity.

The great suburban exodus was for a time, at least in the West, a species movement, a journey of liberation joined by a proletariat that eagerly grasped the immediate fruits of industrial modernity. Suburbia was its vast material expression—an industrially produced landscape that offered the fundaments of a good life to the masses. Contemporary anti-suburban commentary lacks this historical appreciation. It neglects the profound liberation that suburbanisation realised for a proletariat for whom the 'urban village' usually meant a crowded tenement without amenities or privacy.

Suburbanisation was, like all capitalist development, an act of creative destruction—both vastly consumptive, especially of nature, but also productive, of new nature (people, human ingenuity and capacity, lived experience). We too often neglect the latter which speaks to the latent capacity in the suburban landscape to keep creating and producing new forms of species improvement. We must ponder the potential of this dormant capacity and consider what the suburbs might yet become.

With more recent globalisation, the suburban model was broadcast to a willing developing world; offered first, as in the Western experience, to their elites. In the face of critique, suburbia remains what British scholars Mike Hodson and Simon Marvin (2010: 42) term an 'obdurate urbanism': still the heartland and hearth of the Global North, and still desired by many outside it. The work of suburbanisation continues apace, now accommodating the desires of aspirant middle classes in the developing world. China and India are doing what the new worlds did in the 1950s and 1960s by suburbanising, but at much vaster scales and in shorter time frames.

In the fractious 'developing city' however the suburban shift largely takes the form of 'imprisoned freedom', gated villa estates for the elite and isolated tower dormitories for the 'lower orders'. In the contemporary South, the consumerist urban model is carefully cultivated and protected from the indigent masses that supply its most fundamental resource: low paid service labour.

Thus, suburbanisation in the contemporary South is not the mass exodus to material and social freedom that it was earlier in the North. In the South, the 'suburb' denotes a much more fractured urbanism; the gated, guarded estate and its sprawling caricature, the slum. In this context, laissez-faire neoliberalism is governing the translation of the suburban model to a wider world, on much more wretched terms. Žižek believes that suburbia's most objectionable forms, the slums of the South, are once again restive with revolutionary potential.

It would be equally wrong-headed to regard suburbia as a timeless mechanism for improvement. It was also a model of human growth freighted with the very same self-endangerment that threatens us now, but this was not to become clear until late into the twentieth century. The sociologist, John Urry (2011: 64–65) reflected on the 'high carbon lives' that were born and ordained in its car-dependent fabric. As we have observed, the suburb represented and accomplished the dialectic of modern urbanism, creating *and* destroying human possibility. It was simultaneously a landscape of progress for many, including an improving working class, *and* a central expression of the ecocidal process of overaccumulation. Can we imagine it differently, deployed to ecological security and wellbeing, not risk and depletion? We return to this question of imagination shortly.

In his epitaph for the organic, historical urbanism erased by industrial modernisation, David Harvey (2013: xv–xvi) writes: 'The traditional city has been killed by rampant capitalist development, a victim of the never-ending need to dispose of overaccumulating capital driving towards endless sprawling urban growth no matter what the social, environmental, or political consequences'. The ecological legacy of suburbanisation cannot be discounted. Equally, its immense advancement of the life conditions and prospects of the 'lower orders' of western industrialism must stand testament. This dialectic it seems has some time to play out, as a poorer, equally determined world seeks suburban improvement. The Global South aspires to emulate an ideal that has run its historical, and ecological, course. It is surely an urgent human project to rethink and recast this model-machine to prevent its further disastrous replication. We should embrace this project urgently and with positivity, seeing possibility not doom in our current urban failures. As the critic Terry Eagleton (2018: 79) says: 'The true image of the future is the failure of the present'. Before considering the question of future imaginaries, what are the main failures of the present that we must survive and transcend?

The End of the Carnival

The historical suburban model has run its course because its mother ship, capitalism, has run aground on the reefs of contradiction and overreach. Indeed, the whole vessel seemed to crunch to a sickening and deadly halt during the Global Financial Crisis (2008–9) and to continue to founder in the years afterwards. The crisis halted a long phase of neoliberal growth leveraged through mounting private debt, and a progressive decoupling of the material and financial economies. Its successor is still emerging through wildly unsettled global and national political currents, but increasingly it just seems like a new phase of neoliberalism—austerity governance—not the progressive alternative that radicals hoped would be legitimised by the crisis.

The phase of 'Made in China' affluence that preceded the global default was implacably hostile to ecological values. In a new play of species chauvinism, resources—biotic and material—were cast in vast quantities into the furnace of growth. The entropic power of capitalism was marked as never before by a full-scale assault on resource stocks and biodiversity; meanwhile human riches were depleted by cultural homogenisation and relentless commoditisation. It was, however, not the source of the most threatening environmental crises confronting *homo urbanis*, a climate warmed and destabilised by two centuries of growth, fuelled by fossil energy. The industrial order that emerged in the wake of astonishingly clever technical innovations and through an expansion of the human mind generally had one great flaw. It assumed itself freed from nature via access to a carbon legacy assumed infinitely abundant.

This 'Promethean conceit' saw nature as a force to be tamed and shackled to the wheel of progress. Industrial power showed it could be so—at least for a time. There were opponents of Prometheanism who saw the rising volcano of the market, not the growth in the human family, as the trigger for natural depletion and disorder. Long ago Frederick Engels (1959 [1876]: 12) warned: 'Let us not, however, flatter ourselves overmuch because of our human victories over nature. For each such victory nature takes its revenge on us'. Climate change is a spectacular form of revenge. The old criticism of economic growth which neoliberals declared heresy seems to have the angels on its side.

For a long time, the efficiency view dominated. It still does, and its newest manifestation is the rising faith in green technologies to lessen natural dependency and decouple productive activity from its resource and energy foundations. Its urban referents dream of green urbanism, even a 'post-carbon city', made possible through innovation not re-foundation. Blogs are busy with discussion of a 'city fix'; a new era of urban efficiency that rescales resource use within safe limits. In *The Economist* (2012) we read: 'Instead of trying to limit growth, planners should "make room"'. There is nothing new in this unimaginative injunction. Neoliberal urbanism has been making this demand of planning for the last few decades. But it is a death star for *homo urbanis*.

Industrial capitalism proved to be a great innovator, extracting greater yields from fixed inputs—though the record was uneven and often masked the plunder of new resource fields as declining ones were preserved through better husbandry. The main problem was that the drive for efficiency improvement never seemed to dent the relentless growth in resource consumption. Even today, after decades of extraordinary technological advancement and innovation, the ecological burdens of global capitalism continue to increase (Wiedmann et al. 2015). Decidedly, the god of green growth has forsaken us (Smith 2016).

This is partly explained by the 'Jevons Paradox' which posits that improvements in the efficiency of a resource's use tend to increase not decrease the overall consumption of that resource. William Stanley Jevons (1835–82) in his 1865 book *The Coal Question* documented the simultaneous rising efficiency of coal use in England and the growth in aggregate coal consumption. This twin effect has operated ever thus, and often to the immediate benefit of humanity. It has marked an improvement in the overall welfare of human populations, at least in parts of the West. The material power of expanding markets has been greatly intensified by the harnessing of rising energy efficiency to the expansion of aggregate input. Efficiency is reinvested in more growth and consumption, rarely if ever maintaining outputs with fewer inputs. Put simply, efficiency serves the creation of much more with more. It looks benign if we ignore the threat to our species' survival inherent in this trend over the longer term, not to mention the vast majority of the global population who have not seen many, if any, of the spoils of this rampant development project (see Hickel 2017).

A Crisis of Overproduction

The threat of climate warming, already manifest, is primarily a consequence of overproduction not overconsumption, even if these driving forces are, in many respects, two sides of the same coin. The same can be said of other dimensions of the ecological crisis, notably, resource depletion. Consumption of inputs, of final products, follows in the trail of the unstoppable compulsion to expand economic activity and value.

In capitalism the market is a dynamic, self-replicating force. Market relations are characterised by relentless, convulsive expansion not equilibrium or 'steady state' optimality. The unplanned nature of capitalist competition means that, periodically, the output of individual firms, industries, sectors, cannot be sold. Equilibriums are accidents and ever temporary spaces in the long struggle to force growth ever outwards and upwards. Markets obstinately drive output beyond social need and thus ever towards the precipice of overproduction. Harvey (2008: 24) explains:

> Capitalists have to produce a surplus product in order to produce surplus value; this in turn must be reinvested in order to generate more surplus value. The result of continued reinvestment is the expansion of surplus production at a compound rate... The perpetual need to find profitable terrains for capital-surplus production and absorption... presents the capitalist with a number of barriers to continuous and trouble-free expansion.

This unremittingly drives a twin territorial expansion: new territory for the extraction of resources (human and natural) and for the absorption of waste—or in a word, globalisation. In the converging fields of contemporary climate science and climate debate, the question of 'absorption' comes starkly into focus. The constant expansion in productive capacity places ever mounting pressure on the natural environment to supply more raw materials and absorb greater amounts of waste.

Economic globalisation, given new impetus by neoliberalism, produced new terrains for resource extraction but it did not expand the atmosphere. As if in recognition, it now wishes to bury emissions underground through carbon sequestration. Other riskier forms of geo-engineering witness to the increasingly desperate search for some means of mending the rapine of compound growth. Hardly a consequence of straightforward consumption overreach, climate change is a time of profound ecological reckoning which has arisen from historical overburdening of the atmospheric terrain. It is testimony to an economic system that Žižek (2012: 78) describes as '...a beast that cannot be controlled'. It must, however, be brought to heel before it propels humanity, and all we presume to govern, into the abyss.

Consumptive Cities

Increasingly cities, not social and economic structures, are identified as the source of environmental despoliation and resource depletion. This shift is urged by the chorusing of the urban age. The 'consumptive cities' view has different emphases. Enquiry and advocacy seeks to restrain urban environmental overload through better management, improved technical systems, social cooperation and innovation, sustainable design and low-carbon transport. Comparative review points to metropolitan exemplars of the new sustainable urbanism; governance—progressive, entrepreneurial or both—is deemed crucial. Beacon cities—Curitiba Brazil, Portland USA, Vancouver Canada, Freiburg Germany, etc.—are to light the path to a greener urbanity. Colder judgement casts them as cathedrals in a vast desert of neoliberal urbanisation.

Some assessments find refuge in the past, including the 'New Urbanism' which has issued an impressive coda on the quest for urban sustainability. Harvey (1997) sees such misty-eyed urbanisms as a 'communitarian trap'; an attempt by elites to recover in aestheticised, commoditised forms the social relations lost to modernisation. Broader approaches take an open system view, for example, by measuring the environmental footprint of cities, without acknowledging the underlying shaping influences of accumulation and geopolitics in the global ecological crisis. There is recognition that cities export their resource impacts and wastes (including carbon) through the global political economy. Although varying considerably in premise and approach, most such analyses are joined to a broader enterprise—'sustainable urban development'—that seeks to reconcile ecology, including human nature, to economic growth in some form. Much of this literature and advocacy is reactively hostile to the vast fabric in which its readers reside, suburbia, without considering the latent potential capacity of that landscape to adapt and march to a new economic drumbeat.

These assessments are valuable but insufficient. It is undoubtedly true that modern cities are 'over consumptive', but this does not satisfy critical explanation. The 'consumptive city' reifies what we see—the image of a ravenous, belching urban environment—into something it is not, the structural origin of the natural crisis. It neglects the centrality of urbanisation to the creation of value. As French philosopher Henri Lefebvre (2003 [1970]: 117) insisted, urbanisation is 'not only a devouring activity', it hosts and realises production by 'combining markets' (capital, land, labour) and casting aside barriers to accumulation and profit making. Thus, the origin of the present crisis is not 'the city', or even consumption in the first instance, but the endemic problem of overproduction that has plagued capitalism historically, and generated periodic structural defaults. It has also relentlessly, indeed remorselessly driven urbanisation; a principal motive force in the territorial enlargement of the political economy generally.

The dream of green reform is that economic growth can be decoupled from this twin territorial expansion. The insights of industrial ecology would green production. State and civil society would be transformed by a great 'ecological modernisation' of policy and purpose. For decades these dreams have inspired many renovating projects, including in cities which have been stages for new green urbanisms, such as London's Beddington Zero Energy Development. New regulatory frames and voluntary schemes have mandated and starred urban designs with smaller footprints. The margins of efficiency are tightened in some places but in a context of ever massive urbanisation.

Some resources may be used more efficiently but as we have pointed out this husbandry cloaks a greater abandonment, the ever-escalating consumption and degradation of Earth. Our tormented incapacity to live within the sustainable limits of the planet has been relentlessly staged in a world aware of its deteriorating ecology but thus far unable to stem the decline through any means. The spectacle of species impotence has taken on a voyeuristic quality of 'reality television'. We have agonised about the Amazon for years but watched helplessly the inexorable waning of our last great forest.

The global ecological crisis—of declining resource reserves, of failing waste absorption, of biodiversity destruction—betrays a systemic disinterest in reform, whatever its theoretical possibilities. The Club of Rome's *Limits to Growth* thesis, published in 1972, briefly captured the Western imagination (Meadows et al. 1972). The barriers of caution and conservation were subsequently circumvented by the growth path of globalising supercapitalism. And yet, the report was no siren of imminent doom. It looked presciently ahead to 2070, foretelling a collapse in population and production capacity that looks increasingly plausible as business as usual persists despite all warnings. Extensive resource modelling by Graham Turner (2014) and colleagues at Australia's Commonwealth Scientific and Industrial Research Organisation (CSIRO) suggested that the Club of Rome's forecast about species overshoot was largely accurate.

Will a yet-to-be-realised ecological modernisation of capitalism stem the tide of global bankruptcy? This refers to the ever-proliferating ensemble of actions designed to reduce the 'ecological load' of markets, including the heroic ambition to 'dematerialise' accumulation. The economist Tim Jackson's definitive work, *Prosperity without Growth* (2009), exposes the ruse of ecological modernisation. By many indicators, decades of innovation and effort have not even secured the 'relative' decoupling of resource use from economic growth, let alone the absolute declines in resource demands that are so urgently needed (see also, Wiedmann et al. 2015; Ward et al. 2016; Kallis 2017). It is notable that the rising tide of global carbon emissions was not halted by the recent world recession. Reducing or greening consumption runs counter to fundamental expansionary economic forces and raises equity risks—whose consumption is to be reduced? The threat of injustice from responses premised on consumption restraint has been too little debated in the West. It is, however, an established and persistent theme in the global geopolitics of climate response.

What then of urban policy and intervention? Its powers and role must be redefined through a series of premises that recognise the root problem of overproduction. They follow thus. Built environment change is slow and contested. In a developed city, turnover (additions and alterations) in the built stock is typically much less than five per cent per annum. Even if planning could implement rapid change, it is unlikely that this would reduce energy consumption at the scale or in the time frame needed. The relationship between energy use and urban morphology is complex, multivalent and context dependent. The main greenhouse problem is the energy embodied in (and indirectly consumed through) goods and services. Planning is not a frontline mechanism for mitigation. None of this is to deny the project of urban containment in its broadest sense: it responds to and evokes a broader imperative of the age, to craft a new dispensation that enshrines self-limitation as a premise for all human endeavours. If we are to survive the looming social, ecological and economic disruptions to the status quo, the primary goal is not to rebuild our cities but instead learn how to reinhabit a built environment that already exists.

The Limits to Capital

Are we at the threshold of the apocalyptic 'next world' that scientist James Lovelock (2009) speaks of? Put differently, is the human species now at the precipice of natural default and the massive societal change it must surely trigger? These are not new questions. The end of carbon-intensive capitalism has been long predicted: As Beck (2012: 90) reminded us, already, more than a century ago, Max Weber anticipated the end of oil-based capitalism when he spoke of a time when 'the last hundredweight of fossil fuel is built up'.

The contemporary problem of overshoot has two faces: one of over accumulation and thus depletion of natural capital; the other a simultaneous overabundance of financial capital and critical deprivation of social capital ('planet of slums' etc.). The built environment is now central to these twin crises of the age. Urbanisation is at the heart of overproduction and ecological default, but also central to the absorption of excess capital. The real estate sector has its own dynamics, and investment in housing is vital for capital accumulation, as Harvey has explained, yet all this takes place within a paradigm of growth capitalism that shapes and seems to impel these destructive and often exclusive modes of development. The massive contemporary infrastructure development push in world cities reflects both realities—absorption and depletion. The ricocheting spiral of these modalities defines the urban age. This indicates a convulsive instability at the heart of human prospect that contradicts the predictive confidence of popular urban commentary. As debt fuels what seem to be property bubbles in various urban centres—with the Australian capital cities of Sydney and Melbourne being particularly worrying examples—renegade economist Steve Keen (2017) warns that it would be prudent to prepare for the closing of the casino before these bubbles burst. The convulsion suggests a bad ending.

Such a culminating crisis seems imminent. The strengthening testimony of natural science indicates that 'the infernal self-propelling machine of Capital'—in Žižek's (2012: 35) colourful terms—is finally reaching the limits of improvidence. So, can we speak finally of the limits to capital? Could the vertical sprawl of urban intensification be regarded as capitalism's last violent act? The real and awful consequences of the compact city project are finally, if slowly, dawning upon us (Gleeson 2014). As history shows, capital has an infernal power to appropriate and deploy to its own end (valorisation) what begin as progressive causes that seek to restrain its excesses through sound socio-technical innovations. And so it is with the compact city which sought to contain and make safe the heretofore brute and ecocidal nature of capitalist urbanisation. Alas, progressive intent was innocent of capital's intent, which now mocks the compact city ideal through hypertrophic urbanism (inflation of space driven by financial not human logic). As the injuries of urban intensification mount it becomes apparent yet again that, although indubitably an artefact of modernity, capital is exposed yet again as 'a bad friend of progress'.

Harvey (2010: 78) states that '...capitalism has, in the past, successfully circumvented around natural barriers'—the seeming resolution (at least for now) of the peak oil emergency may be the latest instance of this impressive 'Houdini' reflex. Harvey (ibid.) also acknowledges that 'There may be an imminent crisis in our relation to nature that will require widespread adaptations....'. By adaptations he does not mean the technocratic innovations or lifestyle adjustments inherent in green urbanism but wholesale systemic change.

Is Žižek correct? Will natural scarcities and despoliation soon present an absolute, and thus insurmountable, barrier to accumulation that will trigger a final transformative crisis of capitalism? The Right scoffs and many progressives still wish for reform not transformation. The issues reviewed earlier, however, support Žižek. A massive, disruptive adjustment to the human world is inevitable. The next world is already dawning. Humanity will surely survive to see it. Political economic analysis of the causes of the crisis suggests that capitalism will not. As with preceding modes of production it will collapse under the weight of internal contradictions, and perhaps in the face of yet unknown natural obstacles. Humanity will be freer to consider new productive and social relationships. This may not mark transition to a post-growth world of greater wealth but of diminished and reconceived materiality and, with a mixture of struggle and fortune, expanded qualitative relationships.

To a New Settlement

Decades of green censure have done little or nothing to reset the path of consumption, which has yearned for ever higher, ever-more trivial peaks. We may recall the philosopher Erich Fromm's (2009 [1942]) warning that the destructive contradictions of modernity would ever reveal themselves in this manner. The great unheralded cost of individuation was alienation from Earth, kin and community. This rupture would drive an exodus of souls towards the consolations of consumerism and other compensations for the 'terrible burden' of individualism. This flight from desolation has defined the consumerist age of neoliberalism, but it does not explain exhaustively the origins of the current human predicament. Through technological artifice and material restraint small parts of the species have supressed the consumerist drive. But we do not know how to produce less.

Ultimately, the solution to crisis is crisis: a massive suspension of capitalism as prelude to a new economic and social dispensation. It is the new beginning of which philosopher Hannah Arendt (1998 [1958]) believed we are infinitely capable. The energy foundations of capitalism seem set for disruption in coming years and decades as fossil reserves deplete and climate warming ramps up. We enter a chrysalis era—insecure but with latent potential. Urry (2011: 46–47) worried that 'There are rather limited future worlds because of the twentieth-century legacy of high carbon production and consumption'. But humans make history in mysteriously unpredictable ways even with diminished resources, although always, as Marx insisted, the new worlds are stamped with the birthmarks of the old from whose womb they emerge. David Holmgren's (2009) insightful text *Future Scenarios* may well depict the field of divergent human possibilities that will usher in the new dispensation. He speaks of alternative world trajectories, ranging from autocracy and chaos, to Earth stewardship, that will attend the transition that appears inevitable. Likely there will be elements of all these trajectories as the messy future unfolds, and our challenge is to ensure the balance is weighted as far as possible in terms consistent with human and ecological co-existence and mutual flourishing.

Nothing is ordained, however, and it is the task of politics, or collective action more broadly, to choose the next world. As outlined further below, we see urban social movements as humanity's best hope for driving and managing the transition to a new urban and suburban form—a transition that is perhaps already underway, if only in its early stages. The promise of human natality that Arendt reassured us of can be breached but not erased entirely. She firmly believed that the human capacity for renewal would always carry us out of the worst quagmires. Can the great vessel of human ingenuity carry us to new shores? Considering the rising flood of planetary woe, urbanist Mike Davis (2010) asks, 'Who will build the Ark?'

We must set sail for newer, safer shores and resist the sirens of destruction. The urban age is not a time of species affirmation; it is the hour of our gravest peril. It is also the reopening of human possibility. To liberate human prospect, we must cast down not defend the burning barricades of a dying modernity. Urban revolution is upon us again. Unlike the uprisings of the nineteenth century, which tore up slums and tenements of inner cities, this great insurrection must extend to, and in some places, begin from, the suburbs. Its first crucible, however, is not the street or place of assembly but the fundaments and filaments of human imagination. We must imagine a resettled world; a resettled suburbia.

Charting for Degrowth

Resettlement means transformation, of the suburban fabric yes, but also and more importantly, of the fundamental political economy that shapes human activity, especially urbanisation. Transformation in turn necessitates transition, a journey to somewhere different, to a profoundly new human dispensation. To begin this we need a chart to guide change that steers us towards what is possible and necessary and away from the shoals of false hope, in particular the deceptive lures of a reformed capitalism grounded in a 'sustainable' high-energy social system. This requires a careful and discriminatory plotting of the way forward. After all, if the map is poorly drawn and the compass is broken, one is unlikely to arrive at where one needs to go. To avoid that tragic disorientation, we must first 'think globally' about both justice and sustainability, for only then can one know how best to 'act locally'.

The essential contours of the global predicament can be quite concisely stated. There are now 7.6 billion people on Earth, and recent studies from the United Nations suggest we're heading for around 9.8 billion by mid-century and more than 11 billion by 2100. This global population, even if it stopped growing today, is placing tremendous burdens on planetary ecosystems. By all range of indicators (pollution, climatic, deforestation, top toil erosion, resource depletion, biodiversity loss, etc.) the global economy is now in gross ecological overshoot, year-by-year degrading the biophysical foundations of life in ways that are unsustainable (Steffan et al. 2015). Needless to say, modes of production and consumption in the wealthiest regions of the world are by far the most environmentally impactful, although the emerging economies seem to be following (or being forced onto) the same high-impact, fossil fuel-dependent industrial path taken by the richest nations. Let us not pretend that all the talk about 'sustainable development' in recent decades has produced sustainable development.

Despite the global economy being in this overgrown state of ecological overshoot, we also know that billions of people on the planet are, by any humane standard, under-consuming (Hickel 2017). If these people are to raise their living standards to some dignified level of material sufficiency, as they have every right to do, it is likely that this will place further burdens on already overburdened ecosystems. All this and more is radically calling into question the legitimacy of the high-impact forms of urban and suburban life that have evolved in the most developed regions of the world, supported by and seemingly required by the economics of growth that define capitalism.

And yet, despite the fact that humanity is making unsustainable demands on a finite biosphere, all nations on the planet (including or especially the richest nations) are seeking to grow their economies without apparent limit. This is highly problematic, to say the least, because of the close connection between economic growth (in terms of GDP) and rising energy and resource consumption. It is all very well to point to the potential of technology and efficiency improvements to produce 'green growth', but the fact is that as the world gets distracted by such theoretical possibilities, the time for transition is vanishing (Smith 2016).

We frame our forthcoming analysis of suburbia by this 'limits to growth' perspective. We conclude that globalising the high-consumption, energy-intensive ways of living prevalent in the wealthiest regions of the world would be ecologically catastrophic, and reject the theory that all nations on the planet can grow their economies while sufficiently 'decoupling' economic activity from environmental impact by way of technological advancement and efficiency improvements. The extent of decoupling required is far too great (Jackson 2009).

In the same vein, we reject any policy that sees a growing population as a desirable means of keeping the cogs of economic growth turning. Despite all the criticism he has received, Paul Ehrlich (quoted in Hurst 1997) was fundamentally right in stating that 'whatever problem you're interested in, you're not going to solve it unless you also solve the population problem'. That insight applies as much to urban development as other domains of life. At the same time, after siphoning resources away from the rest of the world, it would be inhumane for the rich world to callously close borders now and leave the world's poor—including the growing populations of what are increasingly called 'climate refugees'— to fend for themselves. Clearly this is complex, thorny terrain, which must be negotiated with constant reference to an ethics of solidarity and compassion. One thing is clear: we must oppose the tide of scapegoat racism that seems to being driving the wave of populist nationalism that today calls for the closing of borders at a time when we must be opening our hearts.

Just as there are no simple answers to the vexed population dilemmas, so too with regards sustainable energy transitions. As will be seen, we are generally sceptical about the ability of renewable energy to easily or fully replace the energy services provided by fossil fuels—especially those energy services dependent on the 96 million barrels of oil that are consumed every day. It follows that the most industrialised and energy intensive regions of the world will almost certainly need to adapt to an 'energy descent' future if 100% renewable energy supply is achieved (Odum and Odum 2001). But given the energetic foundations of economic activity, reduced energy supply implies that those energy-intensive societies, such as Australia, will need to go through a phase of planned economic contraction, with the aim of leaving sufficient 'ecological room' for the poorest nations to provide a dignified standard of living for those currently destitute. This will require the rich nations to create new 'post-growth' or 'degrowth' forms of economy, while at the cultural level variously reimagining the good life beyond consumer culture. Tinkering around the edges of growth capitalism will not cut it. Green consumerism is a dangerous mirage.

Granted, most people are not ready to accept these deep implications of the global situation, but only by understanding and acknowledging the true extent of the ecological predicament and the limits of technological and market-based solutions can one understand the arguments developed in this book. It is important to bear this 'limits to growth' perspective in mind when evaluating our position, which might otherwise be interpreted as being too radical. Radical it is, but this is defended on the grounds that it is a response proportionate to the magnitude and urgency of the overlapping crises we face. Given how closely connected urban forms are to their underlying economic modes of production, it should come as no surprise that our book is framed and informed by the macro-perspective of political economy.

The terminology of 'degrowth' has provoked debate (Raworth 2017), but on careful consideration we feel it is the most appropriate term to frame the present enquiry. In a civilisation where growth is widely considered synonymous with 'good' or 'progress', there is certainly a public relations challenge in attempting to undermine this most fundamental metaphor so directly. But therein also lies a key strength. Other terms like 'sustainable development' or the 'green economy' get co-opted so easily, ultimately being rendered meaningless by virtue of meaning anything. Business as usual continues. While degrowth certainly has its own ambiguities, it has the virtue of directly and boldly evoking the need for overall contraction of energy and resource demands in the wealthiest nations. If that it is what is needed, then degrowth clearly lays down that gauntlet in ways that discourse on sustainable development does not. Furthermore, while sustainable development has been interpreted to mean growth, one cannot redefine degrowth to mean growth without degenerating into Orwellian double-speak. We are also encouraged by the fact that over the last decade degrowth has provoked a widespread and necessary debate that is in the process is moving beyond academic circles and beginning to enter public discourse.

In recent decades the 'limits to growth' position more broadly has received a great deal of attention, mostly from economic and ecological perspectives. Recently, the degrowth movement has begun contributing an important range of new political and sociological analyses, offering deeper insight into the alternative paradigm, evaluating transition strategies, policies, and obstacles, while also continuing to update and refine the ecological critique of growth economics in response to those who continue to fetishise growth (see, D'Alisa et al. 2015; Weiss and Cattaneo 2017; Kallis 2017). The purpose of our book, however, is not to review these existing literatures in any depth (see Kallis et al. 2018), but to extend and deepen the understanding of degrowth by examining the concept and the movement from a perspective that has received very little attention—namely, urban theory. What has been written on degrowth and urban theory (see e.g. Lietaert 2010; Xue 2015; March 2018; Lehtinen 2018) has neglected what is our focus herein: suburbia and its (re)inhabitation in an energy and resource constrained world.

Our Project: A Radical Urban Imaginary

We spoke above about the new map we need in order to chart the course of suburban and of course planetary transition, from a terminal capitalism to a new degrowth dispensation. Another way of thinking about this is to realise our need for a new imaginary that 'thinks out loud' the form of, and path towards, a suburbia beyond growth. We use the rather lofty word of imaginary because it does indeed invoke the idea of the loft, a new plateau for thinking about and journeying towards. It denotes transcendence from conventional thinking about cities which the degrowth perspective demands. This current thinking is largely framed by what we term 'neoliberal urbanism', an underlying faith in the ability of markets—reformed, restrained a little perhaps (but not much)—to continue to shape human settlement patterns. Much comes with this thinking that needs immediate abandonment if we are to move forward—hollowed out governance, radical individualism, technocratic determinism, corporate prerogative in the urban process, the mantra of ecocidal growth, an indifference to the injuries of inequality and exclusion, and more besides.

The imaginary we offer in the pages that follow is a sketch outline, with some instructions supplied, for a new suburban deal. We avoid the trap of idealism; that is, casting out ideas without recourse to the material reality that they emerge from and aspire to engage and change. This means our work here is founded in applied scholarship and also the daily urban experiences that shape and inform our lives—lived mostly in suburbia. And we take instruction and inspiration from the work of others that is conducted in the concrete reality of contemporary suburbia. A shining example of this is the work of David Holmgren and his many collaborators on suburban transition, reflected and realised recently in the marvellously instructive and practical manual, *Retrosuburbia: The Downshifter's Guide to a Resilient Future* (Holmgren 2018). Our own offerings, and in particular this book and its imaginary, are different and are expressed through written argument with recourse to the scholarship we are trained and steeped in—the applied investigations of human prospect in an age of sustainability crisis and the forms of urbanisation and urban living that will provide us with passage to a safer world.

Importantly, our imaginary is expressly rooted in the setting that we think and write from, contemporary Australian suburbia. This is to locate us firmly if somewhat peripherally in what might be termed 'new world' suburbia—the extensive, low-density settlements that ring the cores of major and minor cities of North America, Australia, and New Zealand. We address the newer, wealthier regions of the world that were settled by Europeans and later many others, and which quickly embraced and defined the high carbon, low-density suburban model that finds both favour and censure in the rest of the world today.

It is vital to recall that these nations and their suburban landscapes were created through acts of invasion and dispossession that attempted to erase the first peoples who owned and managed these lands for millennia. As part of the transition we advocate, there must be many acts of reconciliation with these surviving first peoples who inhabit our cities and hinterlands. One of these is to respect and draw upon their wisdom in land management and living. In Melbourne, from where we write, indigenous elder Uncle Jack has observed the 'vertical sprawl' of poorly designed high-density housing with a critical wistfulness, urging that 'We need to get back to having our own little piece of dirt to stand on' (quoted in Kermond 2016: 8–9).

Let it be understood then that the suburban imaginary we offer in this book is one created in and firstly for what we referred to above as 'new world' suburbia. We acknowledge further its Australian crucible, cities without the temperatures extremes of North America (certainly the heavy winters) which inevitably conditions the way we think about transition possibilities. Nonetheless, we think there are many postulates, pathways and matters of design in the pages that follow that can be applied with mindfulness to contexts across the suburban landscapes of the new world, and beyond that to the rest of the Global North, especially the countries of Northern and Western Europe. It was the colonialism of the latter that produced the new worlds and changed and disrupted most of the rest of the globe during the centuries of invasion and expansion that immediately preceded and then followed the Industrial Revolution.

Our imaginary engages the Global South by urging a break from the ageing high carbon suburban model that the North has idealised through economic and cultural globalisation in the past half century. Importantly, our degrowth suburbia departs also from the newer offering of the North, the supposedly sustainable model of high-density urbanism that is scarring Australian and many other cities. Just as with indigenous peoples, our imaginary invites a drawing in of wisdom, practical and applied, from the Global South, which has much to teach an increasingly imperilled North about the virtues of self-limitation and the possibilities for good subsistence living.

Our book has been deeply influenced by the work of Ivan Illich, especially his ground-breaking essay *Energy and Equity*, which in the face of conventional wisdom maintained that energy crises in the industrialised world 'cannot be overwhelmed by more energy inputs' (Illich 1974: 10). In this spirit Illich theorised a low-energy, convivial society that inhabited the middle way between under-consumption and over-consumption. For the poorest, Illich (1974: 8) argued, 'the elimination of slavery and drudgery depends on the introduction of appropriate modern technology, and for the rich, the avoidance of an even more horrible degradation depends on the effective recognition of a threshold in energy consumption beyond which technical processes begin to dictate social relations'. Illich saw how a society can be 'just as dangerously overpowered by the wattage of its tools as by the calorific content of its foods' but noted 'it is much harder to confess to national overindulgence in wattage that to a sickening diet' (Illich 1974: 8). He argued that it is necessary to identify the thresholds beyond which energy corrupts, and our theory of suburban transformation is broadly based on Illich's insight that we must 'do so by a political process that associates the community in the search for limits' (Illich 1974: 10).

Chapter Overviews

Having set the scene at some length, we now offer an outline of this book's argument to guide the reader through forthcoming chapters. In this introductory chapter (themed 'Capital'), we have sought to highlight how the suburban form is a function of the underlying political economy of growth and its fossil energy foundations. From this it follows that a new, post-carbon suburbia cannot emerge unless that underlying political economy is transcended or replaced, one way or another. Despite the tired protestations of its defenders, the growth paradigm is proving unable to resolve its various contradictions, especially its ecological contradictions, and thus the crises of growth are destined to intensify, inevitably to unfold most prominently in the cities of our carbon civilisation.

In this book we are less motivated by the increasingly unrealistic goal of avoiding such crises—it seems to us that such an opportunity has already passed. We are motivated instead by the critical and collective task of managing, as wisely, creatively, and as compassionately as possible, the epoch-defining encounter with these urban crises. Our question is whether the descent ahead must be tragic, or whether, instead, there might still be a door, hidden in the wall, through which pathways of descent might still be prosperous. Disconcertingly, this remains an open question.

As globalised capitalism falters, the world is being challenged to reimagine, in order to reinhabit, the built environment—the built environment that is already with us and, for the most part, will remain with us over the next critical decades. We have highlighted new world suburbia as our point of reference, focussing in particular on our own locality of Melbourne, Australia, while acknowledging that in a globalised economy the analysis must, at times, be global in scope. The suburbs will not be knocked down for them to be built again in a 'green' way; instead, the task is to resettle the suburbs according to a new imaginary, which highlights the central inquiry of this book. Fortunately, when approached creatively, the low-density suburban landscape shows itself to be a more promising place to start a transformative retrofit of the built environment than high-density urban areas, in ways we will explain.

We will argue that a degrowth process of planned economic contraction is the most coherent new macroeconomic paradigm for building resilience and solidarity in the face of the urban crises that are developing. Our undertaking is to examine what might become of the suburbs during such a transition, and what can be done in and for suburbia with regards to initiating, driving and managing this ultimately systemic degrowth transformation. Whether this transformation of economic contraction occurs through design or disaster is a thematic question that runs throughout this book, prompting us to shift between utopian and dystopian inflections, in the hope of finding ground upon which to stand and move forward—if not without apprehension, then at least without despair.

In Chapter 2 (themed 'Energy') we seek to establish our premise of forthcoming 'energy descent', a term we borrow from David Holmgren (2009). This premise directly counters mainstream energy narratives that assume that the energy abundance of carbon civilisation can be globalised and maintained indeterminately into the future. The dominant growth paradigm and the suburban form it has produced are both dependent on the vast energy surpluses of fossil fuels, and it is widely assumed that adapting to fossil energy depletion and mitigating climate change will not affect the aggregate energy supply needed to maintain global economic growth. In contrast, we contend that today's energy surpluses cannot be maintained in a carbon-constrained world. Increasing urban and suburban resilience in anticipation of this energy shock is a defining challenge of our age.

In Chapter 3 (themed 'Technology') we examine the ideology of techno-optimism that seems to inform most urban imaginaries today. Technology, markets, and further growth are typically offered as the means for resolving the energy and environmental problems that growth produces. Within that perspective the affluent, mobile, and globally dependent suburban way of life is rarely questioned, because it is assumed that it can be decarbonised with better design, technology, and 'smart growth'. To the extent the suburban form is questioned, vertical sprawl is often considered the solution—or at least it is the solution imposed by the market in a world in thrall to neoliberal urbanism.

Although we categorically defend a world powered by post-carbon energy technologies, we argue that the various limitations of nuclear and renewable energy offer further grounds for thinking that a post-carbon future will be an energy descent future, demanding a societal response that energy analyst Richard Heinberg (2004) calls 'powerdown'. We then narrow our focus by offering a critique of electric vehicles and conclude that a post-carbon suburbia will be a reduced-mobility space, where transport primarily takes the form of walking, cycling, public transport, very infrequent airflight, and more broadly, greatly increased localisation of economy.

Having broadly outlined our energy descent premise and outlined the economic implications in terms of degrowth, we turn in Chapter 4 (themed 'Politics') to consider a necessary socio-political question: if, as we argue, degrowth is the most coherent response to today's overlapping crises, what societal forces, if any, can or should initiate and drive such a radical transformation? In considering this question we acknowledge that we live in an age of almost despairing political paralysis, where governments seem to be in the iron grip of an unimaginative 'growth fetish' (Hamilton 2003). There is much governments could be doing to facilitate the transition to a post-carbon society beyond growth, but in Australia, and elsewhere, governments seem unwilling or unable to transcend the economics of growth and its fossil energy foundations. So if we cannot rely on governments to lead, from where will the sparks of transformation ignite?

This raises important questions about the role grassroots movements and community action may need to play as drivers of societal transformation. In this fourth chapter we present a brief 'theory of change' which underpins our praxis and politics of suburban transformation. We unpack the implications of a paralysed state, which ultimately takes the form of a defence of a post-capitalist politics that is driven 'from below', where citizenries come to regovern their localities through participatory democracy and household and community action (Gibson-Graham 2006). Waiting for governments would be like waiting for Godot—a tragi-comedy of two acts, in which nothing happens, twice, before the curtain closes.

If it is the case that individuals, households and communities must build the degrowth society themselves from the grassroots up, transforming daily life with political and economic ambitions, then the question that follows is what such action might look like and how it might contribute to the mechanics of deep cultural and systemic change. In Chapter 5 (themed 'Praxis'), we present a range of household, neighbourhood, and community strategies that could be undertaken to begin building a new suburbia within the shell of the old. By decarbonising and reducing household energy consumption through solar, biogas, and behaviour change; by disconnecting from fossil energy supply; by practicing voluntary simplicity and localising economy; by cycling, participating in the sharing economy, and reducing waste streams, etc: how far can these grassroots strategies sow the cultural seeds of a new post-capitalist politics and economics?

In examining these issues we reflect critically on the limitations and challenges of household and grassroots action. While it is fashionable to dismiss personal, household and community action as politically naïve and as being unable to deal with the systemic and structural nature of our crises, we argue that the apparent sophistication in this dismissal masks its own naivety in terms of how structures change. We recognise and accept the systemic nature of the crises facing our species but maintain that there will never be a politics or economics beyond growth until there is a culture that demands it, and culture is a product of innumerable small actions and practices. To dismiss the household or community scale, therefore, is to dismiss the foundation of the polis.

Chapter 6 (themed 'Vision') is where we make our most explicit statement of the radical urban imaginary we are developing. Having set up our premises, outlined a theory of change, reviewed the promise and limitations of grassroots and household action, we take this opportunity to present a new narrative of progress based on the notion of 'degrowth in the suburbs'. We envision a suburban future in which complementary socio-cultural movements inspired by notions of degrowth, solidarity, and sufficiency have managed to transform the suburbs from the grassroots up, eventually building new societal structures that support the new, post-capitalist modes of living as the old structures wither away and deteriorate. By turns utopian and dystopian, this narrative chapter is motivated by the aesthetic insight that mobilisation for change always depends upon some vision of what alternative worlds are available, what they might look like, and how they might be realised.

Our book does not set out to answer all questions for all suburban contexts, and we do not provide a complete policy framework for an alternative economic paradigm or urban blueprint. We are seeking to broaden the understanding of suburban futures informed by theories of degrowth and energy descent. Nevertheless, our argument is based on a view of the suburbs that is inextricably linked to the underlying modes of political economy that give shape to the urban form. Accordingly, in Chapter 7 (themed 'Structure') we consider some of the main policy areas that will eventually need to be addressed in order to support and facilitate the transition to a just, resilient, and sustainable suburban future. But as implied above when outlining our theory of change, such regovernance of the city, and regovernance of the economy more generally, is more likely to be an outcome not a driver of suburban transformation, which is why this part of discussion is situated at the end of the analysis not the beginning. We close the book in Chapter 8 by reprising our radical urban imaginary and urging its pursuit in a new suburban movement for change.

References

Arendt, Hannah. 1998 [1958]. *The Human Condition*. Chicago: University of Chicago Press.

Beck, Ulrich. 2009. *World at Risk*. Cambridge: Polity.

———. 2012. *Twenty Observations*. Cambridge: Polity.

D'Alisa, Giacomo, Federico Demaria, and Giorgos Kallis (eds.). 2015. *Degrowth: A Vocabulary for a New Era*. London: Routledge.

Davison, Graeme. 1995. Australia: The First Suburban Nation? *Journal of Urban History* 22 (1): 40–74.

Davis, Mike. 2010. Who Will Build the Ark? *New Left Review* 61: 29–46.

Eagleton, Terry. 2018. *Why Marx Was Right?* London: Yale University Press.

The Economist. 2012. The Laws of the City (23 June 2012). https://www.economist.com/international/2012/06/23/the-laws-of-the-city. Accessed 18 June 2018.

Engels, Friedrich. 1959 [1876]. *The Dialectics of Nature*. Moscow: Progress Publishers.

Esteva, Gustavo. 2010. Development. In *The Development Dictionary: A Guide to Knowledge as Power*, 2nd ed., ed. Wolfgang Sachs, 1–23. London: Zed Books.

Fromm, Erich. 2009 [1942]. *The Fear of Freedom*. London: Routledge.

Gibson-Graham, J.K. 2006. *Post-capitalist Politics*. Minneapolis: University of Minnesota Press.

Gleeson, Brendan. 2014. *The Urban Condition*. London: Routledge.

Hamilton, Clive. 2003. *Growth Fetish*. Crows Nest: Allen & Unwin.

Harvey, David. 1997. The New Urbanism and the Communitarian Trap. *Harvard Design Magazine*. Winter/Spring: 68–69.

———. 2008. The Right to the City. *New Left Review* 53: 23–40.

———. 2010. *The Enigma of Capital and the Crises of Capitalism*. Oxford: Oxford University Press.

———. 2013. *Rebel Cities: From the Right to the City to Urban Revolution*. London: Verso.

Heinberg, Richard. 2004. *Powerdown: Options and Actions for a Post-carbon World*. Gabriola Island: New Society Publishers.

Hickel, Jason. 2017. *The Divide: A Brief Guide to Global Inequality and Its Solutions*. Cornerstone: William Heinemann.

Hodson, Mike, and Simon Marvin. 2010. *World Cities and Climate Change*. Maidenhead: Open University Press.

Holmgren, David. 2009. *Future Scenarios: How Communities Can Adapt to Peak Oil and Climate Change*. White River Junction, VT: Chelsea Green.

———. 2018. *Retrosuburbia: The Downshifter's Guide to a Resilient Future*. Hepburn: Melliodora Publishing.

Hurst, Sam. 1997. *Paul Ehrlich and the Population Bomb*. Documentary. Sydney: ABC.

Illich, Ivan. 1974. *Energy and Equity*. New York: Harper and Row.

Jackson, Tim. 2009. *Prosperity Without Growth: Economics for a Finite Planet*. London: Earthscan.

Jevons, William Stanley. 1865. *The Coal Question*. London: Macmillan.

Kallis, Giorgos. 2017. Radical Dematerialization and Degrowth. *Philosophical Transactions of the Royal Society A* 375 (20160383): 1–13.

Kallis, Giorgos, Vasilis Kostakis, Steffen Lange, Barbara Muraca, Susan Paulson, and Matthias Schmelzer. 2018. Research on Degrowth. *Annual Review of Environment and Resources* 43: 4.1–4.26.

Keen, Steve. 2017. *Can We Avoid Another Financial Crisis?* Cambridge: Polity.

Kermond, Clare. 2016. City of Dreams. *The Age*, August 27.

Lefebvre, Henri. 2003 [1970]. *The Urban Revolution*, trans. Robert Bononno. London: University of Minnesota Press.

Lehtinen, Ari. 2018. Degrowth in City Planning. *Fennia* 196 (1): 43–57.

Lietaert, Matthieu. 2010. Cohousing's Relevance to Degrowth Theories. *Journal of Cleaner Production* 18 (6): 576–580.

Lovelock, James. 2009. *The Vanishing Face of Gaia: A Final Warning*. London: Penguin.

March, Hug. 2018. The Smart City and Other ICT-led Techno-imaginaries: Any Room for Dialogue with Degrowth? *Journal of Cleaner Production* 197 (2): 1694–1703.

Marx, Karl, and Friedrich Engels. 1985 [1848]. *The Communist Manifesto*. Harmondsworth, UK: Penguin.

Meadows, Donella, Dennis Meadows, Jorgen Randers, and I.I.I. William Behrens. 1972. *Limits to Growth*. New York: Signet.

Odum, Howard, and Elizabeth Odum. 2001. *A Prosperous Way Down: Principles and Policies*. Colorado: University of Colorado Press.

Raworth, Kate. 2017. *Doughnut Economics: 7 Ways to Think Like a 21-Century Economist*. White River Junction: Chelsea Green.

Smith, Richard. 2016. *Green Capitalism: The God That Failed*. London: College Publications.

Steffan, Will, Katherine Richardson, Johan Rockström, Sarah E. Cornell, Ingo Fetzer, Elena M. Bennett, Reinette Biggs, Stephen R. Carpenter, Wim de Vries, Cynthia A. De Wit, Carl Folke, Dieter Gerten, Jens Heinke, Georgina M. Mace, Linn M. Perrson, Veerabhadran Ramanathan, Belinda Reyers, Sverker Sörlin. 2015. Planetary Boundaries: Guiding Human Development on a Changing Planet. *Science* 347 (6223). https://doi.org/10.1126/science.1259855.

Turner, Graeme. 2014. Is Collapse Imminent? An Updated Comparison of the *Limits to Growth* with Historical Data. MSSI Research Paper No. 4, August, 1–21.

Urry, John. 2011. *Climate Change and Society*. Cambridge: Polity.

Ward, James, Paul Sutton, Adrian Werner, Robert Costanza, Steve Mohr, and Craig Simmons. 2016. Is Decoupling GDP Growth from Environmental Impact Possible? *PLoS ONE* 11 (10): e0164733. https://doi.org/10.1371/journal.pone.0164733.

Weiss, Martin, and Claudio Cattaneo. 2017. Degrowth—Taking Stock and Reviewing an Emerging Academic Paradigm. *Ecological Economics* 137: 220–230.

Wiedmann, Thomas, Heinz Schandl, Manfred Lenzen, Daniel Moran, Sangwon Suh, J. West, and Keiichiro Kanemoto. 2015. The Material Footprint of Nations. *Proceedings of the National Academy of Sciences* 112: 6271–6276.

Xue, Jin. 2015. Sustainable Housing Development: Decoupling or Degrowth? A Comparative Study of Copenhagen and Hangzhou. *Environment and Planning C. Politics and Space* 33 (3): 620–639.

Žižek, Slavoj. 2010. *Living in the End Times*. London: Verso.

———. 2012. *The Year of Dreaming Dangerously*. London: Verso.

2

Carbon Suburbia and the Energy Descent Future

O hell! What have we here?
A carrion Death, within whose empty eye
There is a written scroll! I'll read the writing.
'All that glitters is not gold;
Often have you heard that told:
Many a man his life hath sold
But my outside to behold:
Gilded tombs do worms enfold.'

—*Merchant of Venice*

'City of Gold' by photographer Andy Serrano is an image that captures the vast, glowing, infinitely sprawling landscape of Los Angeles at night, depicting a constellation of lights from indistinct cars and buildings, a cluster of slowly moving stars against a dark ether, signifying the energy intensity of our infernal civilisation like nothing else. The vista is quite majestical from a distance at night, yet at the same time deeply disturbing to those who know what it means, or might mean, in terms of how growing portions of humanity have come to inhabit our fragile planet in this increasingly urban age. All that glitters is not gold.

© The Author(s) 2019
S. Alexander and B. Gleeson, *Degrowth in the Suburbs*,
https://doi.org/10.1007/978-981-13-2131-3_2

Most readers of this text would have flown into a large metropolis at night and experienced such a panoramic view first hand. Looking out the window, who has not at times been left breathless by the unfathomable reach of the built environment? Is it *still* beneath us? Has it no end? Is it still glowing with various warm energies that give it life? Yes, out to the horizon and beyond! Even from thousands of feet above one can almost hear the city humming, like a magnificent machine made up of millions of moving parts, a network of networks. If we then reflect on the energy intensity of the vehicle in which we fly, it might dawn upon us that even from our seemingly distant perspective on the city we are part of the picture, not spectators but participants. The energy intensity of carbon civilisation—the city of gold—is striking, even if so easily taken for granted. Occasionally we might be confronted by the wastefulness of our ever-growing, poorly designed, energy demanding cities, with their towering cores and far-reaching horizontal suburbs, but given that it is into the mirror we are looking, we generally turn away.

Cities are our most intricate creations. They are the meta-formations within which other expressions of human creativity emerge and develop, and this complexity, like life itself, depends on energy for its sustenance and development. Like all species, we humans expend our energy and that of the Earth to make our homes, increasingly in every remaining corner of the planet. We fell the forests and mine the landscapes to construct our dwellings and build our roads; our houses and water are typically heated with wood or gas; electricity, like a god, gives us light and it powers our abundance of seductive appliances and machines; oil takes us where we desire to be and back again without effort. If a problem arises, we solve it with little or no appreciation of the energy cost, yet the more problems we face and solve, the more energy we need. This is how civilisations take form and evolve, both enabled and constrained by their energetic foundations.

Never has this been truer than in the low-density urban landscapes of new world suburbia, predominantly comprised of stand-alone houses and generally inhabited by high-impact and ever-aspiring consumers, who are both creatures and creators of the growth economy. Suburban affluence is the defining image of the good life under capitalism, held up as a model to which all humanity should aspire. Every aspect of this suburban mode of existence is dependent upon the cheap and abundant fossil energy supplies that have become accessible in the last two centuries, yet this very same fossil dependency is at the same time proving to be a fatal addiction. Fossil fuels are the lifeblood of what we could call carbon suburbia, but what fossil fuels giveth, fossil fuels threaten to taketh away.

Suburban catastrophists like James Kunstler (2005) argue that the suburbs represent the 'greatest misallocation of resources in the history of the world' and that fossil fuel depletion will imminently render this landscape an inhospitable wasteland. But such curdled imaginations fail to see what in Chapter 1 we called suburbia's *latent capacity* to become something new. The well-known documentary 'The End of Suburbia' (Greene 2004) presented a coherent narrative of a post-petroleum future but got at least one thing wrong. There is not a single end to suburbia; there are many ends of suburbia (as we know it), and our undertaking in this book is to chart a course between the Scylla of catastrophe and the Charybdis of false hope, and see whether the descent ahead may yet entail a reconceived prosperity for those communities who are able to navigate these unknown waters mindfully, creatively and in the spirit of solidarity.

Powerdown: Navigating Energy Descent Futures

Throughout history the overconsumption of energy in human settlements was not a prevailing problem—the problem was almost always energy scarcity (Smil 2017). Too many difficulties and desires; not enough energy to solve or satisfy them. Of course, the use of and demand for energy in previous eras caused problems too: deforestation and top-soil erosion are not purely modern consequences of urbanisation and agriculture; there is a long history of homes and factories spewing forth harmful particulates into the air from burning wood and coal; as horses became the dominant mode of urban transportation their manure in the streets became a hazard; and so forth. Environmental change driven by the human exploitation of energy is as old as the mastery of fire, and our energy use always has and always will have negative consequences beyond the benefits it brings. As the gushing waste streams of city life today are trucked out of sight into some mysterious 'other place' we call nature, perhaps subconsciously we hope that our ostensible cleanliness will give us the aura of godliness, entrenching our self-image as masters not servants of nature. It is a Promethean and destructive delusion.

Nevertheless, it seems that we have entered a hyperindustrial age, anticipated by Ivan Illich (1974), in which some of our most pressing problems now arise not from a lack of access to energy but rather from energy overconsumption. Humans certainly enjoy vastly disparate access to energy, with billions around the world still living in conditions of energy poverty, however our species now faces the dual energy crises of fossil energy depletion and climate change, both of which arise not from the under-consumption of energy but from its overuse and overreliance (Friedrichs 2013). But if energy is required to solve problems and satisfy unfulfilled desires, surely we need still more energy than we have today, not less? Then again, what if the overconsumption of energy is now driving the problems that we assume can be solved with even more energy? This is the paradox of energy that is coming to define the twenty-first century, and it is one that presents no obvious resolution.

Energy forecasters today almost always assume that humanity (or the richer economies, at least) will always be able to meet ongoing energy demand in a timely and affordable fashion (e.g. IEA 2017). This flow of energy is critical to maintaining the ongoing pursuit of economic growth, which is an unquestioned goal within dominant economic and political discourse (Purdey 2010; Anderson 2015a). Energy insecurity quickly escalates into national crisis (e.g. the oil shocks of 1973 and 1979) because it threatens the foundations of capitalist accumulation (Thompson 2017). Even slowing energy demand is a source of crisis for the capitalist state because in these moments the inexorable logic of growth is under threat. States frequently step into guarantee security through investment, since the market must not fail given that energy is an essential service and enabling condition for accumulation (Huber 2017).

Urban planning and development take form within and reflect this growth fetish, even if the underlying assumptions about energy are not always conscious. It simply flows from the belief that energy is our fundamental tool for solving problems through continuous economic growth, so if the way we use energy is also causing problems, then it is believed that even more energy and more economic growth will be needed to solve those problems. In mainstream energy discourse the fact that fossil fuels are finite and are being depleted at pace is generally dismissed as a distant concern that will be solved before it arrives. It is assumed that renewable energy or nuclear power will be able to replace fossil fuels without significant social or economic disruption as well as meet growing global energy demand into the distant future.

Analysts point to the promising advances in technology in defence of this energy optimism (Lovins 2011). Sure, they say, new problems will arise that will require the use of energy to solve them, but human beings will be able to meet those energy demands because we are clever and resourceful. Prices and markets will provide the right incentives. According to this narrative, industrial capitalism and urban densification will soon be global—transitions that are clearly well underway—and it is widely assumed that efficiency gains and new energy sources and technologies will mean we can avoid the worst peak oil and climate change scenarios without any paradigm shift in economics or urban planning. Just look to history and you will see that humans have generally managed to meet energy crises in the past by acquiring more energy. The future will be the same, won't it?

One purpose of this book is to challenge this dominant 'cornucopian' energy narrative and consider how today's carbon-intensive cities—focussing on new world suburbia—might be able to prepare for, manage, and perhaps even thrive in an alternative, less idealistic energy future (Odum and Odum 2001). Can the high carbon suburbs 'powerdown' (Heinberg 2004) due to energy constraints and yet create more liveable urban landscapes? In the tradition of Illich, we will argue that they can, and that 'high quanta of energy degrade social relations just as inevitably as they destroy the physical milieu' (Illich 1974: 3). But this means first exposing the fallacy that energy crises can only be resolved by more energy inputs, and dissolving the illusion that freedom and wellbeing depend necessarily on high-energy forms of social organisation. The suburban imaginary developed in this book seeks to lay down roots in that narrow but sufficient range of energy provision that 'separates enough from too much' (Illich 1974: 8), challenging the view that 'clean and abundant energy is the panacea for social ills' (Illich 1974: 5). Indeed, abundant clean energy, without a change in modes of production and distribution, might simply exacerbate the social and ecological contradictions of capitalism—uneven access to energy being a key contradiction.

We begin by reminding readers that fossil fuels, which currently make up 86% of global primary energy consumption (BP 2017), are finite, and therefore carbon civilisation, one way or another, has a time limit. Our one-off fossil energy inheritance is but a brief anomaly in the evolution of the human story, a momentary energy spike from the perspective of deep time (Moriarty and Honnery 2011). Although the timing and trajectory of fossil energy depletion is subject to many uncertainties and controversies—some of which are reviewed below— the fact that fossil fuels are finite and subject to depletion is an undeniable geological reality. This raises questions not only about what a post-carbon suburbia will look like, but perhaps more pressingly, how we should best manage the inevitable and foreseeable contraction of fossil energy production in coming years and decades. Our review of this situation suggests that reports on 'the death of peak oil' have been greatly exaggerated (see Brecha 2013; Chapman 2014; Mohr et al. 2015).

There is also the climate crisis, no longer of the future but the present. The future is now. Climate science overwhelmingly concludes that the burning of fossil fuels is a leading cause of anthropogenic climate change and that any adequate response to this potentially existential threat is going to require, amongst other things, a swift and committed transition beyond fossil energy sources. That is, we need to limit the consumption of fossil fuels even before such limits are geologically enforced, and the question is whether we can muster the wisdom to do this and what the resultant society would look like if we were to succeed. If we fail, then it seems that we will burn—and already things are heating up. Sixteen of the seventeen hottest years in recorded history have occurred since 2001, to say nothing of the increasing regularity and severity of extreme weather events.

And yet we wait. Despite all the sincere-sounding lip service paid to climate change, today's global carbon dioxide emissions of 36 billion tonnes per year are approximately two-thirds higher than they were when the Intergovernmental Panel on Climate Change (IPCC) was established in 1988—and emissions continue to rise (see IEA 2018).

This chapter provides an update to the complex and evolving peak oil situation and unpacks the radical implications of the latest carbon budget analyses (see also, Alexander and Floyd 2018). Our aim is to highlight the truly fundamental challenge these overlapping and connected energy crises pose to the sustainability or even viability of suburbia—more fundamental even than many energy analysts and environmentalist recognise. In the next chapter we consider whether or to what extent alternative energy technologies—specifically renewable and/or nuclear energy—will be able to replace the fossil energy sources of carbon civilisation. Can this be done without rethinking the growth paradigm and the energy hungry suburbs that it has produced?

While we acknowledge a range of promising technological and economic advances in the energy domain, and categorically support the planned transition to a post-carbon society, we also wish to raise critical questions about the various *limitations* of renewable energy and nuclear power. It is our view that these alternative energy sources will be unable to support the energy-intensive suburban way of life as we know it today (see generally, Smil 2015; Moriarty and Honnery 2016; Heinberg and Fridley 2016). This implies that post-carbon suburbs will require not just a 'greening' of their energy foundations, but also a fundamental reimagining of the built environment and the modes of political economy and culture that our cities both shape and are shaped by.

The alternative energy narrative we present maintains that we should be preparing for futures, not of energy abundance, but rather of reduced energy availability, futures in which viable ways of life are characterised by energy sufficiency. This position is based on the inevitability of fossil energy depletion; the near-impossible demands made by recent carbon budget analyses; and the inability of alternative energy sources to fully replace the bountiful energy surpluses and power densities of fossil fuels. Distributive considerations only strengthen the case for rethinking our relationship with energy, implying that in a world of limited energy availability, demand reductions should begin in those areas that currently are consuming the most. With respect to the most energy-intensive societies, all this means we should be planning for energy descent, due to mutually reinforcing geological, ecological and social justice reasons. In this chapter and the next we present a summary case for energy descent, and later chapters explore some of the social, economic, and political implications of this looming reality, as they may play out in new world suburbia.

The Energetic Foundations of Suburbia

One does not need to be an energy determinist or crude reductionist to recognise the fundamental role energy has played, and continues to play, in shaping the rise (and demise) of human civilisations. Energy is not just another resource or commodity: it is the key that unlocks access to other resources and commodities, thereby providing energetic boundaries within which human societies must take form. The energetic foundations of a society delimit the socio-economic forms that a society may take, which is simply to concede that a form of society cannot emerge without sufficient energy supplies to support it, and that a society must be able to meet its *ongoing* energy demands if its specific socio-economic form is to persist. If it cannot, the society will transform or be transformed, voluntarily or otherwise (Tainter 1988; Homer-Dixon 2006).

If agriculture was the first true revolution in energy supply in human history, which created the energy surpluses needed for a complex civilisation to emerge, the second was the wave of industrial revolutions starting in England in the eighteenth century that flowed from harnessing the vast energies embodied in fossil fuels: coal, then oil, and later natural gas. What began with the harnessing of hydropower to mechanise textile production, and was then amplified immensely with invention and refinement of the steam engine, soon developed into a technological and economic explosion that changed the fundamentals of how human beings (or the industrialising societies at least) lived on Earth. It is hard to overstate the significance of this fossil energy revolution and yet so easy to take it for granted, not just in terms of the *magnitude* of energy available in hydrocarbons, but also the *nature* of that energy.

In terms of magnitude, the point is made most emphatically with respect to oil, one barrel of which can enable a quantity of work equivalent to something in the order of 3 years of human labour. When it is understood that in 2017 the global consumption of oil reached around 96 million barrels every day, the scale of energy provided by fossil fuels becomes somewhat easier to comprehend (IEA 2017). Pause for a moment to let those figures sink in, bearing in mind that the vast energy from coal and gas use only makes the scale of energy availability more astonishing still. In the absence of fossil fuels, humanity would need the equivalent of more than 170 billion 'energy slaves' working eight-hour shifts seven days a week year on year to maintain the aggregate energy demands of the existing form of life.

But the magnitude of energy supplied by fossil fuels is one thing; their unique *nature* is another (Smil 2015). More precisely, it is not just how much energy fossil fuels store that make them so extraordinary; it is also the *rate* at which that energy can be converted into useful work (i.e. their power density). The very high power densities of fossil fuels play a key role in the high aggregate rates at which energy services can be provided. The energy equivalent to three years' worth of human labour that a barrel of oil provides can be exploited in a tiny fraction that time. In other words, you can do things with oil that you just cannot do with humans, horses and windmills, such as fly passenger planes, build 100-story buildings, mine thousands of feet into mountains, and transfer the vast cargoes around the world needed to maintain a high-consumption, globalised economy. Add to these remarkable characteristics the virtues of cheapness (at least when environmental externalities are excluded) as well as their historical abundance, and it becomes clearer how and why fossil fuels have come to shape the complex socio-economic form of what we are calling carbon civilisation.

To further emphasise the practical implications of fossil energy we could return to the image of the megalopolis at night—the 'city of gold'—as seen from an aeroplane window. The aircraft itself is entirely dependent on the unique power density of oil, not simply to provide the fuel, but also to make viable the range of complex background activities on which modern aircraft depend: the mining for materials and the production of plastics; the laying of roads and runways; the development and production of computers and communications technologies that coordinate the tens of thousands of daily flights; to say nothing of the broader investment in education required to train the engineers, computer scientists, pilots, and so forth.

In this chain of dependencies, it is not long before one arrives at the combine harvester that plays a key role in feeding much of the population. These machines, also powered by oil, take the Neolithic innovation of freeing up human labour for 'non-food specialisation' and amplify its effects through the industrialisation of agriculture. If in the past essentially every member of hunter-gather societies were required to be 'food specialists', in advanced industrial societies today the percentage of the population required to be farmers has dropped to as low as 2%. During this demographic transition people were displaced from the land by machines and into the factories and offices of the built environment. It is this image of mass migration that perhaps most vividly illustrates the tight interrelationship between the intensification of socio-political complexity and the urbanisation of modern life in the industrialised world.

Beneath the plane lie the immense, glowing suburbs—the defining manifestation of carbon civilisation on the ground. No form of human settlement has ever been more energy intensive to produce or more energy intensive to maintain. Again, consider the long and diverse chains of extraction and production on which suburbia depends, not only for its creation but also to support the high-consumption living standards widely practised therein: the underlying energy infrastructure like oil and gas pipelines and the electricity grid; the range of mining activities which siphon resources from the global periphery to the urban and suburban landscapes; the carbon-based transport of materials like metals, stone, and wood to the factories; and the final consumer commodities shipped and trucked to the shopping malls, via a vast and complex network of global trade routes and practices; the manufacture of private automobiles which transport people to and from work, leisure, and tourist activities; the production of houses, kitchen gadgets, plastics, computers, pharmaceuticals, appliances, and clothing; the heating of water, and the heating and cooling of space; and, thanks to hydrocarbon-derived fertilisers, the abundant provision of food from all around the world, no matter the season, free from blemishes due to the liberal use of hydrocarbon-derived pesticides and herbicides, etc. (Moriarty and Honnery 2011).

The list above has no end, because in our increasingly globalised and interconnected world economy everything seems dependent on everything else—but nothing is more fundamental than the fossil fuels that make everything else possible (Huber 2017). Just look around the space in which you are reading: it may not always be obvious, but essentially every artefact you see will have a history saturated with fossil energy, especially oil.

This is carbon civilisation.

The Finitude of Oil and the Fate of Suburbia

We have highlighted some of the ways in which suburbia has been enabled by the vast and unprecedented energy surpluses provided by fossil fuels. This point is also apparent in the close correlation between energy use and economic growth, as measured by GDP (Fig. 2.1). This tight linear relationship draws attention to the dependence that all economic activity has on energy, and that sharply increasing energy supply has been required to enable the unprecedented growth and industrialisation of economies over the last two centuries (Ayres and Warr 2009). Today's globalised modes of production, distribution, and consumption—and the suburban way of life in particular—simply would not have been possible without the cheap energy surpluses provided by fossil fuels.

However—to restate the obvious—there is only a limited amount of fossil fuels in the ground, and in the last two centuries humanity has been extracting these historically cheap, seemingly abundant, but ultimately finite resources with ravenous enthusiasm. This raises questions about what may happen as these non-renewable energy sources continue to deplete in coming years and decades, even as demand is expected to grow.

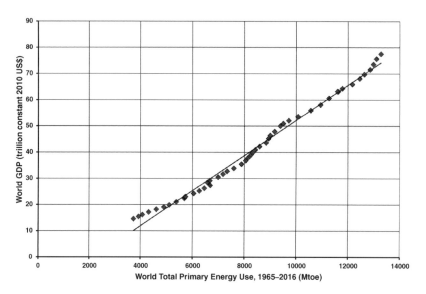

Fig. 2.1 World GDP versus total primary energy use, for the period 1965–2016. The strong correlation between GDP and energy use is apparent, with $R^2 = 0.9907$ for the linear trend line shown ($y = 0.0067x - 14.935$) (*Data sources* World GDP, World Bank; Energy use, BP Statistical Review of World Energy 2017)

Peak oil is the most widely discussed phenomenon in the context of fossil energy depletion, referring to the point at which oil production reaches its maximum rate, to be followed by a production plateau and eventual decline. This phenomenon has been observed in every oil well ever drilled; it has been experienced in most oil-producing regions of the world already; and in coming years the entire global oil industry will also experience a production peak and decline (Mohr et al. 2015).

This global peak will arrive not because oil is running out, as such, but because the easy-to-produce oil has already been discovered and extracted, leaving only reserves of increasingly marginal value (e.g. deep water or arctic oil, tar sands, shale oil, etc.). These marginal reserves are costlier to extract, both financially and energetically. As the best reserves deplete, producers must run faster and faster—or drill ever-more, in ever-less ideal places—merely to stay in the same place (Murphy 2013). Eventually producers will not be able to maintain supply rates however hard they try, and the flow of oil will stop growing or 'peak' and subsequently fall, despite the fact there will still be considerable quantities of oil left to produce.

The primary concern of the peak oil school is that the peak and decline of global production arrives while demand keeps on growing (Heinberg 2011). And demand is certainly growing and indeed accelerating, with the rate of growth in 2017 being twice that of the preceding decade (IEA 2018). According to basic economic principles, a constrained supply coupled with increasing demand will drive rapid increases in prices, and given how much oil is used today, and given how hard and costly it is to substitute oil with other energy sources, expensive oil places a huge financial burden on dependent economies, with destabilising effects.

When oil gets expensive, everything dependent on it gets more expensive, like transport, mechanised labour, industrial food production, and plastics, amongst a host of other things. This pricing dynamic siphons discretionary expenditure and investment away from the rest of the economy—or out of the national economy altogether—causing debt defaults, economic stagnation, recessions, or even longer-term depressions (Thompson 2017). Carbon civilisation was built with cheap and abundant fossil energy, especially oil, and the growth paradigm which has driven and maintained this mode of existence is similarly dependent. Take away these cheap energy inputs and the viability of this socio-economic form—epitomised by new world suburbia—is imperilled.

Concerns about peak oil have fallen from prominence in recent years, as the shale boom in the US produced an unexpected oil glut in global markets, leading to the significant price drop in mid-2014, from over US$100 to around US$50–60 where it sat in late 2017, rising to around US$70 by mid-2018. This has indeed been an extraordinary phenomenon, which energy and financial analysts across the board failed to predict, even if the dynamics are well understood. Incremental production increases from the Canadian tar sands have also taken pressure off oil markets. Nevertheless, a close reading of the current situation indicates that the shale boom has not debunked but merely delayed, or more accurately disguised, the unfolding dynamics of peak oil. The mood of complacency this has induced is disturbing.

Peak Oil: Not Dead, Only in Remission

There are many powerful reasons to think that peak oil is not dead but only in remission. Growth in oil production since 2005 has been primarily dependent on shale production in the US (Murphy 2013), but even the relentlessly optimistic US Energy Information Agency (EIA) and the International Energy Agency (IEA) think US production will peak around 2025, suggesting a global peak is only a few years away at most. A new study from the Massachusetts Institute of Technology (Montgomery and O'Sullivan 2017) indicates US shale production could peak sooner, even as global demand is expected to grow to 2040 and beyond. The rigorous work of geologist David Hughes (2018) also casts doubt on more optimistic estimates.

The profitability of shale is also highly uncertain, evidenced by the fact that no less than 134 US oil production and exploration companies have filed for bankruptcy since the price crash of mid-2014. Indeed, the *Wall Street Journal* reported in 2017 that over the preceding decade the shale oil industry in the USA has spent $280 billion more on investments than it has generated from operations. How long can this capital sink continue? If shale cannot make profits, the so-called boom may go bust sooner than most analysts think, even if there are vast technically recoverable resources. This is uncertain and contested territory.

Despite demand for oil being at historic highs and continuing to increase, discoveries of oil are the lowest since 1947. In 2016, the IEA reported that discoveries were less than one-tenth of what was consumed. Like a household spending ten times what it earns, the unsustainability of this situation should be obvious. An oil crunch awaits. Moreover, a recent HSBC report (Fustier et al. 2016) concludes that between 64–81% of existing fields are in decline, making it ever harder to maintain existing levels of supply, especially as new discoveries dry up. The energy-return-on-investment of oil is also in terminal decline (Murphy 2013), meaning that more energy is being invested in the energy sector per unit of oil produced, leaving less surplus for the rest of the economy.

All this has implications for the future of oil supply. Amongst the most lucrative industries of the twentieth century, the profitability of oil seems to be turning sharply, as the cost of finding and producing oil is relentlessly on the rise while the depressed price of oil is sitting at a level that is decimating profits of previous eras. As profitable projects become harder to find, the industry is investing less in building future capacity, raising further concerns about a near-term oil crunch. Increasing oil consumption in member states of the Organisation of the Petroleum Exporting Countries (or OPEC) is also making it harder to maintain the same level of global exports, as the OEPC nations keep more oil for themselves. Accordingly, the rest of the world should not expect to maintain the same share of global supplies.

Beyond the geology and economics, there are also geopolitical, environmental and social justice concerns that cannot be dismissed. Huge portions of oil production today take place in politically unstable regions of the world and this means we are only one war or terrorist attack away from significant supply disruptions—hardly an implausible scenario (Amhed 2017). Climate change (discussed further below) means that we should essentially be embracing peak oil now *by choice* and learning to manage with a sharply declining oil supply to have any chance of maintaining a safe climate. And then there are distributive questions, always the last aspect to receive attention (see Gardiner 2011; Ekanayake et al. 2015). If there is only a finite supply of oil that can be economically or sustainably consumed, then we need to ask how that oil should be used, for what purposes, and for whose benefit.

For these types of reasons, peak oil is proving to be a more complex phenomenon than theorists originally anticipated. It is not being experienced as a precise 'moment' or 'event', but rather as a dynamic interplay between various forces that have provoked some adaptive adjustments (such as demand destruction or increased investment in shale) in incremental and multidimensional ways. There may never be a 'shock moment' of peak oil's arrival; instead, peak oil may continue to play out as a gradual, unplanned and largely misunderstood transition to a new set of energy and consumption patterns that are less oil dependent, giving rise to social, economic, and ecological impacts that no one can predict with any certainty. The evolving interrelationship of geological, geopolitical, economic, environmental, cultural, and technological variables has continued to surprise analysts—both the cornucopians, who claim there is nothing to worry about, and the doomsayers, who think collapse is imminent, as well as everyone in between.

No doubt there will be more twists still to come in this energy tale. But what seems clear is that the consequences of peak oil are not going away. Whether production peaks in three years or ten years is of little consequence; a post-petroleum future is inevitable, so it makes sense to prepare our oil-hungry cities for this momentous energetic fate. One of the key issues to be explored throughout this book is what a post-petroleum suburbia might look like and how best to make such a transition. Given how long this transition is likely to take (Smil 2010), the uncertainty over when exactly global production will peak becomes far less important than the fact that it is plainly foreseeable. We must figure out how to leave oil before oil leaves us. The viability of suburbia depends on it.

It will now be shown, however, that humanity's problems run even deeper than peak oil and the depletion of fossil energy. Arguably the more pressing problem is not how little fossil energy we have available—but how much.

Unburnable Carbon

Geological timescales often span tens of thousands or even tens of millions of years or more. Today, however, we live in the Anthropocene, the first epoch in which collective human actions can be viewed as constituting forces of geological significance (Steffan et al. 2015). The Anthropocene is barely three hundred years old, a consequence of industrialisation and the carbon civilisation which fossil fuels enabled, and no environmental disturbance more clearly represents the Anthropocene than climate change (Hamilton 2017). Human activity on the planet is now so imposing that we are destabilising something as fundamental as the climate system, with the future inhabitability of Earth by humans being threatened by impacts such as ongoing global warming, sea level rise, and the increased regularity and severity of extreme weather events (droughts, floods, storms, etc.). In the cosmological context of the human story, this environmental disruption is occurring strikingly fast, yet it will have consequences for centuries, millennia even. Understanding the suburban impacts of climate change as well as the ways suburbia might be transformed to mitigate and adapt to this phenomenon are central themes of this book. This calls for a frank look at the latest climate science and its economic implications.

Scientists are now able to predict within a range of probabilities the likely temperature rise that would result from a certain amount of further GHG emissions. This is the foundation of what is called 'carbon budget analysis', a term that has entered the lexicon of climate scientists over the last decade. A carbon budget essentially refers to the maximum amount of carbon emissions that can be released into the atmosphere if the goal is to prevent global temperatures from rising a specified level above a pre-industrial baseline. We know that existing reserves of fossil fuels far exceed what the climate can tolerate if they are all burned, so most will need to stay in the ground—by choice (see Carbon Tracker and Grantham Institute 2013). What, then, is our budget? That is a complex question, without a single answer (Hausfather 2018).

The size of any carbon budget is dependent on a range of parameters, each of which will contribute to making the carbon budget higher or lower, and thus easier or more challenging to keep within. Key parameters include: What temperature rise above pre-industrial levels are we trying to avoid? What probability of success or failure is considered justified? What assumptions are being made about the role of carbon-capture-and-storage (CCS) and negative emissions technologies (NETs)? And how should the carbon budget be shared between and within nations, to ensure distributive equity in an age of ecologically imposed energy constraints? Obviously, the choice of different parameters will have socio-economic implications, and this draws the scientific analyses into more normative, value-laden, or 'politicised' spaces.

In recent decades, a maximum 2 °C temperature rise above pre-industrial levels has been commonly assumed to represent a 'safe' threshold, beyond which humanity would enter increasingly 'dangerous' territory (Anderson and Bows 2011). However, there is a growing recognition amongst scientists that a temperature rise of 2 °C is far too risky, and this emerging consensus came to inform the Paris Agreement of 2015, in which almost all nations of the world committed to keeping temperatures 'well below' 2 °C and 'to pursue efforts to limit the temperature increase … to 1.5°C'.

Indeed, even at 1.5 °C above pre-industrial levels, the science indicates that many low-lying islands and coastal cities are at grave risk of being submerged; the Great Barrier Reef will likely be dead; food security will be seriously threatened for significant portions of the global population; and melting permafrosts may well release enough methane to trigger further temperature rises even if anthropogenic emissions have declined or ceased (see Spratt and Dunlop 2017). In what Ulrich Beck (2009) termed a 'world at risk', even the affluent suburbs of the new world lie in the destructive path of the furies of climate change, especially from 'heat stress events' that are already occurring with greater regularity in North America, Australia, and elsewhere.

Given these risks, what probability of success should humanity consider appropriate when formulating a carbon budget? Would you cross the road if you had a 50 or 66% chance of doing so safely? Would you do so if you had an 80% chance? A 95% chance? Probably not, and yet it seems the world is basing climate policy on far lower expectations of success. The IEA tends to assume a 50% chance of avoiding 2 °C; the IPCC develops 1.5 and 2 °C scenarios based on 50 and 66% chances of success, but no higher. This normalises a one-in-two or one-in-three chance of failure.

Why such low probability expectations of success? Sadly, the answer is political and economic, not scientific or moral. For instance, if world leaders concluded on reviewing the evidence that an 80% chance of remaining below 1.5 °C was the most justifiable climate goal, they would then discover that there is in fact no carbon budget left (Rogelj et al. 2015), just as there is no carbon budget if a 90% chance of avoiding 2 °C is assumed (Spratt and Dunlop 2017). Public acknowledgement of this would constitute a form of global emergency declaration, signalling the need for radical transformation of societies to manage the swiftest decarbonisation possible. But rather than accept this implication, mainstream political and economic analyses essentially 'self-censor' their own work to avoid questioning the dominant paradigm of growth capitalism (Anderson 2015a).

It is also worth noting that there are some worrying ambiguities in the very language of a '1.5°C scenario'. If such a scenario assumes a 50% chance of success, what is typically missed is that this means a 33% of exceeding 2 °C and a 10% chance of exceeding 3 °C (Spratt 2016). So if there is 10% chance of exceeding 3 °C and thereby most likely causing outright chaos, it doesn't seem right to call this a 1.5 °C scenario. But such is the politics of language, glossed over by most people, including many in the scientific community (Anderson 2015a).

Several of these so-called 1.5 °C carbon budget scenarios based on low chances of success (e.g. 50% or 66%) have been published (see Hausfather 2018). Even some of the relatively unambitious scenarios show that based on current emissions of around 36 billion tonnes per year, such a budget will be blown in about 4 years. Other recent studies indicate a 1.5 °C budget may already be blown (Rogelj et al. 2018). Given that emissions are still increasing—in 2017 they increased approximately 1.4% over 2016—any carbon budget is shrinking at pace; and again, if a higher probability of success is aimed for there is no carbon budget left. This has led climate commentator David Spratt (2014), with good reason, to talk of the 'myth' of burnable carbon. It has even led some climate scientists (e.g. Peters 2018; Geden 2018) to question the use of carbon budgets, given that the variety of possible formulations is distracting the world from seriously beginning the task of deep decarbonisation.

The Moral Hazard of Possible Technological Solutions

Another critical question concerns what assumptions should be made about the role of CCS and NETs in mitigating climate change. CCS involves capturing carbon dioxide produced in coal or gas power stations and burying it underground; NETs include things like planting up large areas of land with carbon-sequestering trees and plants; seaweed and algal farming; biochar; and ocean fertilisation. Some NETs can even be combined in an approach called 'biomass energy carbon capture and storage' (BECCS), which involves planting carbon-sequestering trees and eventually burning the wood to produce electricity while capturing and storing the emissions.

The more carbon that is captured or sequestered, the more fossil fuels the world can burn—and vice versa. The worrying aspect of this parameter lies in the fact that currently CCS is not commercially viable and the NETs tend to be unproven, expensive, slow to implement, not currently deployable at the scale needed, and have implications for competing land uses, such as food production and biodiversity. So inherently uncertain assumptions must be made about the future viability, feasibility, or even desirability of these strategies. Put otherwise, decision-makers must make value-laden judgements about how much we are prepared to gamble on mitigation strategies that presently are highly uncertain, speculative, or high risk.

It seems we are gambling wildly. Of the 116 2 °C scenarios included in the IPCC Fifth Assessment Report (AR5), 101 of them involve sucking vast amounts of carbon out of the atmosphere, chiefly via BECCS (Vaughan and Gough 2016). It is estimated that this scale of 'negative emissions' would require land between one and three times the size of India, and as much water as is currently used for global agriculture (Anderson 2015b). As of early 2018, no national climate policy mentions BECCS. There is currently one working project in the world, a relatively small, repurposed corn ethanol plant in Decatur, Illinois. Worryingly, it seems that international political discourse on climate has come to rely on a technology that is theoretically coherent but at present is for all practical purposes non-existent. This was not mentioned in the Paris Agreement.

Climate scientists Kevin Anderson (based at the Tyndall Centre for Climate Research) and Glen Peters (based at the Centre for International Climate and Energy Policy) call CCS and NETs an 'unjust and high-stakes gamble' and 'a moral hazard' (Anderson and Peters 2016) because such mitigation strategies are a way of deferring stronger decarbonisation, on the dubious assumption that vast amounts of carbon can be captured and sequestered in the future. Again, the hope is that the more carbon that can be captured or sequestered, the less pressure there is to reduce fossil fuel use. This is a nice prospect in theory, but unfortunately it is just the latest means of gambling with the climate, delaying stronger decarbonisation. Efforts to quantify future potential for carbon dioxide absorption by forests and reduction by CCS are subject to irreducible uncertainty and hence must be regarded as speculative. They may be politically attractive, but reliance on them cannot claim scientific legitimacy.

And what if it turns out CCS never becomes a viable technology? In 2017 one of the few CCS pilot projects shut down as budget estimates blew out. What if land, food, or water pressures, or forest fires, mean assumed carbon planting never eventuates or never succeeds at the scale necessary? These are very real possibilities, but if we act today as if CCS and NETs will be successful and they end up failing, then the carbon budget for a safe climate will be blown, perhaps catastrophically, meaning even more challenging (probably unrealisable) decarbonisation strategies will be required.

Anderson and others make a compelling case that it would be better to assume that CCS and NETs will not scale up significantly, and act on that basis. If it turns out some such technologies can scale up, then all the better. Mainstream analyses, however, do not proceed on that basis because it would shrink the available carbon budget so drastically that mitigation strategies would clearly be incompatible with the dominant economic growth paradigm. Essentially all mainstream pathways for atmospheric carbon mitigation, including those based on the IPCC assessments, make extremely bold assumptions about CCS and NETs, in the tortured hope that world economies can grow themselves out of the climate problem. That the economics of growth might be causing this problem seems unthinkable, or at least, unspeakable.

The Politics and Economics of Deep Decarbonisation

Although the science underpinning carbon budget analysis is increasingly robust, most scientists, politicians, economists, and the broader public, have been slow to recognise the radical socio-economic and political implications. Suppose, for example, that the world settled on a carbon budget that was framed by a relatively unambitious carbon goal, based on a 50% chance of keeping temperature rise under 2 °C. Suppose further that the models assume that emissions in the developing nations somehow manage to peak in 2025 and decline thereafter at an unprecedented rate of 7% p.a. Based on these assumptions—which, it should be noted, are extremely favourable to most 'developed' economies—Kevin Anderson and Alice Bows (2011) have shown that those developed nations would need to decarbonise at 8–10% p.a. in order to keep within their available carbon budget. Note further that those figures were published in 2011, and since then the world has been emitting about 36 billion tonnes of carbon dioxide each year, meaning that today the decarbonisation rates would be steeper still.

Even prominent climate economists such as Nicholas Stern (2006) argue that economic growth in terms of GDP is incompatible with decarbonisation rates over 3 or 4% p.a., and let us not forget that despite the movement towards renewable energy technologies, global emissions continue to rise, not fall. Accordingly, efficiency alone cannot be expected to achieve sufficient decarbonisation, and renewables or nuclear (discussed in the next chapter) cannot be scaled up fast enough. As a consequence, emission reductions of 8–10% must be supplemented by significantly reduced demand for energy services dependent on fossil fuels. The close connection between energy use and economic growth means that significantly reduced energy services will result in less physical production and consumption (Ayres and Warr 2009; Anderson 2013). That is precisely the conclusion mainstream analysts and politicians are desperate to avoid. But that is the implication of even unambitious carbon budget analyses.

Here is the most challenging aspect of these calculations. The above carbon budget analysis—based on merely a 50% chance of avoiding a 2 °C temperature rise above pre-industrial levels—is no longer in line even with mainstream political and economic rhetoric. If, for example, humanity aimed for a 50% chance of avoiding a 1.5 °C rise, or a 66 or 80% chance of avoiding a 1.5 °C, then obviously the decarbonisation rates outlined above would not be 8–10% p.a. but far higher, requiring even deeper demand reductions and making continuous economic growth even less compatible with a safe climate. And if we were to ask whether capitalism would (or even could) give up growth to avoid climate catastrophe, we need only look at the world today to find our answer. Within the current system, growth is beyond question.

A Just Transition to a Post-carbon Suburbia Implies Energy Descent

The implications of all this are clear but radical: if the world is serious about keeping within a carbon budget for a safe climate, the rich nations must not just vastly increase the energy efficiency of each unit of economic output, but simply extract and consume far less energy. Achieving a safe climate therefore means accepting the inevitability of energy descent within energy-intensive societies and working within such conditions even before energy descent is imposed upon us from fossil energy depletion. We must voluntarily embrace peak oil at once! This means initiating a swift transition to a post-petroleum world, but that of course is an utterly transformative agenda in a world addicted to oil. And the distributive implications must never be lost sight of: if the most energy-intensive forms of human existence are found in the suburbs of the wealthiest nations, then elementary moral reasoning dictates that it is there where the first and deepest energy reductions should be made. This social justice imperative, in itself, is a very compelling argument for the embrace of energy descent in carbon suburbia and the development of a new political economy of energy.

Given how central energy and materials are to economic growth, it seems the only coherent response to peak oil, the climate crisis, and social justice imperatives, is for the wealthiest nations to develop modes of economy that do not depend on economic growth, which implies transcending capitalism and embracing degrowth. That is the premise of this book, and if it seems that we have laboured energy analysis (given that this is a book about the suburbs), it is only because the prospect of energy descent finds no place within mainstream energy and economic analysis, to say nothing of urban theory. Nonetheless, critical reason demands that we commit to fashioning an equitable post-carbon suburbia, and that necessitates a depreciation of the increasingly lethal rhetoric of growth.

References

Ahmed, Nafeez. 2017. *Failing States, Collapsing Systems: Biophysical Triggers of Political Violence.* New York: Springer.

Alexander, Samuel, and Josh Floyd. 2018. *Carbon Civilisation and the Energy Descent Future.* Melbourne: Simplicity Institute.

Anderson, Kevin. 2013. Avoiding Climate Change Demands De-growth Strategies. https://kevinanderson.info/blog/avoiding-dangerous-climate-change-demands-de-growth-strategies-from-wealthier-nations/. Accessed 1 Mar 2017.

———. 2015a. Duality in Climate Science. *Nature Geoscience* 8: 898–900.

———. 2015b. Talks in the City of Light Generate More Heat. *Nature* 528: 437.

Anderson, Kevin, and Alice Bows. 2011. Beyond 'Dangerous' Climate Change: Emission Scenarios for a New World. *Philosophical Transactions of the Royal Society* 369: 2–44.

Anderson, Kevin, and Glen Peters. 2016. The Trouble with Negative Emissions. *Science* 354 (6309): 182–183.

Ayres, Robert, and Benjamin Warr. 2009. *The Economic Growth Engine: How Energy and Work Drive Material Prosperity.* Cheltenham, UK: Edward Elgar.

Beck, Ulrich. 2009. *World at Risk.* Cambridge: Polity.

BP. 2017. BP Statistical Review of World Energy 2017. https://www.bp.com/content/dam/bp/en/corporate/pdf/energy-economics/statistical-review-2017/bp-statistical-review-of-world-energy-2017-full-report.pdf. Accessed 28 Feb 2018.

Brecha, Robert. 2013. Ten Reasons to Take Peak Oil Seriously. *Sustainability* 5 (2): 664–694.

Carbon Tracker Initiative and Grantham Research Institute. 2013. Unburnable Carbon 2013: Wasted Capital and Stranded Assets. http://carbontracker.live.kiln.digital/Unburnable-Carbon-2-Web-Version.pdf. Accessed 1 Mar 2018.

Chapman, Ian. 2014. The End of Peak Oil? Why This Topic Is Still Relevant Despite Recent Denials. *Energy Policy* 64: 93–101.

Ekanayake, Primal, Patrick Moriarty, and Damon Honnery. 2015. Equity and Energy in Global Solutions to Climate Change. *Energy for Sustainable Development* 26: 72–78.

Friedrichs, Jorg. 2013. *The Future Is Not What It Used to Be: Climate Change and Energy Scarcity.* Cambridge, MA: MIT Press.

Fustier, Kim, Gordon Gray, Christoffer Gundersen, and Thomas Hilboldt. 2016. Global Oil Supply: Will Mature Field Declines Drive the Next Supply Crunch? *HSBC Global Research Report*, September. https://drive.google.com/file/d/0B9wSgViWVAfzUEgzMlBfR3UxNDg/view. Accessed 1 Mar 2018.

Gardiner, Stephen M. 2011. *The Perfect Moral Storm: The Ethical Tragedy of Climate Change*. Oxford: Oxford University Press.

Geden, Olliver. 2018. Politically Informed Advice for Climate Action. *Nature Geoscience*. https://doi.org/10.1038/s41561-018-0143-3.

Greene, Gregory. 2004. The End of Suburbia: Oil Depletion and the Collapse of the American Dream. Documentary. Produced by the Electric Wallpaper Company.

Hamilton, Clive. 2017. *Defiant Earth: The Fate of Humans in the Anthropocene*. Crows Nest: Allen and Unwin.

Hausfather, Zeke. 2018. How Much 'Carbon Budget' Is Left to Limit Global Warming to 1.5C? *Ecologise*, April 18. https://www.ecologise.in/2018/04/18/how-much-carbon-budget-is-left-to-limit-global-warming-to-1-5c/. Accessed 20 June 2018.

Heinberg, Richard. 2004. *Powerdown: Options and Actions for a Post-carbon World*. Gabriola Island: New Society Publishers.

———. 2011. *The End of Growth: Adapting to Our New Economic Reality*. Gabriola Island. New Society Publishers.

Heinberg, Richard, and David Fridley. 2016. *Our Renewable Future: Laying the Path for One Hundred Percent Clean Energy*. Washington: Island Press.

Homer-Dixon, Thomas. 2006. *The Upside of Down: Catastrophe, Creativity, and the Renewal of Civilisation*. Washington: Island Press.

Huber, Mathew. 2017. Petrocapitalism. In *The International Encyclopedia of Geography*, ed. Douglas Richardson, Noel Castree, Michael Goodchild, Audrey Kobayashi, Weidong Liu, and Richard Marston. Hoboken: Wiley.

Hughes, David J. 2018. Shale Reality Check. *Drilling into the US Government's Rosy Projections for Shale Gas and Tight Oil Production Through 2050*. Post Carbon Institute. http://www.postcarbon.org/publications/shale-reality-check/. Accessed 20 June 2018.

Illich, Ivan. 1974. *Energy and Equity*. New York: Harper and Row.

International Energy Agency (IEA). 2017. World Energy Outlook 2017. https://www.iea.org/weo2017/. Accessed 1 Mar 2018.

———. 2018. Global Energy and CO2 Status Report 2017. http://www.iea.org/publications/freepublications/publication/GECO2017.pdf. Accessed 20 June 2018.

Kunstler, James. 2005. *The Long Emergency: Surviving the Converging Catastrophes of the Twenty-First Century.* New York: Grove/Atlantic.

Lovins, Amory. 2011. *Reinventing Fire: Bold Business Solutions for the New Energy Era.* White River Junction: Chelsea Green.

Mohr, Steve, Jianliang Wang, Gary Ellem, James Ward, and Damien Guiurco. 2015. Projection of World Fossil Fuels by Country. *Fuel* 141: 120–135.

Montgomery, Justin, and Francis O'Sullivan. 2017. Spatial Variability of Tight Oil Well Productivity and the Impact of Technology. *Applied Energy* 195: 344–355.

Moriarty, Patrick, and Damon Honnery. 2011. *Rise and Fall of the Carbon Civilisation: Resolving Global Environmental and Resource Problems.* London: Springer.

———. 2016. Can Renewable Energy Power the Future? *Energy Policy* 93: 3–7.

Murphy, David. 2013. The Implications of the Declining Energy Return on Investment of Oil Production. *Philosophical Transitions of the Royal Society A.* https://doi.org/10.1098/rsta.2013.0126.

Odum, Howard, and Elizabeth Odum. 2001. *A Prosperous Way Down: Principles and Policies.* Colorado: University of Colorado Press.

Peters, Glen. 2018. Beyond Carbon Budgets. *Nature Geoscience.* https://doi.org/10.1038/s41561-018-0142-4.

Purdey, Stephen. 2010. *Economic Growth, the Environment, and International Relations: The Growth Paradigm.* New York: Routledge.

Rogelj, Joeri, Gunnar Luderer, Robert Pietzcker, Elmar Kriegler, Michiel Schaeffer, Volker Krey, and Keywan Riahi. 2015. Energy System Transformations for Limiting End-of-Century Warming to Below 1.5C. *Nature Climate Change* 5: 519–526.

Rogeli, Joeri, Alexander Propp, Katherine Calvin, Gunnar Ludererer, Johannes Emmerling, et al. 2018. Scenarios Toward Limiting Global Mean Temperature Increases Below 1.5C. *Nature Climate Change* 8: 325–332.

Smil, Vaclav. 2010. *Energy Transitions: History, Requirements, and Prospects.* Santa Barbara: Prager Publishers.

———. 2015. *Power Density: Key to Understanding Energy Sources and Uses.* Cambridge: MIT Press.

———. 2017. *Energy in Civilization: A History.* Cambridge: MIT Press.

Spratt, David. 2014. The Real Budgetary Emergency and the Myth of 'Burnable Carbon'. *Climate Code Red,* May 22. http://www.climatecodered.

org/2014/05/the-real-budgetary-emergency-burnable.html. Accessed 1 Mar 2018.

———. 2016. Unravelling the Myth of a 'Carbon Budget' for 1.5C. http://www.climatecodered.org/2016/09/unravelling-myth-of-carbon-budget-for.html. Accessed 1 Mar 2018.

Spratt, David, and Ian Dunlop. 2017. *What Lies Beneath: The Scientific Understatement of Climate Risks*. Breakthrough Institute. https://docs.wixstatic.com/ugd/148cb0_56b252a7d78b485badde2fadcba88d00.pdf. Accessed 1 Mar 2018.

Steffan, Will, Katherine Richardson, Johan Rockström, Sarah E. Cornell, Ingo Fetzer, Elena M. Bennett, Reinette Biggs, Stephen R. Carpenter, Wim de Vries, Cynthia A. De Wit, Carl Folke, Dieter Gerten, Jens Heinke, Georgina M. Mace, Linn M. Perrson, Veerabhadran Ramanathan, Belinda Reyers, and Sverker Sörlin. 2015. Planetary Boundaries: Guiding Human Development on a Changing Planet. *Science* 347 (6223). https://doi.org/10.1126/science.1259855.

Stern, Nicholas. 2006. *Stern Review on the Economics of Climate Change*. Cambridge, UK: Her Majesty's Treasury; Cambridge: Cambridge University Press.

Tainter, Joseph. 1988. *The Collapse of Complex Societies*. New York: Cambridge University of Press.

Thompson, Helen. 2017. *Oil and the Western Economic Crisis*. London: Palgrave Macmillan.

Vaughan, Naomi, and Claire Gough. 2016. Expert Assessment Concludes Negative Emissions Scenarios May Not Deliver. *Environmental Research Letters* 11 (9): 095003. https://doi.org/10.1088/1748-9326/11/9/095003.

3

Light Green Illusions and the 'Blind Field' of Techno-optimism

Temples were amongst the earliest form of built environment, pointing to the fact that religion, faith and superstition have always played a defining role shaping the urban landscape, both physically and culturally. Even today, at the centre of most towns and cities, one almost always finds a temple or church of some denomination, where people throughout history have gathered in search of metaphysical consolation or guidance. Like religion but in different ways, technology has also shaped and continues to shape the nature and development of towns and cities—the way we build; how we transport ourselves and our goods; the products and services that can be provided; how we entertain ourselves and communicate, etc. These things are all a function of the state of technological development, and together our technologies, as well as the cultural practices they both engender and reflect, help weave the fabric of urban life. In short, human beings are historically embedded creatures of faith and technology—but increasingly, it seems, we have become urban creatures whose faith *is* technology.

While faith in traditional religions may be on the wane in many places, secular alternatives are arguably on the rise. A new religiosity has emerged in the form of neoclassical economics, with its evangelists

© The Author(s) 2019
S. Alexander and B. Gleeson, *Degrowth in the Suburbs*,
https://doi.org/10.1007/978-981-13-2131-3_3

providing structure and purpose to our increasingly globalised economic order. Politicians across the globe are dedicated parishioners, and the broader congregation of citizenries fall quietly (or at least helplessly) in line. 'God's away on business', as poet-musician Tom Waits would assert. Nevertheless, despite what many feel as God's absence, redemption is still offered to us through technology, which promises to cure all social and environmental ills, including the energy crises reviewed in the previous chapter.

Consoling though it might seem, this attitude towards technology functions to deflect attention away from any need to rethink the ecocidal economics of growth or the high-impact consumerist modes of production and consumption that are causing contemporary ills, leaving us hacking at the branches of our troubles when we should be aiming for the roots. But it seems that it is too confronting to question such fundamentals. Instead, supreme faith is invested in technologists, architects, and designers—our saviours—who we trust will be able to resolve all problems through innovation without us having to change much in the way we live our lives or inhabit our cities. It is all extremely convenient and non-confronting. Too good to be true, one might say.

So deeply entrenched as to be invisible, this techno-optimistic worldview creates what Henri Lefebvre (2003 [1970]: 23) would call a 'blind field' in our vision of future possibilities. It is a paradigm that conceals more than it reveals, privileging technological solutions to contemporary problems while marginalising or obscuring other modes of action or response (Huesemann and Huesemann 2011). This blind field can even set humanity off in the wrong direction, by hiding alternative paths and posing the wrong questions, suggesting that perhaps truth today may come in the form of new questions, rather than new answers to old questions.

The faith of techno-optimism is neatly summed up by eco-modernists Ted Nordhaus and Michael Schellenberger (2012: n.p.) when they write: 'The solution to the unintended consequences of modernity is, and has always been, more modernity—just as the solution to the unintended consequences of our technologies has always been more technology'. Wrapped in the language of modernity and technological advancement, Nordhaus and Schellenberger in fact express old answers to old questions, reflecting an out-dated zeitgeist that we wish to unsettle.

To question humanity's relationship to technology, however, is not to be anti-technology, regressive, or primitive, but rather to be *for* 'appropriate technology' or what Ivan Illich called 'convivial technology'—a term he used to designate the embrace of 'responsibly limited tools', consciously selected for the mutual advancement of human and ecological flourishing (Illich 2009 [1973]: xii). We share his concern that, left unchecked, the current trajectory of technological modernisation, given form by the demands of profit-maximisation under capitalism, will 'carry us past the last turnoff from a hyperindustrial Armageddon' (Illich 1974: 8). That turnoff approaches, if it has not already passed. When we read that in the last forty years alone the populations of invertebrate species on the planet have declined by half (Carrington 2014), talk of 'the Sixth Great Extinction' seems more justified by the day (Kolbert 2014).

Of course, there are good reasons to place considerable trust in scientists and engineers. Through the advancement of science and technology, human beings have been able to produce electricity, cure diseases, split the atom, travel into space, invent computers and the internet, and map the human genome, amongst an unending list of things that often seem like miracles. Notably, these scientific and technological advancements have also assisted in the unprecedented expansion of our productive capacities, primarily through harnessing the energy in fossil fuels and developing machines to augment human labour. This has allowed many people, primarily in the rich nations, to achieve lifestyles of material comfort or even abundance that would have been unimaginable even a few generations ago. Increasingly all seven-and-a-half billion people on the planet seem set on achieving these high-consumption lifestyles for themselves, and at first consideration the universalisation of affluence seems a coherent and plausible pathway of progress. Indeed, from the perspective of those living destitute and crowded lives in the slums of the Third World, the suburban way of life would justly seem to be a highly attractive model of the good life.

But all that glitters is not gold. No matter how awesome the advancement of science and technology has been as a means of raising material

living standards, there are also well-known social and environmental dark sides that flow from this mode of development. Urbanisation
depends on the natural environment for resources, well beyond its
physical footprint, siphoning resources from the global periphery into
the urban and suburban centres. As economies and populations have
expanded, especially since the industrial revolution, more pressure has
been placed on Earth's finite resources, ecosystems, and waste sinks.
Today, we face a series of overlapping social and ecological crises owing
to the heavy burden our energy and resource hungry cities are placing
on the planet, in ways and to an extent it is presently unnecessary to
review. It quickly gets too depressing to digest. And yet, technology has
given us powers that our species needs to develop the wisdom to wield.

Optimists believe, however, that just as technology may have been a
significant driver of environmental problems historically and today, so
too does it provide the primary solution. From this view, humanity will
be able to solve environmental problems primarily through technological advancement and better design, while continuing to focus attention
on economic growth. Prices and market mechanisms will facilitate this
process by providing the right incentives and allocating resources efficiently. By implementing this 'green growth' approach—both to economies in general and cities in particular—it is widely believed humanity
will be able to eliminate global poverty and raise living standards for all
(including, or especially, the richest), without destroying the necessary
ecosystem services that sustain life as we know it.

In its most extreme form, this faith in the ability of human beings to
control nature has led to some in the eco-modernist school to talk of
the 'good, or even great, Anthropocene' (Breakthrough Institute 2015:
6). Just as our godly powers have allowed us to destabilise the climate,
deforest the planet, and decimate biodiversity as the urban age took
hold, this school of thought assumes that only more technology and
more capitalism will allow us to bend nature to our own purposes. The
lack of species self-awareness astounds. The human imagination is man-
ifestly capable of more creative responses than this.

Nevertheless, there can be no doubt that the promise of technology is
seductive—material abundance for all through economic growth, while
solving environmental problems. But is this promise credible? If not,

what are the implications, especially for the suburban dream? If there are limits to technological salvation, does that imply a suburban dystopia awaits? Or might this be a false dualism, obscuring alternative pathways into the future?

In this chapter, we continue excavating the foundations of carbon suburbia by critically examining the techno-optimism upon which it rests. We have seen that fossil energy depletion, climate mitigation, and distributive justice, all present radical challenges to the future viability of suburbia as we know it, but the techno-optimism that pervades our age is quick to offer non-confronting technological solutions to these challenges. According to this line of reasoning, if fossil fuels are causing problems then the suburban way of life we know today can still survive, provided that 'green energy' comes to replace the fossil energy foundations of the economy.

The same attitude shapes thinking about urban and suburban mobility: if the internal combustion engine—the definitive enabling mechanism for suburbia—is causing problems, then we do not need to give up the private motor vehicle or the way of life it enables, we just need to drive electric cars. This chapter examines the plausibility of these technological solutions to current crises and concludes that today's optimism is dangerously misguided. In doing so we begin exploring a view of suburbia's future that currently sits behind the blind field of techno-optimism, in the hope of highlighting alternative and more plausible future scenarios (of energy descent) that are currently obscured by faith in machines. While it is too late to allow ourselves to be immobilised by despair, we argue that it is also too late to be a techno-optimist. Instead, we seek to carve out and inhabit a space between glitter and doom.

Losing faith in techno-optimism, therefore, is not a cause for despair—it just implies that responding adequately to current crises means rethinking the nature of the underlying cultures of consumption and the macroeconomics of growth which currently shape (and are shaped by) suburbia. We should not assume that doing so implies some sort of 'regression'. This is not an attack on science, progress, or innovation. We subscribe to all three values. But it will require exposing some light green illusions about what a sustainability transition might involve, and rethinking what 'progress' might mean in an age when the perfect storm of ecological and social crises gathering on the horizon means that the future does not look how it used to look. These issues will need some unpacking.

Nuclear Energy: Limited Potential as Carbon Mitigation Technology

We turn first to consider whether or to what extent alternative energy sources can solve the overlapping energy challenges reviewed in the previous chapter. While we are, as noted, wholly in favour of transcending fossil fuels and initiating a swift decarbonisation of current modes of economy, we now offer a critical assessment of the potential of various alternative energy sources to fully replace the vast energy foundations of carbon civilisation with 'green energy'. This contradicts the widely held techno-optimism that shapes thinking about energy futures today, even amongst most environmentalists. We begin with a very brief consideration of nuclear power before moving on to renewable energy technologies. We conclude by outlining some key implications of our analysis, both economically and in terms of the future of urban and suburban landscapes, issues that we develop in more detail in later chapters.

One way to think about whether nuclear energy could or should be the primary means of replacing fossil energy is to consider how many nuclear power plants would be needed to do this. American Physicist Joshua Pearce (2008) did the calculations and concluded that to meet global energy demand in 2004 via electricity, the world would need approximately 14,500 nuclear power plants of 1 GW capacity. To meet anticipated energy demand in 2050, the world would need to build 26,000. To put those figures in context, currently (as of early 2018) the world has 449 nuclear power plants, with only 60 new ones under construction. Furthermore, a huge number of existing nuclear plants are due for decommissioning in coming years.

While technology will continue to improve, the sheer scale of the nuclear rollout nevertheless points to its greatest challenge: the seemingly impossible timeline it faces as a climate mitigation technology. Given that it generally takes 10 years or more to get approval and build a single nuclear power plant, rollout rates that would make a globally material difference on the climate front stretch the limits of plausibility. Any significant scale up might also soon face a crisis of expertise, which could further increase the chance of accidents. In any case, since Fukushima, global enthusiasm for nuclear, which was already quite weak, has waned further, suggesting a nuclear renaissance should not be relied on, especially as renewables continue their advance.

As well as these barriers and concerns, Australian energy analyst Joshua Floyd (2017: n.p.) explains that:

> expansion of currently commercial nuclear technology appears hamstrung by crippling capital costs, calling the economics into question at time when the costs of renewables are unambiguously on the decline. Generation IV 'intrinsically safe' reactors that greatly reduce waste concerns and massively expand the scope of current fuel reserves look promising on paper, but significant R&D remains, with the most advanced efforts at pilot stage only. Practical fusion power continues to be at best a theoretical possibility many decades in the future, despite many billions of dollars of past and ongoing investment.

On balance, then, it is our non-dogmatic view that nuclear energy is going to play a continuing role in global energy systems for decades ahead, but we see its role as most likely being limited to a minor fraction of total final energy supply. It will probably continue its relatively flat levels of electricity production, perhaps increasing its significance in some nations, but quite plausibly declining in overall capacity in coming years as old generators are decommissioned faster than new generators come online. Given that any serious climate response means decarbonising the global economy over the next couple of decades or less, the pressing timeline for a nuclear rollout seems too tight for this technology to be relied on to a much more significant extent, given how long it takes bring a single power plant online.

Can Renewable Energy Fully Replace Fossil Fuels?

The limitations of nuclear point towards futures in which powering human societies almost entirely with renewable sources appears to be our present best bet. In overall energy terms, it looks like wind and solar photovoltaic (PV) will need to do most of the heavy lifting. Questions of whether it's *feasible* to power human societies in this way then naturally come to the fore.

There's a rich irony here: it's of course *absolutely* established that 100% renewably powered societies are feasible, by the simple fact of viable non-industrial human ways of life over the vast majority of our species' existence. A great diversity of distinct human social forms demonstrates the adequacy of energy flows from the sun for successful functioning. But renewable energy feasibility research overwhelmingly has a narrower focus. In essence, it asks whether currently commercial and close-to-market renewable energy conversion technologies can support industrial, growth-orientated societies and economies functionally equivalent to those in place today.

In response to this question we hear a lot about the polarised perspectives holding that current renewable technologies *absolutely can* or *absolutely cannot* provide the scope and scale of energy services currently provided by fossil fuels. There is a broad middle ground though that tends to have a lower public profile. These are the many serious and highly informed investigators who support the transition to renewable energy to whatever extent is possible, and who at the same time regard the nature of future energy systems—and often, the forms of economy and society that they enable—to be uncertain.

Many in this middle ground share a commitment to thinking critically about the roles and prospects for renewable energy conversion technologies (McKay 2009). Thinking critically is not the same as being a 'renewable critic' or 'anti-renewables'. It involves carefully considering the contexts and foundations for knowledge claims, and questioning assumptions. We hope that the following critical inquiry into the potential and limitations of renewable energy is received in that spirit—as seeking to deepen the understanding of an area that is presently, and for some time may remain, highly uncertain.

This echoes our approach to suburbia and in fact informs it. Just as we reflect critically on the renewable energy technologies we ultimately support, so too do we position ourselves as critical urbanists, whose approach should not be interpreted simplistically as being 'anti-sub-urbs'. Again, we are motivated to think critically about the suburbs due to their latent capacity to be transformed into something more compatible with social and ecological wellbeing, but that first means getting to grips with the fundamental energy systems and flows that would underpin and shape such a transformation. We are of the view that currently the energy analyses shaping contemporary urban theory are often unconsciously shaped by overly optimistic assumptions about the feasibility of replacing fossil energy supplies with renewable energy flows. If societies cannot simply 'green' the supply of energy but must significantly reduce overall demand, then it follows that thinking about suburban futures may need to head in radically new directions.

Renewable Energy: The Potential and Limitations

The first point we make is abstract but critically important. When people question the viability of fully replacing fossil fuels with renewable energy, one often hears in response that *of course* it is possible. After all, humans already know how to convert the sun's energy into electricity, and merely one hour of sunlight striking the Earth provides energy equivalent to a year's worth of human use. The sheer scale of solar energy's *theoretical potential* is so vast that most renewable advocates seem to assume that transitioning the global economy to renewables *must* therefore be perfectly feasible.

But this assumption blinds many people to the range of practical obstacles that will greatly limit the *practically realisable potential* of renewables (Smil 2010). Granted, we already have the technical capacity to generate electricity via wind turbines, solar panels, biofuels, etc., but the proportion of this that can be realised in practice, once a wide range of geographical, engineering, environmental, economic and socio-political factors are considered, is far less certain (Moriarty and Honnery 2016). Theoretical potential is not enough to change the world's energy systems.

One only needs to consider the limited progress to date, which is often overlooked in the flurries of techno-optimism. In December 2017, the International Energy Agency (IEA 2017a) reported that solar, wind and geothermal energy together constituted merely 1.5% of global final energy supply. This tiny fraction is no cause for despair, but it calls on us to be brutally honest about the challenges of a 100% renewable energy transition and how slowly we are moving down that path. After all, it has been thirty years since the IPCC was established!

What this suggests is that we need to remove the rose-coloured glasses of techno-optimism—we need to look behind and beyond the blind field—and that means increased knowledge humility as well as thinking more critically about the challenges of converting our fossil energy systems into renewable energy systems (Heinberg and Fridley 2016). When a report concludes that a 100% renewable energy transition is technically feasible and economically affordable, the wide range of assumptions upon which the conclusion rests are typically overlooked or unstated—assumptions that are sometimes or often highly questionable, uncertain, or speculative. The media quickly celebrate the optimistic results, usually uncritically—as do many environmentally conscious energy experts. But if any one of those assumptions turns out to be flawed, the conclusion is called into question. If many or all the assumptions are dubious or unverifiable, then the uncertainty or implausibility of the conclusion compounds.

Indeed, when serious critics have examined the high-level models that claim 100% renewable energy is technically feasible and economically affordable, it seems that there are so many uncertainties and questionable assumptions informing the models that they often lack the scientific legitimacy they claim. Peer-reviewed analyses sit on both sides of this contested debate (see e.g. Jacobson et al. 2015; Clack et al. 2017). But environmentalists generally do not want to hear this, and in an age of Twitter the time and effort required to unpack highly complex feasibility studies seems too much. The quality of public debate is poor. Justifiably opposed to fossil fuels and cautious about or opposed to nuclear, the green movement (broadly speaking) is quick to believe what it wants to believe, and a central tenant of mainstream environmentalism today is an almost religious faith in the ability of renewable energy to resolve looming climate and oil crises without interfering with economic growth and high-consumption lifestyles. This position was restated in 2015 by Stephen Hatfield-Dodds, Chief Scientist at Australia's CSIRO, who insists that climate change can be solved without rejecting consumerist social values or economic growth (Hatfield-Dodds 2015). Around the world green politics exemplifies this contradiction starkly.

When the prospects of a 100% renewable energy transition are discussed, the first objection that is typically raised concerns the fact that the electricity supply provided by PV and wind is intermittent. That is, PV panels only produce electricity when the sun is shining; wind turbines only spin when the wind is blowing. On a calm night, therefore, renewable energy infrastructure reliant on these sources alone will generate little or no electricity. But of course, in today's industrial societies, demand for electricity will remain, irrespective of weather conditions. With fossil fuels, there is no problem in this regard, because coal or gas sit waiting to be burned as demand fluctuates, no matter the weather. But imagine a winter night when the wind is not blowing, in a society that doesn't use fossil fuels. People come home from work at 6 p.m., turn on the lights, television, and heater, have a shower, bath the children, cook dinner, put on some washing, etc. Energy demand across society can peak at a time when solar is producing absolutely nothing, and if the wind isn't blowing, where is the energy supply coming from?

Sometimes the response is to note that the sun is always shining *somewhere* or the wind is always blowing *somewhere*, so all we need is to distribute renewable electricity generation capacity sufficiently widely and then transmit that electricity to where it is needed. For example, Europe could just import electricity from the Sahara, as the Desertec project envisions. But to the extent that wider distribution of generating assets can increase supply reliability to a sufficient level (which is highly questionable), this has two major drawbacks: first, transmitting electricity long distances increases losses (reducing overall system efficiency and increasing costs); and secondly, and more significantly, this strategy requires replicating generation and transmission capacity across multiple regions (also increasing costs). Sourcing energy, whether via electricity or fuels, from distant regions also reduces resilience, as a community or city has less control of its essential energy services, especially if the energy is coming from politically unstable regions (Ahmed 2017).

A further response to the intermittency challenge is simply to note that batteries, pumped hydro plants, or hydrogen, can store energy, which can be used later, when needed. That is, we can produce surplus energy when the sun is shining and the wind is blowing, store it, and use that surplus to meet demand when it exceeds primary generation. This is technically feasible of course, but it significantly increases costs, even taking into account the continuing developments in battery technology and manufacturing. As a crude indicator, just call around and inquire how much it would cost for your household to go completely off-grid for energy, including disconnecting from fossil gas, while also having the capacity to charge an electric car (or two). Similarly, imagine that same call was made by a factory owner producing electric cars, who was hoping to take the factory off-grid. One would discover that transitioning a household to be entirely self-sufficient in meeting energy needs from renewable sources is one thing, quite challenging enough; transitioning the means of production to 100% renewable energy sourced in the vicinity of the points of use is another challenge altogether.

The issue here simply concerns the sheer scale of the storage challenge: we are talking about storing energy for periods of days or even weeks, for entire regions or countries. Suppose there is a calm, cold, and cloudy month in winter, when renewable generation is at a minimum while demand is high. This extended period of bad weather might only happen once every few years, but since industrial societies in their current forms are reliant on electricity supply being available on demand, 24/7, running such a society with 100% renewable electricity would need sufficient storage to cover the occasional long period of calm and overcast weather. Vast expenditure is required merely to cover weather events that might happen very rarely. That said, battery storage will be part of a post-carbon (energy descent) future, even if its primary function may be to assist stabilising the grid rather than enabling widespread disconnection.

But now we arrive at what is perhaps the biggest obstacle in the way of a 100% renewable energy transition within a growth economy. Even if it is possible to convert existing *electricity* supply to renewable energy, what must be recognised is that electricity is only about 18% of global final energy supply (IEA 2017a). If the challenge of meeting base load and peak load electricity is difficult and expensive even when this is merely 18% of global final energy demand, imagine the magnitude of the challenge if the other 82% of demand (especially that portion currently met via oil) is converted to electricity. Oil analyst Robert Hirsch and his colleagues are right to describe the challenge of peak oil mitigation as first and foremost being a liquid fuels transportation challenge (Hirsch et al. 2010). The climate challenge is similar: how can a globalised industrial economy continue without oil?

It is of course theoretically conceivable that today's oil-dependent global transport systems come to run on electricity or biofuels instead of petroleum products, and that other key oil-intensive tasks, like mining and agriculture, do the same. And it is theoretically conceivable that such a society also builds such vast energy storage systems that it can still meet energy demand over a few weeks of overcast and calm weather when the renewable energy infrastructure is barely producing. But again, theoretical potential and practically realisable potential are two very different things.

This points to the fact that the real challenge of creating a post-carbon society is how to solve the liquid fuels problem—that is, how to stop consuming 96 million barrels of oil every day, without globally integrated transport systems grinding to a halt (Friedmann 2016). Running the extensive global mining operations solely or mostly on renewable electricity seems similarly implausible, as does any hope of electrifying a global fleet of heavy cargo trucks or transitioning to 100% biofuel aeroplanes in any credible timeframe. Biofuels seem destined to play a minor role only in solving the liquid fuels crisis (Murphy 2013), particularly due to their low EROI and the fact that they compete with food production. There is likely to be a place for liquid biofuels in a post-carbon society, but that role is likely to be very limited.

There is a further disconcerting problem underlying such a renewable energy transition that most advocates do not like to acknowledge: currently the production of renewable energy technologies are inextricably dependent on the fossil fuels they are trying to replace. Yet again, it is theoretically conceivable that in the future all the processes involved in the production of renewable energy systems—including mining, manufacture and transport—can be powered by renewably generated electricity. But between present reality and the realisation of such a vision lies a vast landscape of engineering, economic and institutional challenges that humanity has hardly begun to confront. Today there is not a single solar panel or wind turbine that has not depended on fossil fuels for its manufacture and throughout its production and supply chain (Zehner 2012). Just look at a large wind turbine with the tiny human engineers standing on the top: this is decidedly a product of carbon civilisation! While it is quite feasible that many factory operations eventually come to be run on renewable electricity, there are many links in the chain of production that will prove technically very difficult or economically prohibitive. This is not an argument against renewable technology of course. Instead, it is a further argument for creating a society that requires as little energy as possible to flourish (Illich 1974), rather than assuming that energy-intensive societies can transition to renewable technologies without much difficulty.

We hasten to reiterate that the reflections above must not be interpreted as being anti-renewables. We have taken pains to clarify that it is our desire that the world is run primarily or wholly on renewable energy as soon as possible, but given the many limitations of renewable energy, we have argued that any such transition will mean significantly reduced energy supply compared to advanced industrial societies today (Moriarty and Honnery 2012; Heinberg and Fridley 2016). Not only is the *magnitude* of the supply likely to be reduced, which itself will have deep socio-economic implications, the *nature* of renewable energy supply will be sufficiently different to the incumbent supply system that a post-carbon society will need to undergo fundamental changes and adaptations in its economic, political, social and cultural characteristics (Smil 2015).

We freely admit that our energy prognosis could prove to be wrong. Certainly, our critical and sobering review will be controversial and resisted by those with techno-optimistic tendencies. But in these first two chapters we have presented a range of mutually reinforcing reasons to suggest that energy descent is a highly plausible future for any developed nation that seeks to transition to a post-carbon society. Given the risks of not being prepared for energy descent, we contend it makes sense to anticipate this probable energy future (Holmgren 2009; Fleming 2016a).

In particular, what is needed is a new urban discourse that is prepared to consider the possibility that futures of energy abundance may not be compatible with geological limits, carbon budget constraints, distributive justice, or the limitations of alternative energy sources. Yet, to date this call has fallen mostly on deaf ears, unable to be heard over the green noise of techno-optimism; the message unable to be seen because it sits behind or within a blind field. The result is that non-confronting light green illusions are conjured up that obscure any realities that might challenge the fundamentals of the Western-style industrial form of life (Zehner 2012). Those alluring phantoms must be exorcised if there is to be any prospect of making genuine progress towards an ecological civilisation.

A Critique of Electric Vehicles: Driving Down the Wrong Road More Slowly

The extraordinary technological advances that have been made in recent years and decades have flared techno-optimistic visions of green-tech cities, but for the reasons canvassed above, this frenzy has deflected attention away from the momentous obstacles that still lie in the way of any smooth or swift transition to post-carbon cities. Rather than rely on some dubious hope of 'greening' the high-energy demands of the most energy intensive societies today—let alone globalising this way of life—we have argued that it would be more prudent to embrace the prospect of energy descent and aim for some conception of energy sufficiency, which implies self-limitation and moderation (Trainer 2010).

After all, as a society reduces its energy demand, meeting that demand from renewable sources will become proportionately easier. But embracing energy sufficiency would require changing the nature of society and urban landscapes in ways that techno-optimists seem unwilling to consider. In this penultimate section of the chapter we briefly consider a further example of this refusal: the apparent inability to think beyond the private motor vehicle on the assumption that electric vehicles are the future of post-carbon transport. We contend that this is another example of the 'blind field' of techno-optimism at work.

Private motor vehicles with their internal combustion engines (ICEs) are the embodiment of carbon civilisation and indeed are defining of the capitalist mode of production. As political and cultural theorist Matthew Patterson (2007: 92) observes, '[a]cross a wide range of political/economic discourses the car has been seen to play a fundamental role in the promotion of economic growth in the twentieth century [and twenty-first century], and thus in the reproduction of capitalism as a system'. Not only are cars still produced according to Henry Ford's philosophy of assembly line efficiency, but they are also marketed according to the philosophy of Alfred Sloan—president and later chairman of General Motors from 1923 to 1956—who succeeded in increasing automobile sales with strategies of planned obsolescence and marketing techniques designed to evoke desire based on differing spending abilities of different classes.

Today the automobile remains a symbol of self and social status, and as suburbs have expanded ever-more broadly across the landscape, often without adequate public transport, the private car has become a virtual necessity for many households to manage city life. From the scathing pen of Andre Gorz (1980: 74) we read: 'From being a luxury item and a sign of privilege, the car has thus become a vital necessity. You have to have one so as to escape from the urban hell of the cars. Capitalist industry has thus won the game: the superfluous has become necessary'. This is especially so where house prices and sprawling developments have pushed people ever further away from their places of work. As Graeme Davison (2004: 21) notes, cars have become 'the mobile embodiment of a middle-class suburb family life'.

It scarcely needs stating, however, that this defining suburban commodity—the car—whatever its conveniences, has had and continues to have devastating environmental and social consequences. There are now over one billion cars on the road and counting, each of which is made up of roughly two tonnes of materials and depends on carbon-intensive petroleum products for manufacture, operation, and disposal. It has been estimated that manufacturing one average car produces 29 tonnes of waste (Pinderhughes 2004: 138). There are also the social costs of road accidents, noise pollution, and building and maintaining the vast networks of roads; the mental health implications of commuting in heavy traffic; and even the geopolitical incentive to invade oil-rich nations to meet and secure high domestic oil requirements. The social addiction to private motor vehicles, therefore, seems to be coming at incredibly high costs—costs that are not always obvious or accounted for in cost-benefit analyses.

Nevertheless, the addiction is spreading not retracting. Most of the global population lives in the so-called developing countries, meaning that the largest wave of motorisation is yet to come. Of today's roughly one billion cars on the road, only two million (or a measly 0.2%) are EVs. The IEA (2017b) estimate that by 2040 there will be two billion cars on the road, 280 million of which may be electric, leaving more than 1.7 billion ICEs still on the road. Is this the path of sustainability? Or might we be failing, at our own peril, to think beyond the private motor vehicle itself? Gorz (1980: 74), again, warned of a pernicious paradox we have yet to resolve:

> The car has made the big city uninhabitable. It has made it stinking, noisy, suffocating, dusty, so congested that nobody wants to go out in the evening anymore. Thus, since cars have killed the city, we need faster cars to escape on superhighways to suburbs that are even farther away. What an impeccable circular argument: give us more cars so that we can escape the destruction caused by cars.

With a dangerous lack of critical reflection, it seems the dominant view today is that the solution to the environmental impacts of carbon-dependent cars is simply to transition to electric vehicles. This places hope in a convenient technological solution that seeks to avoid the necessity of any significant behavioural, cultural or economic shifts. In theory, this response is coherent, but the eco-credentials of electric vehicles are far more complex, and at a systemic level they are arguably slim to non-existent. Wherein lies the truth?

Advocates are right to argue that EVs have no tailpipe emissions, reducing urban air and noise pollution relative to conventional ICE vehicles, and if batteries are charged with renewably generated electricity, there are no direct emissions from the process of driving. Because no petroleum products are required to propel EVs, they also hold out the prospect of decreasing reliance on oil in an era when it is likely to become ever harder for supply to keep up with demand, thus increasing resilience in the face of potential supply disruptions and expensive oil. At first examination, then, there is much to like about EVs.

The full picture tells quite a different story, however, one full of intricacies that tarnish this glossy first impression. First, EVs are significantly more energy and resource intensive to produce than conventional cars, primarily due to the battery component and the related mining of resources and production of various advanced components. The Union of Concerned Scientists report (Nealer et al. 2015) that an EV has between 15–68% more emissions associated with production than a conventional car. Furthermore, we noted above that the production of an ordinary car produces an estimated 29 tonnes of waste on average, and given that EVs are even more energy and resource intensive to produce, one shudders at the thought of building an entire new fleet of private motor vehicles to meet the expected demands over coming decades. Does sustainable development really mean building two billion EVs? To our mind this is a dangerous failure both of reason and imagination.

But leaving the production impacts to one side, even the proclaimed climate benefits of EVs are questionable. An EV is only 'zero-emissions' in operation (i.e. while driving) if the battery was charged with zero-carbon electricity—and given the reliance on fossil fuels for their manufacture and deployment, no renewable electricity source can actually claim this status. If the battery is charged with electricity generated via fossil fuels, then an EV hardly contributes to decarbonisation and might even increase emissions over an ICE vehicle. Even a house with solar panels still draws electricity with grid-average societal emissions if car batteries are charged during the morning or evening when there is little to no sun. The problem, therefore, is that most electricity is still generated using fossil energy, and while a shift to low-carbon sources is clearly underway, the transition, as we have seen, is painfully slow, despite the media reports. Given that EVs are expected to have the largest markets in the highly populated developing nations, whose electricity is especially dependent on fossil energy, the potential climate benefits of EVs are very modest indeed.

More precisely, in 2017 the IEA published their annual World Energy Outlook (IEA 2017a) and optimistically concluded, as noted above, that by 2040 there could be 280 million EVs on the road (up from 2 million today), but it concluded that this only makes a 1% difference to global carbon emissions. Furthermore, the IEA does not believe that EVs are going to induce an oil 'peak demand' in the foreseeable future, expecting any reductions in oil consumption due to EVs to be negated by increase in oil use in other areas of the global economy (shipping, trucks, aviation, petrochemical industry, etc.). These conclusions from a mainstream energy institution are devastating to the self-image of EVs, whose enthusiasts hold up them up as commodities capable of saving the climate and building resilience in the face of peak oil concerns.

If all that wasn't enough, the very economics of EVs as a climate and oil mitigation strategy are also highly problematic. To begin with, EVs are still extremely expensive relative to comparable ICE vehicles. Even as batteries come down in price, EVs remain essentially a luxury item for relatively wealthy environmentalists and will remain in this category for some time (which is not so much a criticism as an important qualification).

But even if more people could afford them, just think through the opportunity costs of replacing one or two billion conventional ICE vehicles with EVs over coming decades. How much will be spent on EVs if this full transition is achieved? How much will one or two billion

EVs cost and is that the best use of money if decarbonising the economy (or the transport sector in particular) is the goal? If the world is serious about decarbonising the transport sector, we argue that EVs should not be held up as the primary means of doing so.

Please do not misunderstand us. EVs are certainly going to play some, no doubt increased, and quite possibly significant, role in global transport. And to the extent that a household is genuinely locked in to car dependency, an EV may be a better option than continuing with an ICE, if electricity sources of manufacture and operation are decarbonised sufficiently. But even in that situation, there is a great risk of this being a grossly sub-optimal investment from a societal perspective. Structural incentives are needed to direct the capital that might otherwise go into EVs towards utility-scale decarbonisation of electricity supply and electrified public transport. Given the extent of the challenges that lie ahead, the world needs to invest its limited financial resources in optimal directions (fully costed), and for the reasons reviewed above, it is highly questionable whether EVs should receive the high praise they so often do as an eco-product. They are arguably problems disguised as solutions, deepening an already catastrophic path dependency.

We are similarly sceptical about the prospects for driverless vehicles, which is exactly the type of utopian innovation that makes techno-optimists froth at the mouth with excitement. Just as nuclear energy is likely to play a small role in the energy matrix in the future, driverless vehicles are almost certainly going to play a role in urban transport over coming years and decades. But to think that this is a 'solution' to urban transport or that driverless vehicles are on the cusp of disrupting urban transport is delusional. Yes, there will be more driverless vehicles in the future, but in time frames relevant to climate change—say, the next decade or two—driverless vehicles will be of little consequence and, in short, such technologies really only serve to entrench a mode of transport that has only marginal relevance to a post-carbon urban landscape.

And there is serious potential for such vehicles to make the impacts of high-power personal mobility on the urban environment worse not better. At present, most private vehicles spend the vast majority of their lives parked and stationary. What might the consequences be of unshackling the vehicle fleet from its reliance on drivers to keep it in circulation? Will we see increased traffic, as vehicle use is maximised by autonomy? The dynamics here are complex—this could well lead to a decrease in private ownership and mass expansion of shared use, offsetting the impacts of the increased hours of active use over a vehicle's operating life. But it is this very complexity that means we cannot anticipate where such changes will end up taking us. Linear predictions based on a narrow view of isolated benefits will almost certainly be wrong.

Fortunately, all these comments in criticism need not sound so depressing. The essence of sustainable transit is quite simple. We need to transition to the unexciting but eminently low-carbon modes of transport: walking, cycling, and electrified public transport powered by renewables. That is to say, the basic goal is relatively clear. And Illich (1974: 60) reminds us that equipped with a humble bicycle, the human being 'outstrips the efficiency of not only all machines but all other animals as well'. Indeed, we can move many times faster than the pedestrian while only using a fraction of the energy. This evokes the efficiency implicit in the notion of 'convivial technology', which informs our vision of a degrowth society.

However, as Gorz (1980: 77) implored: 'never make transport an issue by itself. Always connect it to the problem of the city'. His point is that transforming systems and practices of transportation requires addressing, not just transport itself, but also a range of policy, structural, economic and cultural shifts—both locally and globally. Modes of transport take place and take form within broader structural constraints, and it may be that a post-carbon transport system cannot emerge until those fundamental structural constraints are themselves transformed.

In this chapter our contention has been that techno-optimists are hoping to avoid the need for such fundamental shifts. By promoting their dubious if not counter-productive approach of technological modernisation they merely make it harder to achieve a just and sustainable world by entrenching the cultural attachment to the private motor vehicle, albeit in electrified form. As Lewis Mumford warned long ago: 'The right to access every building in the city by private motor vehicle... is actually the right to destroy the city' (quoted in Kimmelman 2012: n.p.). This critical perspective finds new evidential support in the work of urbanists, Elizabeth Taylor and Jonathan Laskovsky, whose analyses show just how much urban space is dedicated to cars and parking, and how wasteful and inefficient the use of that space is (Laskovsky and Taylor 2017). For example, parking in Melbourne's city centre alone demands 460 hectares. For such urban space to be reclaimed and repurposed, what is needed is a radical urban imaginary that dares to think beyond the private motor vehicle in order to envision and enable convivial urban landscapes that are made for people and communities, not cars.

Energy Descent, Relocalisation, and the Low-Mobility Future

The argument of this book has a long way to go, but key premises have begun to emerge. We have argued that the dual challenges of climate change mitigation and fossil energy depletion strongly suggest that the most energy intensive societies of the developed world should embrace or at least prepare for a future where there is less energy available than there is today. While we have defended a post-carbon transition to renewable energy, and called for radically increased urgency in this regard, our review of the situation has led us to conclude that renewable energy technologies will be unable to fully replace the fossil energy foundations of carbon civilisation, certainly not in the time available to avoid blowing the ever-shrinking carbon budget. In other words, a post-carbon future is likely to be an energy descent future, whether that future is chosen to mitigate climate change or imposed upon us by force of the geological depletion of fossil resources. Distributive imperatives—how to equitably share the energy we have available—only make this case for energy descent stronger in the affluent West, amongst the world's highest energy consumers.

One of the key implications of all this is that the globalised modes of production and consumption that fossil fuels have enabled—exemplified by suburban affluence—will need to be transcended if the goal of decarbonisation is ever taken seriously. While complete economic localisation may be neither likely nor desirable, considerable 'relocalisation' of production seems necessary (Norberg-Hodge 2016; De Young and Princen 2012). It is all very well to talk of decarbonising our electricity supply, but carbon civilisation depends most fundamentally on ships and cargo trucks to transport commodities and resources all around the world on a daily basis, and neither cargo ships nor long haul cargo trucks show any prospect of being decarbonised in the foreseeable future (Friedmann 2016). Even light trucks that transport goods within cities and which show some prospect of electrification are currently so expensive that they seem unlikely to scale in the time frame required to make a material contribution to climate mitigation. So, an energy descent future will almost certainly mark the end of globalisation as we know it. As post-carbon theorist David Fleming (2016b: 173) wrote: 'localisation stands, at best, at the limits of practical possibility, but it has the decisive argument in its favour that there will be no alternative'.

Just as with the nature of the globalised economy, so too with lifestyles. The energy descent future is likely to be a low-mobility future, compared to what is taken for granted today (Moriarty and Honnery 2008). Running commercial aviation affordable to the general public on biofuels is a pipe dream, and production passenger aircraft running on electricity will not be available with sufficient size and performance to secure the industry's viability in the foreseeable future (if ever). So one of the most confronting cultural challenges presented by a post-carbon society is the fact that it is inconsistent with the global lifestyles we are familiar with today, where many people take regional and international flights multiple times a year. Electric cars, we have shown, are no solution to the problem of private motor vehicles, so even the day to day existence of city life is likely to involve reduced mobility, in terms of total passenger kilometres, even if public transport improves. Technological innovation will doubtless continue, but technology alone cannot save us on the timescales dictated by global warming, and one must not forget that new technologies are a two-edged sword, which can both help solve as well as exacerbate ecological problems.

These conclusions contradict popular visions of future energy abundance, green growth, and unconstrained private urban mobility—visions that still inform and shape urban and suburban development today. Cheap energy inputs over the twentieth century gave rise to a global economic order, which today demands around 96 million barrels of oil every day to function. Resources are mined and transported with oil; goods and commodities are produced and again transported with oil to urban and suburban centres; consumers go to the malls in their oil-dependent cars to purchase oil-dependent products only to return to their suburban homes where electricity use is still reliant on coal and gas-fired generation. It is assumed that these vast energy and commodity supplies will remain affordable and capable of decarbonisation. It is assumed that the energy foundations of carbon suburbia are secure. It is assumed that economic growth can be maintained indefinitely and globalised despite the finitude of our one, fragile, already overburdened planet.

To be sure, analysts and politicians sometimes recognise and acknowledge the social justice and environmental problems with this mode of development. But in the next breath they will insist that the consumer way of life can and should be globalised, provided we do so in a 'green' way, which technology, markets, and policy reforms will supposedly enable us to do. Politicians, business leaders, and consumers themselves, are quick to embrace this convenient, non-confronting vision of sustainable development. Thus business-as-usual more or less prevails.

As Slavoj Žižek (2010) would say, these hopeful tropes about 'sustainable capitalism' act relentlessly to 'normalise the apocalypse'. The techno-optimistic mythology retains its iron grasp on people's imaginations and shapes the politico-economic order of globalised capitalism, and in consequence the ecosystems upon which humanity rely are being brutally degraded; inequality within and between nations is increasing; billions remain in destitution; and all the while there is a growing and disconcerting sense that even those who are living the suburban dream have not often found the meaning, community, and contentment they were promised in the glossy advertisements (Hamilton and Denniss 2005).

Given the close connection between energy consumption and economic growth, the most challenging and fundamental implication of energy descent is a necessary transcendence of the growth paradigm, since less energy means less capacity to produce and consume. If reduced production and consumption occur in unplanned ways within an economy dependent on growth, this is properly called recession, and it will generally lead to a range of harmful societal effects, including increased unemployment, debt defaults, social conflict, economic instability, and possibly longer-term depressions or even economic collapse.

However, if that energy descent future is anticipated and managed wisely, the process of planned economic contraction, increased localisation, broader distribution of wealth, and judicious deindustrialisation can be called degrowth, and there is no reason to think that the economics of sufficiency this implies is incompatible with a 'prosperous way down' (Odum and Odum 2001; Alexander 2015). Indeed, in an age of pressing ecological limits, degrowth may well be the only economic paradigm consistent with human and ecological flourishing. The remainder of this book explores how these questions, challenges, and possibilities might play out in the suburban terrain, and how or whether activity within that context might help turn this apparent 'crisis of progress' into an opportunity for suburban renewal. Before turning to the question of praxis, however, in the next chapter we consider the politics of change.

From where will the sparks of transformation ignite?

References

Ahmed, Nafeez. 2017. *Failing States, Collapsing Systems: Biophysical Triggers of Political Violence*. New York: Springer.

Alexander, Samuel. 2015. *Prosperous Descent: Crisis as Opportunity in an Age of Limits*. Melbourne: Simplicity Institute.

Breakthrough Institute. 2015. *An Ecomodernist Manifesto*. http://bit.ly/2yKa-Wwi. Accessed 20 June 2018.

Carrington, Damien. 2014. Earth Has Lost Half of Its Wildlife in the Last Forty Years, Says WWF. *The Guardian*, October 1. https://www.theguardian.com/environment/2014/sep/29/earth-lost-50-wildlife-in-40-years-wwf. Accessed 20 June 2018.

Clack, Christopher, et al. 2017. Evaluation of a Proposal for Reliable Low-Cost Grid Power with 100% Wind, Water, and Solar. *PNAS* 114 (26): 6722–6727.

Davison, Graeme. 2004. *Car Wars: How the Car Won Our Hearts and Conquered Our Cities*. Crows Nest: Allen & Unwin.

De Young, Raymond, and Thomas Princen (eds.). 2012. *The Localization Reader: Adapting to the Coming Downshift*. Cambridge, MA: MIT Press.

Fleming, David. 2016a. *Lean Logic: A Dictionary for the Future and How to Survive It*. White River Junction, VT: Chelsea Green.

———. 2016b. *Surviving the Future: Culture, Carnival and Capital in the Aftermath of the Market Economy*, ed. Shaun Chamberlin. White River Junction: Chelsea Green.

Floyd, Joshua. 2017. Uncertainty Is the Best Tool to Navigate Toward Our Post-carbon Future. *Insurge Intelligence*, August 10. https://medium.com/insurge-intelligence/uncertainty-is-the-best-tool-to-navigate-toward-our-post-carbon-future-a5e4d45d45a1. Accessed 20 June 2018.

Friedmann, Alice. 2016. *When the Trucks Stop Running: Energy and the Future of Transportation*. New York: Springer.

Gorz, Andre. 1980. *Ecology as Politics*. Boston: South End Press.

Hamilton, Clive, and Richard Denniss. 2005. *Affluenza: When Too Much Is Never Enough*. Crows Nest: Allen & Unwin.

Hatfield-Dodds, Stephen. 2015. Study: Australians Can Be Sustainable Without Sacrificing Lifestyle or Economy. *The Conversation*, November 5. https://theconversation.com/study-australians-can-be-sustainable-without-sacrificing-lifestyle-or-economy-50179. Accessed 20 June 2018.

Heinberg, Richard, and David Fridley. 2016. *Our Renewable Future: Laying the Path for One Hundred Percent Clean Energy*. Washington: Island Press.

Hirsch, Robert, Roger Bezdek, and Robert Wendling. 2010. *The Impending World Energy Mess: And What It Means to You*. Toronto: Apogee Prime.

Holmgren, David. 2009. *Future Scenarios: How Communities Can Adapt to Peak Oil and Climate Change*. White River Junction, VT: Chelsea Green.

Huesemann, Michael, and Joyce Huesemann. 2011. *Techno-fix: Why Technology Won't Save Us or the Environment*. Gabriola Island: New Society Publishers.

Illich, Ivan. 1974. *Energy and Equity*. New York: Harper and Row.

———. 2009 [1973]. *Tools for Conviviality*. New York: Marion Boyars Publishers.

International Energy Agency (IEA). 2017a. World Energy Outlook 2017. https://www.iea.org/weo2017/. Accessed 1 Mar 2018.

————. 2017b. *Global EV Outlook 2017*. https://webstore.iea.org/global-ev-outlook-2017. Accessed 20 June 2018.

Jacobson, Mark, Mark Delucchi, Mary Cameron, and Bethany Frew. 2015. Low-Cost Solution to the Grid Reliability Problem with 100% Penetration of Intermittent Wind, Water, and Solar for All Purposes. *PNAS* 112(49): 15060–15065.

Kimmelman, Michael. 2012. Paved, but Still Alive. *New York Times*, January 6. https://www.nytimes.com/2012/01/08/arts/design/taking-parking-lots-seriously-as-public-spaces.html. Accessed 20 June 2018.

Kolbert, Elizabeth. 2014. *The Sixth Extinction: An Unnatural History*. New York: Henry Holt.

Laskovsky, Jonathan, and Elizabeth Taylor. 2017. A Lot of Thought: The Space of Car Parks and Shopping Centres in Australian Cities. In *Proceedings of Automotive Historians Australia Automotive Histories: Driving Futures*, ed. Harriet Edquist, Mark Richardson, and Simon Lockrey, 1–18, Sept 1–2, 2016, Melbourne, Australia.

Lefebvre, Henri. 2003 [1970]. *The Urban Revolution*. Minneapolis: University of Minnesota Press.

McKay, David. 2009. *Sustainable Energy Without the Hot Air*. Cambridge: UIT.

Moriarty, Patrick, and Damon Honnery. 2008. Low-Mobility: The Future of Transport. *Futures* 40: 865–872.

————. 2012. Preparing for a Low-Energy Future. *Futures* 44 (10): 883–892.

————. 2016. Can Renewable Energy Power the Future? *Energy Policy* 93: 3–7.

Murphy, David. 2013. The Implications of the Declining Energy Return on Investment of Oil Production. *Philosophical Transitions of the Royal Society A*. https://doi.org/10.1098/rsta.2013.0126.

Nealer, Rachel, David Reichmuth, and Don Anair. 2015. *Cleaner Cars from Cradle to Grave*. Union of Concerned Scientists. https://www.ucsusa.org/sites/default/files/attach/2015/11/Cleaner-Cars-from-Cradle-to-Grave-full-report.pdf. Accessed 20 June 2018.

Norberg-Hodge, Helena. 2016. *Ancient Futures*. Totnes: Local Futures.

Nordhaus, Ted, and Michael Shellenberger. 2012. Evolve: The Case for Modernization as the Road to Salvation. *Breakthrough Journal* (Spring). https://thebreakthrough.org/index.php/journal/past-issues/issue-2/evolve. Accessed 20 June 2018.

Odum, Howard, and Elizabeth Odum. 2001. *A Prosperous Way Down: Principles and Policies*. Colorado: University of Colorado Press.

Patterson, Matthew. 2007. *Automobile Politics: Ecology and Cultural Political Economy*. Cambridge: Cambridge University Press.

Pearce, Joshua. 2008. Thermodynamic Limitations to Nuclear Energy Deployment as a Greenhouse Gas Mitigation Technology. *International Journal of Nuclear Governance, Economy and Ecology* 2 (1): 113–130.

Pinderhughes, Raquel. 2004. *Alternative Urban Futures: Planning for Sustainable Development in Cities Throughout the World*. New York: Rowman and Littlefield.

Smil, Vaclav. 2010. *Energy Transitions: History, Requirements, and Prospects*. Santa Barbara: Prager Publishers.

———. 2015. *Power Density: Key to Understanding Energy Sources and Uses*. Cambridge: MIT Press.

Trainer, Ted. 2010. *The Transition to a Sustainable and Just World*. Sydney: Envirobook.

Zehner, Ozzie. 2012. *Green Illusions: The Dirty Secrets of Clean Energy and the Future of Environmentalism*. Lincoln: University of Nebraska Press.

Žižek, Slavoj. 2010. *Living in the End Times*. London: Verso.

4

Resettling Suburbia: A Post-capitalist Politics 'From Below'

We closed the last chapter by pointing to a crisis of progress unfolding at the energetic core of carbon civilisation. This book will not outline a comprehensive resolution for this crisis—indeed, it probably has no 'solution', as such. Instead, our motivation is to reflect on what may be the most appropriate responses to this crisis, in and for the suburban context, given the world as it is but with an eye on what it could yet be. The narrative of progress that has defined urban 'development' in recent decades places imaginative constraints on what might become of the cities and suburbs of carbon civilisation. Therefore, any attempt to resettle the built environment will have to overcome these constraints in order to enable and empower the political agency upon which societal transformation always depends. The realisation of a new suburban imaginary might ultimately depend on a remapping of political terrain and political strategy in ways that we will explore in this chapter. In short, our vision of degrowth in the suburbs needs a 'theory of change' to ground and inform its praxis.

Across the globe today, economic growth in terms of GDP is the most prominent metric from which a general trajectory of progress is inferred (Purdey 2010). Money can be viewed as a claim on the product

© The Author(s) 2019
S. Alexander and B. Gleeson, *Degrowth in the Suburbs*,
https://doi.org/10.1007/978-981-13-2131-3_4

of surplus energy, and societies employ money in solving their problems, suggesting that more money allows more problems to be solved. Yet, the expansion of physical economic activity, as well as the ongoing urbanisation of growing global populations, entails increased rates of energy use. As discussed in the first two chapters, this energy–economy relationship is evidenced historically by the close correlation between economic activity measured in terms of GDP and energy use. Provided energy surpluses continue to grow, economies and cities have been able to grow and complexify (Homer-Dixon 2006). On the surface, then, it is quite understandable why more money and energy are overriding goals of most, if not all, contemporary societies: these things are apparently required for 'progress'. More important still is the deeper systemic logic: capitalism can never be a steady state entity and must grow or collapse (Smith 2016). We have cast this as the growth model of modern progress, and its hegemonic status has never been as dominant and imposing as it is today.

But what might happen if a society or a city finds itself (by choice or by force of circumstances) with less energy to invest in economic growth and, at the same time, having to bear the complexification that growth brings and requires? Two broad pathways lie ahead: either, the society tries to maintain the existing, growth-orientated socio-economic form but solve fewer problems due to the declining energy budget (a phenomenon typically characterised as societal decay or collapse, depending on the speed of decline); or, the society rethinks the range and nature of the problems it is trying to solve, and then reprioritises its investment of available energy in order to create new, less energy intensive socio-political and economic forms. In our urban age, the latter implies radically less energy and resource demanding cities.

It seems clear enough, however, that the wealthiest nations—our primary focus in this book—embody the former strategy. This is evidenced by their unremitting hunger for energy and resources, more technological solutions, and yet more economic growth (Wiedmann et al. 2015). Other nations of the world seem committed to following suit, in large part, it would seem, due to forced integration into the neoliberal global order by way of military and corporate coercion from the dominant powers (Fotopoulous 2016). This military-industrial growth paradigm is globalised on the rarely questioned assumption that more energy will be available in the future to fund increased complexity, which is the message relentlessly pushed by mainstream energy analysts and institutions, and indeed a hidden assumption (or resigned acceptance) of most urban planners. As we have argued already, the forms carbon-hungry cities have taken are a function of the underlying political economy of growth that shape them, from which it follows that until that growthist macroeconomic vision is transcended, the prospect of post-carbon suburbs, or post-carbon cities more generally, will remain elusive. With dangerous myopia, it seems that currently the pursuit of post-carbon cities is taking place within a mode of political economy that will never permit their realisation.

The carbon and resource-intensive consumer class that is so widely aspired to around the world today—typified by a suburban lifestyle—has no future. Earth's ecosystems are trembling under the weight of one or two billion high-end consumers, so it is nothing short of delusional to think that our planet could sustain four, six, eight or ten billion people living this way. Affluence as we know it simply cannot be globalised. There are limits to what Earth will tolerate. Technology alone will not save us. We must choose an energy descent future, and if we do not, it is coming anyway. As Henry David Thoreau (1984: 153) would put it, with his inimitable wit: 'When a dog runs at you, whistle for him'. In other words, we must learn to embrace our energetic fate.

Democracy, Energy Descent, and the Post-capitalist Politics of Degrowth

The central implication of our analysis so far is that the most coherent response to the crises of our time is for high-impact societies to embrace a radical strategy of degrowth, given the likelihood of forthcoming energy descent and the fact that the irresolvable ecological contradictions of growth capitalism seem destined to intensify as economies pursue more growth in the hope of solving the problems growth is causing. We do not argue that this voluntary transformation of overgrown economies is likely, only that, by force of reason and evidence, some such transition will be necessary if there is to be any ecological reconciliation with Earth, and thus it is a goal deserving of our collective pursuit, irrespective of the prospects of success.

Indeed, we acknowledge the slim chances of degrowth being widely embraced by governments or civil societies. But this admission is not fatal to the case for degrowth. If, in the face of compounding evidence, nations continue to pursue economic growth without limit, and thereby intensify the collision with ecological limits, then we argue that the degrowth values and practices of sufficiency, solidarity, and self-limitation, remain justified (even more justified!) as a means of building resilience in the face of forthcoming shocks. Today more than ever before humanity must aim for regenerative forms of social organisation that build rather than deplete the foundations on which they rely. The only responsible course of action is to act appropriately, in light of the best evidence, and in an age of gross ecological overshoot, we contend that the imperative for degrowth is undeniable.

This raises the question of what social, political and economic mechanisms might drive such a transition beyond growth, and the conventional answer to this question is that governments must be the prime movers. But can degrowth in the suburbs emerge from the 'top down' within a capitalist system ruled by profit-maximisation? If not, where might the revolutionary movement for change emerge and how might it operate?

This line of inquiry is especially complicated given that in radical thought the traditional locus of revolutionary potential has been in the working class. But this class has in many ways subscribed to the ideology of growth, in the sense that the proletarian struggle since industrialisation has been for a greater, more equitable share of a growing economy pie, especially higher wages—and quite understandably so. Capitalism tends to concentrate wealth in grossly unjust ways, as economist Thomas Piketty (2014) has famously established in recent years with reference to vast historical data. This historical struggle for distributive equity has been a just and necessary struggle.

The demand for higher wages, however, can render the working class complicit in the ecocidal drive for ongoing economic growth that has no viable future in an age already marked by planetary overshoot. Thus a socialist revolution that does not transcend the ideology of growth is no revolution at all, since an overgrown growth economy whose spoils are more fairly distributed is still unsustainable. It follows that in an age of increasingly severe ecological limits, traditional theories of change must be reconsidered (Albert 2004; Gibson-Graham 2006; Alexander and Burdon 2017).

The working class struggle must be grounded in ecological context and revise its demands and strategies accordingly, as eco-Marxists and eco-socialists are beginning to do (Sarkar 1999; Foster 2000; Baer 2017). But rather than appealing for a 'top down' transition led by the state, we will argue that an eco-city must emerge 'from below', led by the broad consuming class that occupies suburbia. These change agents will include workers, who increase their participation in non-monetary or informal economies as times of crisis deepen, as well as members of the more affluent middle classes, who withdraw from the vapidity of consumer culture and act in solidarity with others who are building new, fairer and more localised economies within the shell of a global capitalist system clearly in decay. It should be clear that this is not in any way to dismiss the material groundings of systemic change; it is only to invite political strategists to be open to reimagining modes of transformation for the present era of severe ecological limits.

It is these questions concerning the politics of transformation in an age of ecological limits which we direct attention to in this chapter. We seek to develop a coherent 'theory of change' before exploring its practical application in subsequent chapters. More specifically, we will outline a post-capitalist politics of degrowth that underpins our vision of suburban transformation, without attempting to review the various political literatures, from neo-Marxism, to Saul Alinksy, to theorists of the Occupy movement, that in recent decades have attempted to rethink or radicalise democracy for the modern era. While we acknowledge key theorists and positions in places, we do not review the entire radical canon. Instead, our goal is to apply critical insights of democratic theory, practice, and strategy to the specific case of a suburban politics for degrowth.

This is a political question in ecological context that has yet to receive detailed attention within the degrowth movement but which is necessary to the present undertaking and informs forthcoming chapters. Counter-intuitively, perhaps, it is our view that the substantive issue of 'what' is to be done is best explored after having gotten to grips with the procedural or strategic question of 'how' change in this context is best achieved.

The Growth Imperative, Capital, and the Political Problem of 'Empire'

To initiate this inquiry into a theory of change, it is necessary to unpack why the political economy of growth has acquired its hegemony and why hopes of an enlightened government or state leading a degrowth transition from the top down seem slim to non-existent (irrespective of how necessary such a transition may be). These inquiries are important because understanding the nature of the growth imperative has implications on political strategy for change, including a political strategy for suburban transformation. As we have argued, a 'degrowth capitalism' (to be distinguished from capitalism in recession) is a contradiction in terms. It is worth exploring the rationale for this observation a little further.

The first reason is that, within capitalism, corporate firms must seek to maximise profits and productivity or risk being destroyed by more ambitious and ruthless market competitors. Even if business owners feel they might have 'enough' to maintain a decent and secure livelihood, they will be driven to grow their business whenever possible, and fill all available gaps in the market, to avoid competitors taking that advantage and potentially putting them out of business. This provides an existential incentive to maximise profits and productivity without limit. Thus, at the microeconomic level, the golden rule of capitalism is: grow or die (Smith 2016).

Similarly, there is a related growth imperative created by debt-based monetary systems, especially but not exclusively under capitalism.

Currently money is predominately loaned into existence by private banks as interest-bearing debt, and in order to pay back the debt plus the interest, this implies an expansion of the monetary supply. Banks only lend to people or institutions that they think will be able to pay back the debts incurred, and those most likely to make the most profit get given credit first. This lending system inherently gives capitalism a pro-growth structure since money—and the power it brings—is most readily available to the firms most likely to make the most profit (Trainer 2011). Given the trillions of dollars of debt that has been taken on across the globe in recent decades, capitalism (more than ever) requires growth for stability, for otherwise debts stop being repaid and the system collapses, which is what almost happened in 2008. At the macroeconomic level, then, we see that the same golden rule of capitalism applies: grow or die.

Furthermore, the powers-that-be—say, the largest corporations and governments that are doing financially well within the capitalist system—would not tolerate a deliberate transition to a post-growth or degrowth economy. At least since Marx there has been a line of critical theory that conceptualises the state as merely a tool for securing and advancing the interests of the richest agents or institutions in society. To illustrate this perspective, recall when a relatively fringe Occupy Movement in 2011 began to challenge undue corporate influence on democratic processes and make noise about wealth inequality. Soon enough the executive branches of government bore down upon the activists and stamped out the spectacle of opposition with extraordinary brutality. Mainstream media (as profit-maximisers) made little effort to understand the movement or to condemn the state violence, since it was not in their interests to do so. Governments in particular seek a growing economy, because that implies a larger tax base to draw from to implement their range of policies. Given that a degrowth economy would directly undermine the economic interests (as conventionally measured by money) of the most powerful corporations and institutions in society, one should expect merciless and sustained resistance from these vested interests if a degrowth movement ever began gaining ascendency. Capitalism will not lie down like a lamb at anyone's request. It will fight for existence all the way down.

Indeed, even if a government *wanted* to pursue a degrowth agenda, there are global and national economic forces at play which would obstruct such an agenda being rolled out. Call this the problem of 'Empire', a concept developed by post-Marxist, political theorists Michael Hardt and Antonio Negri (2000). Not only are nation-states today constrained by numerous international trade agreements and powerful global institutions, but the free flow of capital around the globe has given new power to an imperium of transnational corporations that can now move their financial resources from country to country with unprecedented ease. If governments were to create unattractive financial conditions (e.g. by raising corporate taxes or the minimum wage), corporations could threaten 'capital flight', and just knowing that capital flight is possible can insidiously constrain government action through fear, even in the absence of an explicit threat.

A strong case can be made that all this has led to economic forces becoming more autonomous from political controls, and consequently that political sovereignty has declined. But as Hardt and Negri (2000: xi) have argued, '*The decline in sovereignty of nation-states… does not mean that sovereignty as such has declined*'. Sovereignty, they argue, has just taken on a new, globalised form—the form of Empire—which can be understood as a decentralising and deterritorialising apparatus of power which is 'composed of a series of national and supranational organisms united under a single logic of rule' (Hardt and Negri 2000: xii).

The logic of rule to which they refer, of course, is the capitalist logic of profit maximisation, and nation-states dare not step out of line. Recent theories of the 'deep state' and 'dark money' offer further support for this view, implying that, today more than ever before, there are hidden or non-transparent political, institutional, and financial forces that function undemocratically to entrench and globalise the neoliberal world order and undermine any progressive antagonists who attempt to explore post-growth alternatives (Fotopoulous 2016).

In today's globalised world order, it is hard to even comprehend what complex portfolio of national policies could produce a stable and flourishing degrowth economy from the 'top down'. Some bold policy formulations have been attempted (see Cosme et al. 2017), and yet deep questions remain, especially about economic and financial stability during any transition. For example, how would the stock markets react if a government announced a policy agenda that would deliberately aim to contract the economy for environmental reasons and distribute the shrinking economic pie more broadly for social justice reasons? More specifically, how would the stock markets react if a government, in pursuit of sustainability and global equity, introduced a diminishing resource cap that sought to phase out the most damaging industries and reduce energy and resource consumption by 80% of current Australian levels over the next ten years?

One can be sure there would be utter turmoil, bursting financial and property bubbles, capital strikes and flight, a shattering 'consumer confidence', all ultimately leading to an economic crash far greater than the global financial crisis of 2008. After all, how would debts be repaid in a contracting economy? As financial analyst Michael Hudson (2012) famously quipped: 'debts that can't be paid, won't be'. The point is that it may well be impossible to implement a smooth 'top down' transition to a degrowth economy, even if a strong social movement developed that wanted this. The growth-dependent, heavily indebted market economies we know today would be unable to adjust to the types and speed of the foundational changes required. As noted in Chapter 1, in an age when capitalism has attained near complete hegemony, growth-orientated societies just do not know how to deliberately create a macroeconomy that produces less—and yet, that is precisely what seems to be necessary.

Finally, to make matters more challenging still, there is also the geopolitical risk of being a leader in a degrowth transition, as this may involve fewer funds available for military forces, weakening a nation's relative power globally. Can we imagine powerful nations like the US, Russia or China voluntarily embracing degrowth if that meant reduced geopolitical security or influence? This is a classic prisoners' dilemma situation, which applies as much to capitalist governments as socialist ones: it may well be in the interests of even the most powerful nations to embrace degrowth in order to avoid ecosystemic collapse, but in the distrustful world of geopolitics, nations end up choosing courses of action which are ultimately not in their, or anyone else's, or the planet's, best interests. Again, the logic here is simple: grow the economy for military strength, or risk being invaded and destroyed. In the end perhaps this is one of the most compelling of the various growth imperatives, but all of these issues radically call into question the feasibility of a 'top down' transition to a degrowth economy. A 'great disruption' of some form may be a necessary or inevitable part of the transition beyond growth, a disconcerting issue to which we will return in later chapters.

The central point however is that nation-states have *various* growth imperatives built into their structures, meaning that governments should not be relied on to be the prime drivers of any degrowth transition. This calls for a further reconsideration of conventional Marxist theory, in so far as taking control of the state may not necessarily be the best way to initiate the transition to a just and sustainable low-energy future, for a socialist state may find itself locked into unsustainable growth just as capitalism is. Put otherwise, a post-growth state may only ever be the outcome, not the driving force, of a movement for degrowth.

The Politics of the Household Economy: Driving Suburban Change 'From Below'

The line of reasoning just sketched out presents a deep challenge to the notion of suburban transformation in the spirit of degrowth—or any post-growth agenda—insofar as it questions the coherency of such a transformation being initiated and driven by governments which are under the spell of growth fetishism. At the same time, that challenge sets up one of the theoretical points of distinction of this book. If conventional representative democracy in advanced capitalist societies is unable to accommodate the degrowth imperative by virtue of politicians and dominant institutions being locked into the growth model, then it follows that the emergence of degrowth in the suburbs will have to depend on a post-capitalist politics of participatory democracy (Gibson-Graham 2006).

We locate these new politics of change in the suburbs, traditionally the crucible of the growth order, which is one reason we firmly claim our imaginary to be radical—certainly radically out of kilter with the conventional political wisdom of contemporary Western democracies. Perhaps in the age of Trump and of generally widening political and social distemper, this misalignment, while radical, is not as uncommon as it might have been a decade ago. We live in an age of unsettlement that is centred in the cities and their troubled heartlands and hinterlands, and it is perhaps therefore timely to think of, *and from*, suburbia in profoundly new ways.

Theories of urban development typically look to governments, local and national, to take the lead in transforming urban landscapes to promote sustainability and wellbeing. This is especially so when the problems requiring a coordinated response—such as climate change—are deep, urgent, and often 'wicked'. Nevertheless, in many parts of the world today, including Australia, recent and current government policies provide little hope that the range of structural changes necessary to create more sustainable, post-carbon cities will emerge from the top down. Despite paying lip service to sustainability issues, most political actors still operate firmly within the out-dated growth paradigm where new roads, new coal mines, or fracking for oil and gas are touted as solutions to urban transport and energy problems, and too often we see cities continuing to eat away at their surrounding greenways with conventional, expansionist, poorly designed housing developments. Business-as-usual more or less prevails, for reasons primarily owing to the growth imperatives we have just described. Political actors mistake the poison of growthism for the cure, and when the poison doesn't cure anything and, indeed, often makes things worse, they assume they mustn't have had enough of it. In the words usually attributed to Horace Walpole: 'the world is a comedy to those who think, and a tragedy to those who feel'.

So far as governments are failing to act coherently in the face of today's ecological and energetic emergencies, it becomes ever-more important to look towards grassroots movements and practices as the key to urban renewal 'from below'. This political positioning is fundamental to the suburban imaginary we will develop in this book, which calls for and rests on a democratic renaissance of sorts, whereby people reclaim the right of self-governance from their distant, so-called representatives. This means re-localising political power through participatory and collective action, rather than waiting for governments to solve problems which they are either unable or unwilling to solve.

Indeed, the broad suburban consuming class—although heterogeneous in its constitution—presents itself today as having the potential to become a transformative social movement. As outlined above, we see this social class as constituted both by workers struggling to 'get by', as well as more affluent 'post-materialist' suburbanites who are increasingly disillusioned and alienated by the unfulfilled promises of consumerism, and who seek an alternative and more meaningful way of life (Inglehart and Welzel 2005). In ways we will develop in this book, we see these social forces combining—potentially at least—to reweave a fraying economy from the grassroots up, reconstituting the economic and social fabric of suburbia in new ways and on new terms (Albert 2004).

Thus a post-capitalist politics is one in which the power of people acting collectively is able to outweigh the undemocratic influence of money in politics, and this includes social resistance to ongoing vertical sprawl masquerading as 'green growth'. More fundamentally, our post-capitalist politics recognises that governments are in the thrall of a growth fetish, so any economics beyond growth must be driven into existence by mechanisms that utilise but transcend the ballot box. To be clear, this does not mean that governments will not have a key role to play in mitigating the range of crises currently unfolding on the global stage, only that waiting for a top down solution would involve waiting while the ship of growth capitalism drifts over the cliff into the dark abyss below—like Thanatos, unable to resist its own death-drive.

Re-accomplishing Democracy Through Participation

A new suburbia, we argue, depends on this new, post-capitalist political orientation, which implies a renewal of participatory democratic spirit. It was with characteristic insight that the great American philosopher, John Dewey (1981–90: 299), wrote: 'Every generation has to accomplish democracy over again for itself'. His point was that, at each moment in history, citizens and nations inevitably face unique challenges and problems, so we should not assume the democratic institutions and practices inherited from the past will be adequate for the conditions of today. Our ongoing political challenge, therefore, is to 'accomplish' democracy anew, every generation.

It seems the world's democratic societies today have forgotten Dewey's lesson. Too often it is assumed instead that democracy is something that has been achieved already, once and for all. Why do we need to reinvent it? Indeed, in the wake of each democratic election it is easy to be seduced back to the comfortable unfreedom of the shopping mall or withdraw into the existential numbness of social media or television, believing that, having voted, one's political work is done. The task of governing is now in the hands of our so-called representatives. That's surely what political participation means in market capitalistic society.

This is, of course, an impoverished, even dangerous, conception of democracy, which democratic societies today propagate by way of casual apathy at their own peril. It is government *of* the people, certainly, but not government *by* the people, and increasingly not government *for* the people. With respect to urban development, this emasculation of democracy plays out in terms of capital overriding the interests of people and planet—a process we have called hypertrophic urbanism.

It may be that an ecological blindness is in fact an inherent feature of the very structure of representative democracy. Unable or unwilling to look beyond the short-term horizon of the next election and constrained by the undemocratic but often hidden influence of money in policy formation, politicians are essentially prohibited from taking a geological or eco-centric view of things, which is necessary for the preservation of the biosphere. To avoid making hard decisions, environmental costs are pushed into the future, all glossed over by a techno-optimism that promises ecological salvation through technology, innovation, design and market mechanisms.

From this perspective there is no need to question consumer lifestyles or conventional growth-orientated modes of urban and suburban development. One consequence of this non-confronting myth is that the voices of future generations fall on deaf ears—rendering democracy decidedly 'unrepresentative' in this glaring way, to say nothing of the holocaust of biodiversity whose victims had no voice at all. We surely need to rethink the neoliberal politics of representative democracies in and for the Anthropocene (Purdy 2015).

In regressive political contexts, such as contemporary Australia, it is at the household and community levels where people generally have most agency—most freedom to influence their world—so it is at this grassroots level where we will examine what could be done, here and now, to embrace, or at least prepare for, an energy descent future in the spirit of degrowth. People may not feel like they have much influence over the decisions of their members of parliament, or the decisions of big business or other global institutions, all of which are fatally infected with growth fetishism. But within the structural constraints of any society there nevertheless resides a realm of freedom through which individuals and communities can resist and oppose the existing order and make their influence felt (Holloway 2002; Trainer 2010; Holmgren 2018).

It is in those cracks which permit a degree of urban autonomy and self-governance where we argue people must thrust the crowbar of oppositional activity in the hope of leveraging their influence. However small those acts of opposition or renewal might seem in isolation, when they form part of a large social movement or cultural shift, their cumulative impact can reshape society 'from below' and ultimately form a tidal wave of transformative significance, washing away the old imaginary, or aspects of it, and clearing space for the new. A brief glance at the history of (partially successful) urban social movements shows this to be true—civil rights, women's rights, gay rights, etc. The future may hold further confirmation in new domains of life—suburban transformation, perhaps—if only we choose it.

Through this process of participatory democracy and grassroots action there might just be a chance to 'crack capitalism', as political theorist John Holloway (2010) puts it, and out of the rubble of capitalist decay build something new by reinhabiting the built environment in better, more ecologically viable and more humane ways. We say that there might just be a chance in the sense that it is the only hope. This is not to say that the household or community levels are necessarily the ideal spheres of societal transformation (a question we leave open); it is only to acknowledge that if governments will not embrace degrowth—or, more specifically, if governments will not attempt to initiate a degrowth transformation in the suburbs—then the household and community levels are the *only* remaining spheres of transformative potential.

We feel this perspective could be easily misunderstood, so a word of clarification is in order. We are not suggesting that strong top-down governance of cities and their suburbs would not be desirable. On the contrary, it is perfectly clear to us that governments, local and national, could do many things to advance the causes of justice and sustainability, and in Chapter 7 we share some of our thoughts on this. We acknowledge, furthermore, that acting only at the grassroots (or microeconomic) level is problematic, since voluntarily reducing energy and resource consumption in a market society can function to reduce pressure on markets and hence induce price reductions. Those pricing dynamics can then lead to *increased* consumption by those actors in society who are not attempting to create a degrowth society and who happily exploit the access to cheaper commodities. This 'wicked problem' has lead Blake Allcot (2008) to highlight the legitimate concern that frugality in some sectors of society might lead to a consumption 'rebound effect' elsewhere. Accordingly, in order to affect structural reduction in energy and resource use, there ultimately needs to be some mechanisms to limit aggregate use—and this needs cooperation by formal political and economic institutions.

Nevertheless, our position is that growth fetishism has such a strong hold on the branches of government that efforts directed towards producing strong top-down policy for a degrowth economy will essentially be ignored by policy makers—unable to make it through the filter of pro-growth capitalist ideology—and thus those efforts for progressive top-down change could well be wasted. Oppositional movements do not, of course, have a surplus of energy or resources to waste or misdirect, so if it is the case that the zebra of growth capitalism will not change its stripes, it arguably follows that people should not dedicate their efforts towards convincing it to do so, no matter how desirable that top-down change may be. Rather, people should dedicate their efforts towards areas with the greatest leverage—with the greatest potential to effect positive change—and we have come to suspect that, with respect to degrowth, the areas that have the greatest leverage lie amongst the grass-roots of social movements and culture, not parliament or the courts—at least at this early stage in the transformation (Alexander 2013).

The socio-cultural domain may have special disruptive potential due to the fact that other spheres of transformation can be understood as tools or means, whereas the socio-cultural sphere can be understood to be the source of goals or ends. This difference is important because until there is a culture shaped by the values and vision of living on a 'fair share' ecological footprint, available tools or means for societal change (e.g. legislation, technology, capital, etc.) are likely to be misdirected, and perhaps even be employed in counter-productive ways. In much the same way as the tool of 'fire' can have a positive or negative impact on our lives, depending on how it is used and how much of it there is, the tools of technology, business, and politics can advance or inhibit the transition to a degrowth society, depending on the social values and desires that shape their implementation and development. For these reasons, the urban socio-cultural sphere can be considered fundamental, in the sense that it provides the ends towards which available means are directed.

Another way to think about the importance of the socio-cultural sphere is in terms of sequencing; that is, in terms of what order various transformations may need to take place on the path to a degrowth society. By the time business, the state, and technology are capable of 'disrupting' the status quo, it may be that a revolution in social values would need to have already taken place, in order to have driven such transformation in the first place and been receptive to it. Again, this is not meant to downplay the undeniable importance of technological, economic, and political innovations on the path to a new, ecologically viable and socially just way of life. A coordinated, multi-faceted approach is both necessary and desirable. But insofar as technology, business, and politics are a reflection of the culture in which they are situated, it would seem that disruptive innovation in the socio-cultural sphere may need to be the prime mover, so to speak, which would then enable or ignite further disruptive innovations in other spheres of life.

Putting faith in the emergence of a new cultural consciousness and new social practices is of course a two-edged sword. Culture can either create the driving force for a new economy, through progressive grass-roots action, or be responsible for the extant economy being maintained and entrenched, by way of apathy, distraction or inaction. Furthermore, to suggest that the nature of a political economy, and the urban form a political economy produces, are merely reflections or products of culture is a contestable and, in many ways, an overly simplistic proposition. Public (and specifically urban) policy, for example, rather than always being shaped or enabled by culture in a uni-directional way, sometimes takes the *lead* in societal development and is influenced by forces *other* than culture—for better or for worse. The same can be said of the spheres of business and technology, both of which *shape* culture as they are *shaped by* culture, in a dialectical fashion.

Nevertheless, any transformative politics, technology, or business model needs to be complemented, and probably preceded by, a co-relative transformation in the socio-cultural sphere. This suggests that we must carefully consider not only what social conditions would best facilitate the realisation of a degrowth economy, but also what role social or cultural movements might have to play in producing those conditions. For even if notions of degrowth were to gain widespread acceptance within a culture, it seems highly unlikely that a degrowth economy would emerge unless people had some idea of what needed to be done at the household and community levels to bring about such an economy. In other words, it is not enough merely to offer a critique of existing *structures* of growth capitalism; it is equally important to explore the question of *how one ought to live* in opposition to those structures. Again, we draw on the words of Holloway (2010: 254):

> Revolution is not about destroying capitalism, but about refusing to create it... To think of destroying capitalism is to erect a great monster in front of us, so terrifying that we either give up in despair or else conclude that the only way in which we can slay the monster is by constructing a great party with heroic leaders who sacrifice themselves (and everyone around them) for the sake of the revolution... To pose revolution as the destruction of capitalism is to distance it from ourselves, to put it off into the future. The question of revolution is not in the future. It is here and now: how do we stop producing the system by which we are destroying humanity [and the planet]?

Resistance and Renewal: Contemporary Urban Social Movements Bubbling Under the Surface

The theory of change presented in this chapter maintains that there will be no realisation of degrowth visions of the economy and society—including suburban transformation—until there is a confluence of engaged and active grassroots social movements that demand degrowth (or something like it) and are prepared to drive a new world into existence. Currently our concern is that representative democracy in advanced capitalist societies has created a largely apolitical culture that is too often sedated by the promise of rising affluence, in which citizens vote once every few years and otherwise leave the task of governance to developers and their political representatives. It is a passive politics that works relentlessly in the interests of capital.

It is quite clear to us, of course, that no movement for degrowth is currently capable of inducing the revolutionary changes that degrowth would require, certainly not in Australia. Nevertheless, in closing this chapter it is worth acknowledging some of the contemporary social movements that, while far from representing an organised movement for degrowth in the suburbs, do hint at aspects of what a transition politics could look like if radicalised over coming years and decades. (Obviously, the vocabulary of degrowth does not need to be used for a movement to contribute to degrowth's emergence.) Furthermore, we hold some uneasy confidence that as the dominant growth economies continue to collide with ecological limits in coming years the case for degrowth will only become clearer to more and more people, which will act as a mobilising force.

Urban social movements can be defined as 'urban-orientated mobilizations that influence structural social change' (Castells 1983: 305) and which seek to 'undermine social hierarchies which structure urban life and create, instead, a city on the basis of use values, autonomous local cultures and decentralized participatory democracy' (Mayer 2006: 202). We use the term broadly to include social mobilisations that self-identify as a movement, as well as local eruptions of community engagement and significant cultural shifts made up of only loosely connected participants. The premise we seek to defend and build upon is that through 'self-organization of independent actors' urban social movements raise 'radical possibilities for living different urban lives in reconfigured urban economies' (Bulkeley 2013: 11). As Manuel Castells (1983: 294) argues: 'without social movements, no challenge will emerge from civil society able to shake the institutions of the state through which norms are enforced, values preached, and property preserved'.

In Australia we could begin a grounded survey of promising urban social movements by turning to the relatively small but vocal networks of concerned citizens in the large cities that operate under the banner of 'Save our Suburbs'. This social movement is focussed on resisting the destructive renewal of urban consolidation and overdevelopment and seeks to mobilise communities with the aim of establishing planning and design policies that maintain or improve neighbourhood amenity; are environmentally sensitive and sustainable; and are genuinely democratic and consultative in nature. This network is often demonised by planners and progressives who wish to push for market-based compaction. There is also a risk that the movement reflects a class of privileged actors who, far from being motivated by hopes of contributing to the common good, merely seek to maintain the clean and spacious affluence of their own often expensive and thus exclusive suburban contexts.

Nevertheless, we see in this movement the seeds of something more progressive—at least potentially. The problem with current modes of urban development—especially poorly designed infill apartments on suburban subdivisions—is that the outcome often functions to inhibit or render impossible the very modes of suburban sufficiency that are implicit in the vision of degrowth. Until suburban communities mobilise in the face of capital and reclaim the right to shape their own suburban futures, suburbia is likely to continue being shaped and reshaped by developers who are driven by profit-maximisation, not the desire to see the suburbs transform in ecologically viable and socially convivial ways.

The 'Transition Towns' Movement (now generally referred to as 'Transition Initiatives') is another nascent social experiment that emerged on the scene over a decade ago—first in the UK and now across many nations of the world—and which remains bubbling under the surface in many cities without managing to fulfil its ambitious goals (Hopkins 2008, 2011). Whereas the more-established Ecovillage Movement has generally sought (or been required) to escape the urban context to establish experiments in alternative living, the Transition Movement, motivated by similar concerns, tends to accept the challenge of transforming city life from *within* the urban boundary. Both the promise and the failings of the movement are instructive.

The fundamental aims of Transition Initiatives are to respond to the overlapping challenges of climate change, peak oil, social isolation, and economic instability by decarbonising and re-localising the economy through a community-led model of change based on permaculture design principles. As well as decarbonisation and relocalisation, another central goal of the movement is to build community resilience, a term which can be broadly defined as the capacity of a community or society to withstand shocks and the ability to adapt after disturbances. There is obviously a huge overlap here with the concerns reviewed in earlier chapters of this book. Notably, within the Transition Movement crisis in the current system is typically presented not as a cause for despair but as a transformational opportunity, a prospective change for the better that should be embraced rather than feared.

Rather than waiting for governments to lead, communities in this movement are embracing the 'power of just doing stuff', as it is expressed by the movement's most prominent spokesperson, Rob Hopkins (2013), based in Totnes in the UK. In doing so, the movement runs counter to the dominant narrative of globalisation, representative democracy, and economic growth, and instead offers a positive, participatory, highly localised but more humble vision of a post-carbon future, as well as an evolving roadmap for getting there through grassroots activism. In the words of post-growth economist, Tim Jackson, this international grassroots movement is 'the most vital social experiment of our time' (quoted in Hopkins 2011).

Recently, David Holmgren, whose Australian-based work has significantly shaped the Transition Movement both in theory and practice, has called for such grassroots movements to 'retrofit the suburbs' (Holmgren 2012, 2018). This process would involve individuals and communities acting locally—with or without government support—to try to radically transform their urban and suburban landscapes by thinking creatively about how to make the best of an infrastructure that is often poorly design from social and environmental perspectives.

Defining activities include attempts to (re)localise food production and connect with local farmers; increase home-based economies; relearn the skills of self-sufficiency; practise frugality and voluntary simplicity to reduce consumption; organise sharing and barter schemes beyond the formal economy; take the energy efficiency of their homes and lifestyles into their own hands; as well as attempt to decarbonise energy use not only through household and community-based renewable energy systems but also by minimising energy consumption through behaviour change (e.g. cycling more and driving less). More than one thousand Transition Initiatives in over 40 countries have been established over the last decade, seeking to practice these and other 'retrofitting' strategies. This movement, marginal though it remains, has been able to celebrate many inspiring successes (Hopkins 2015).

Nevertheless, promising though it is, the Transition Movement thus far has failed to scale up to a degree needed to disrupt the momentum of growth capitalism. It is important to be balanced in this critique, however, since it is quite clear that *every* strategy has failed to create a just and sustainable post-capitalist world. It is easy to dismiss permaculture and Transition Initiatives as being of trifling significance—as modes of resistance that are easily accommodated by capitalism. And such dismissal is not without some justification. Indeed, like the 'Save the Suburbs' movement, the Transition Movement also seems to be at risk of being overrepresented by the 'usual suspects'—the generally white, privileged, and educated people that find it easier than others to find the time for social and environmental activism. It is hard to imagine a post-capitalist world coming into existence through activism unless a movement manages to engage the working classes more broadly than the Transition Movement has thus far been able to do.

But again, the failures of the Transition Movement to date do not necessarily mean that the general theory of transformation it seeks to practice is flawed. After all, how can we seriously expect a new world to emerge if local communities—including the range of working classes in the twenty-first century—do not come together themselves to create it? Even if aspects of the transition will require progressive state policy, surely such policy will never manifest until the social conditions are conducive to its emergence.

Furthermore, marginal though the Transition Movement is, it is important to remember that the first 'sit in' during the Civil Rights Movement
would also have been dismissed as dreamy and of no consequence, and
the same could be said of every social movement of significance. But as
the Australian singer Paul Kelly reminds us: 'From little things big things
grow'. The more interesting question, therefore—especially in a context
of 'top down' political paralysis—is what might happen if the Transition
Movement radicalised and scaled up? Might the Transition Movement, or
something resembling it, still be needed if urban and suburban landscapes
are to be transformed in radically progressive ways?

Even though the Transition Movement may have already had its
'15 min of media fame', it is heartening to note that there is a broader
emergence of grassroots social and ecological activism and activity that
in many ways advances its ambitions, even if the language of Transition
Initiatives (or degrowth) is not used. These include the range of local
food movements and initiatives, from local farmers markets and community gardens, to larger urban agriculture projects or more symbolic
acts of guerrilla gardening. It includes the participants and organisers of
emerging sharing economies, as well as the growing pool of climate activists (including 'Lock the Gate' groups), divestment organisers, and progressive unions. It includes the energy frugal households quietly moving
towards solar, one by one undermining the fossil fuel industry and subtly
disrupting the status quo, as well as the artists, musicians, storytellers and
film makers that are helping tell new stories of prosperity. Thus the tenta-
tive hope we place in the Transition Movement really extends well beyond
those formally engaged with the movement, and includes a far broader
movement of people and communities engaged in 'transition activities'.

We admit that these movements for change remain marginal, especially in cultures and economies, such as Australia, still dominated by
materialistic and growth-orientated conceptions of progress. But one
way or another, that old story of progress is coming to an end in coming years due to its irresolvable ecological and financial contradictions.
Perhaps it has already come to an end, such that we find ourselves today
in a sort of limbo, in-between stories, without a new narrative in which
to lay down roots. Or, then again, perhaps a new narrative—or rather, a
confluence of new narratives—is already with us, and our political duty

today, as ecological citizens on a shared planet, is to participate in their emergence and to live them into existence.

Certainly, we must conceive of this action at a transformative scale. To succeed, there must be solidarity across the suburban fabric: a 'save our suburbs' or Transition Initiative which radicalises and organises to become a mutually supporting mosaic of richer and poorer localities and demographics. From this could emerge a movement to 'renew our suburbs' which transcends the impulse to defend the status quo in the face of rampant urban capital and forwards to a new urban imaginary.

Getting on with the Work of Resettling

The task of the next chapter is to explore what it might mean to resettle the suburbs in the spirit of degrowth, here and now, even if it is clear that often people will find themselves locked into reproducing capitalism against their wishes. As David Harvey (2013: xvi) argues, reclaiming the city 'cannot occur without the creation of a vigorous anti-capitalist movement that focuses on the transformation of daily urban [and suburban] life as its goal'. Thus, it is to the transformation of daily suburban life that we now turn. We do so not only to understand what progressive steps can be taken within existing structures, but also to highlight the structures that currently constrain and disenfranchise many people today, even in affluent societies. Too many cultural theorists fail to see the constraints on action imposed by the structures of political economy, whereas too many political economists fail to see how the structural change that is necessary must be grounded in a new cultural consciousness. Our goal is to synthesise these perspectives, both of which, we maintain, are necessary to any coherent politics of deep societal transformation in the direction of degrowth.

In exploring these issues we endeavour to reconceive the notion of revolution, leaving behind the idea of revolution as being some historical or future 'event' where disgruntled citizenries storm the Bastille. There is no Bastille to storm anymore, since the politico-financial nodes of global capitalism, or Empire, are so widely dispersed and decentralised that the system can evade a centralised confrontation of the old revolutionary kind. So revolution, as such, is no longer a goal to be achieved. Instead, revolution today—a suburban revolution, in particular—must take the form of a frame of mind grounded in a way of life: as an ongoing transgressive engagement with the present, in the flow of revolt, with ambitions of building new worlds within the shell of the old.

References

Albert, Michael. 2004. *Parecon: Life After Capitalism*. London: Verso.

Alexander, Samuel. 2013. Voluntary Simplicity and the Social Reconstruction of Law: Degrowth from the Grassroots Up. *Environmental Values* 22 (2): 287–308.

Alexander, Samuel, and Peter Burdon. 2017. Wild Democracy: A Biodiversity of Resistance and Renewal. *The Ecological Citizen* 1: 45–54.

Allcot, Blake. 2008. The Sufficiency Strategy: Would Rich-World Frugality Lower Environmental Impact? *Ecological Economics* 64: 770–786.

Baer, Hans. 2017. *Democratic Eco-socialism as a Real Utopia*. New York: Berghahn.

Bulkeley, Harriet. 2013. *Cities and Climate Change*. London: Routledge.

Castells, Manuel. 1983. *The City and the Grassroots: A Cross-Cultural Theory of Urban Social Movements*. Berkeley: University of California Press.

Cosme, Ines, Rui Santos, and Daniel O'Neill. 2017. Assessing the Degrowth Discourse: A Review and Analysis of Academic Degrowth Policy Proposals. *Journal of Cleaner Production* 149: 321–334.

Dewey John. 1981–90. *The Later Works: Volume 13*, ed. Jo Ann Boydston. Carbondale: Southern Illinois University Press.

Foster, John Bellamy. 2000. *Marx's Ecology: Materialism and Nature*. New York: Monthly Review Press.

Fotopoulous, Takis. 2016. *The New World Order in Action: Globalization, the Brexit Revolution, and the 'Left'*, vol. I. San Diego: Progressive Press.

Gibson-Graham, J.K. 2006. *Post-capitalist Politics*. Minneapolis: University of Minnesota Press.

Hardt, Michael, and Antoni Negri. 2000. *Empire*. Cambridge: Harvard University Press.

Harvey, David. 2013. *Rebel Cities: From the Right to the City to Urban Revolution*. London: Verso.

Holloway, John. 2002. *Change the World Without Taking Power*. London: Pluto Press.

———. 2010. *Crack Capitalism*. London: Pluto Press.

Holmgren, David. 2012. Retrofitting the Suburbs for the Energy Descent Future. *Simplicity Institute Report 12i*: 1–8.

———. 2018. *Retrosuburbia: The Downshifter's Guide to a Resilient Future.* Hepburn: Melliodora Publishing.

Homer-Dixon, Thomas. 2006. *The Upside of Down: Catastrophe, Creativity, and the Renewal of Civilisation.* Washington: Island Press.

Hopkins, Rob. 2008. *The Transition Handbook: From Oil Dependency to Local Resilience.* White River Junction: Chelsea Green.

———. 2011. *The Transition Companion: Making Your Community More Resilient in Uncertain Times.* White River Junction: Chelsea Green.

———. 2013. *The Power of Just Doing Stuff: How Local Action Can Change the World.* Cambridge: UTI/Green Books.

———. 2015. *21 Stories of Transition.* Totnes: Transition Network.

Hudson, Michael. 2012. Debts That Can't Be Paid, Won't Be. http://michael-hudson.com/2012/04/debts-that-cant-be-paid-wont-be/. Accessed 20 June 2018.

Inglehard, Ronald, and Christian Welzel. 2005. *Modernization, Cultural Change, and Democracy: The Human Development Sequence.* Cambridge: Cambridge University Press.

Mayer, Margit. 2006. Mauel Castells' The City and the Grassroots. *International Journal of Urban and Regional Research* 30 (1): 202–206.

Piketty, Thomas. 2014. *Capital in the Twenty-First Century.* Cambridge: Harvard University Press.

Purdey, Stephen. 2010. *Economic Growth, the Environment, and International Relations: The Growth Paradigm.* New York: Routledge.

Purdy, Jedediah. 2015. *After Nature: A Politics for the Anthropocene.* Boston, MA: Harvard University Press.

Sarkar, Saral. 1999. *Eco-socialism or Eco-capitalism: A Critical Analysis of Humanity's Fundamental Choice.* London: Zed Books.

Smith, Richard. 2016. *Green Capitalism: The God That Failed.* London: College Publications.

Thoreau, Henry David. 1984. *The Journal of Thoreau (Volume I).* Layton: Peregrine Smith Books.

Trainer, Ted. 2010. *Transition to a Sustainable and Just World.* Sydney: Envirobook.

———. 2011. The Radical Implications of a Zero-Growth Economy. *Real World Economics Review* 57: 71–82.

Wiedmann, Thomas, Heinz Schandl, Manfred Lenzen, Daniel Moran, Sangwon Suh, J. West, and Keiichiro Kanemoto. 2015. The Material Footprint of Nations. *Proceedings of the National Academy of Sciences* 112: 6271–6276.

5

Unlearning Abundance: Suburban Practices of Energy Descent

'Collapse now and avoid the rush.'
—John Michael Greer

To this point, our argument has been predominantly abstract and 'big picture', deliberately so, in order to lay the foundations for a radical urban imaginary and a social movement that might prosecute it. In this chapter we shift perspectives and move the concrete examination of life in suburbia to the centre of our analysis. It is here, as we have just argued, where the struggle for a post-capitalist economics and politics will play out most significantly—or rather, *must* play out—in the form of degrowth practices that seek to resettle suburbia from the grassroots up.

Degrowth for Whom?

At once we need to highlight a critical tension raised by this shift in perspective—a tension that speaks to the complexity of any praxis and politics of degrowth. On the one hand, this new paradigm categorically entails a significant reduction in the energy and resource demands of

© The Author(s) 2019
S. Alexander and B. Gleeson, *Degrowth in the Suburbs*,
https://doi.org/10.1007/978-981-13-2131-3_5

the wealthiest societies, so it is important to grasp what such down-scaling might look like in terms of lived experience. The forthcoming analysis considers that question in some detail. On the other hand, it is clear that there are many people, even in affluent societies like Australia, who are in precarious financial situations, struggling simply to feed and clothe their families, and who certainly do not experience their consumption practices as being excessive and superfluous (Bauman 2004). Degrowth for whom, one might fairly ask?

This raises structural and distributive issues concerning class, privilege, and property ownership. These issues entail a critique which has been levelled at the permaculture, ecovillage, sustainable consumption, and 'simple living' movements regularly, and it has some bite in the context of degrowth too. Although the practices reviewed below will need to be a part of any convivial emergence of degrowth in the suburbs, many (but not all) of the practices depend on the ownership of land or access to secure housing, which are privileges far from being universally provided.

Access to affordable land and housing is fundamental. This draws the analysis into radical and controversial territory, because broadening societal access to land and housing implies a revision of property rights and market structures which sit at the conceptual heart of capitalism. Options for radical reform will be considered in Chapter 7 but for now the point is simply that some of the practices reviewed in this chapter are not easily embraced by those unable to secure ownership of, or secure access to, housing and land. As populations grow and put more pressure on cities, this problem of ownership and access to affordable housing threatens to intensify, unless there are some bold policy interventions aimed at broadening the distribution of wealth, power, and property in society.

In the same vein, tenure is profoundly important. There are obvious reasons why people renting will not invest in solar panels or water tanks in a transient or insecure rental property. That is, renting implies what urban theorist Anitra Nelson (2018: 102) calls an 'unsettled temporariness'. Even digging up the lawn and growing food can depend on the permission of landlords. Furthermore, retrofitting a house can be expensive and many households may not have discretionary expenditure to invest in solar panels, efficient appliances, water tanks, etc., especially if trying to get into the housing market which may well imply oppressive mortgage obligations.

It would be naïve, therefore, to suggest that personal or household action alone can resolve the problems outlined in previous chapters. But that does not mean that the following program of action is not a necessary part of the picture of transformation. It just means that there are deep structural, financial and cultural obstacles that lie in the way of such a grassroots transition scaling up.

In light of these complexities we will argue that the urban social movements needed for degrowth to emerge must ultimately work towards structural change, so that the freedom to practice degrowth does not remain limited to those relatively privileged sectors of society that are currently able to 'choose' their material living standard to some extent. Nevertheless, we also recognise the latent transformative potential of those who have the agency to downshift their material living standards, here and now (Holmgren 2018). These relatively high-consumption suburbanites—prosperous working and middle classes—will have to play a lead role creating the social conditions needed for a politics of degrowth to emerge, and this chapter will focus predominately on that class capacity. But this focus on suburban homeowners can only be the start of a degrowth transformation, and ultimately this constituency must commit to and collaborate with broader social movements of solidarity, resistance, redistribution and transition.

Enough, for Everyone, Forever: Towards an Economics of Sufficiency

What, then, might degrowth look like at the level of the suburban household? What does it mean for a household to plan for economic contraction and embrace an energy descent future? Does this necessarily imply hardship, deprivation, and sacrifice? Or, if negotiated wisely, could such a managed descent give rise to an alternative form of prosperity? This raises practical questions about what suburban households can actually do to begin building the new economy within the shell of the old, but it also highlights the question of what role socio-cultural transformation needs to play in reclaiming the city for the post-capitalist struggle for degrowth (Gibson-Graham et al. 2013).

Some of the practices and attitudes reviewed in this chapter will come as no surprise, such as retrofitting a house for increased energy efficiency; a material ethics of frugality and sharing; household investment in solar panels; mending and making things rather than always buying; radically reducing waste; cycling; re-localising food production via backyard gardening and urban agriculture; and connecting with local farmers and producers, etc. Such 'old ideas' will not excite those who fetishise 'the new', but we argue that such practices deserve cursory restatement because they have a necessary and significant role to play creating the socio-cultural conditions needed for a degrowth society to emerge. In other words, there will be no politics or macroeconomics beyond growth until there is a culture of sufficiency that wants it, so we must understand what material and energy sufficiency would look like in a suburban context.

We also review other potential features of a retrofitted suburbia that have received far less attention in mainstream sustainability discourse, including domestic biogas production, disconnecting from fossil gas, composting toilets, solar ovens, peer-to-peer sharing, the gift economy, and re-commoning public and private space. Many of these practices are particularly suited—sometimes *only* suited—to the suburban landscape, in ways we will explain. We do not present such a brief survey as a universalisable or complete blueprint to be applied independent of context. By considering a range of such practices, and highlighting their underlying principles of motivation, it is hoped that we can begin to discern a new, post-carbon suburban imaginary that embodies the precepts of degrowth.

Remember, the central message of our argument so far is that sustainability in the suburbs (and more broadly) cannot be achieved merely through techno-efficiency improvements and the decarbonisation of consumer lifestyles. The extent of decoupling required is simply too great. Of course, all societies do need to exploit appropriate technologies and design innovations in order to produce and consume more efficiently. But to have any positive effect, efficiency has to be grounded in an ethics, economics and ultimately a politics of sufficiency and self-limitation, and in overconsuming and overproducing societies, including Australia, that means a radical but voluntary demand-side reduction in energy and resource use. Efficiency without sufficiency is lost, as demonstrated by the increasing resource demands of growth capitalism over recent centuries (Kallis 2017).

Such a demand-side reduction will involve the ethical renegotiation of our relationships with the material world, as well as a vast and growing politics of collective action to support and realise it (Read et al. 2018). The rejection of materialistic values and practices is generally referred to as voluntary simplicity, otherwise known as 'downshifting' or just 'simple living' (Alexander 2009). That means unlearning consumerist cultures of consumption which are so easily taken for granted and normalised in developed nations, and relearning creative frugality. But it also means creating the range of societal structures to support rather than inhibit post-consumerist, sufficiency-based ways of living. Even though it is currently out of intellectual and political fashion, we maintain that there is an utterly indispensable literature on sufficiency, moderation, self-limitation and frugality that must inform any coherent sustainability-justice agenda (Westacott 2016; Alexander and McLeod 2014). Degrowth is one of the few politico-economic paradigms that seek to make sufficiency central to a new way of life.

We reemphasise that we are not oblivious to the range of deep structural obstacles that make the following household practises and behaviour changes harder than they need to be (and depending on context and situation, sometimes impossible). We are perfectly yet uncomfortably aware that there are many people—the homeless, landless, and even precarious renters and those burdened by basic mortgages with precarious jobs—that are experiencing harsh economic insufficiency or at best a crude, enforced sufficiency. To argue for material balance and moderation must not be interpreted as rationalising destitution. A post-growth society must meet all basic human needs for food, clothing, shelter, education and healthcare—while recognising that the very notion of 'needs' is complex and, beyond basic biophysical requirements for subsistence, the distinction between need and want is inevitably culturally dependent (Jackson et al. 2004).

All this complicates the advocacy of certain practices of low-impact living and calls for caution against moralism and 'middle-class broadcasting'. As the Kantian dictum goes: ought implies can. While embracing more frugal and low-impact household practices is a strategy available to wide segments of affluent societies, there are also many people who are structurally 'locked in' to high-consumption lifestyles for one reason or another, in ways to be discussed, just as others can be 'locked out' (Sanne 2002). In both cases, the injunction to 'consume less' is not helpful, pointing to the necessity of a systemic response, albeit one driven 'from below'. Accordingly, redistribution of resources and ensuring economic security for all are not just desirable but necessary societal goals, given that inequality and poverty are amongst the most potent barriers to realising an economy of sufficiency.

We hope readers will see that the political naivety that reflects poorly on some accounts of sufficiency and 'simpler living' is, for the most part, at least, absent in this book. Indeed, one of the purposes of the following household analysis is to lay the groundwork for a more focussed structural and macroeconomic lens later in the book. We want to understand what the barriers are to deep green sustainability practices and how ordinary people can contribute to their deconstruction.

Building upon the post-capitalist politics argued for in the last chapter, let us remember that 'economy', according to Aristotle, meant the good management of the household, and for him the household was the foundation of the *polis*. In our age of governmental paralysis and failure of nerve, this Aristotelian perspective might again highlight the necessity of a political strategy which begins with the intentional transformation of daily life in the suburbs. As Theodore Roszak, author of *Where the Wasteland Ends* (1972: 422), stated:

> There is one way forward: the creation of flesh and blood examples of low-consumption, high-quality alternatives to the mainstream pattern of life. This we can see happening already on the counter-cultural fringes. And nothing – no amount of argument and research – will take the place of such living proof. What people must see is that ecologically sane, socially responsible living is *good* living; that simplicity, thrift and reciprocity make for an existence that is free.

Suburban Practices of Energy Descent

Our survey of household actions and attitudes begins by focussing on the question of energy, to outline how some suburbanites are already practicing energy descent. After reviewing these practices of energy descent, we consider some broader homesteading activities consistent with the imaginary of suburban degrowth.

The Necessity of Demand Reduction

Although it is a message that does not contain any sexy new buzzwords, the most important thing any household can do to decarbonise their energy use is simply to reduce energy demand. After all, as previously argued, a transition to 100% renewables will be proportionately easier to achieve if demand is significantly reduced. Since the industrial revolution, energy has been so cheap that it's made it easy to be wasteful and careless in energy use. That wastefulness provides a source of grounded hope, however, because it means there are huge opportunities for demand reduction in ways that do not imply any reduction in wellbeing. Trimming the energetic fat, so to speak, requires both behavioural changes and investments in household retrofitting activities for increased efficiency and self-provision (Sorrell 2015).

In terms of behaviour change, households can practice a range of unexciting energy rituals, including: turning lights off when leaving the room; taking short showers; never using (or having) a clothes dryer; rarely using air-conditioning; washing clothes only when genuinely needed; closing curtains and windows on very hot days to keep the heat out; putting warm clothing on in cool temperatures before turning on any heating (and only heating the rooms being used); watching TV or online entertainment sparingly; unplugging appliances when not in use; and a long list of tiny other things too mundane to mention. Mainstream environmentalism has been on top of this 'light green' advice for decades, but while these things are necessary they are far from enough to achieve sustainability.

In terms of retrofitting a house, options include: investing in efficient appliances (like a small fridge) and solar panels, and progressively electrifying all gas appliances; putting extra insulation in the walls and roof to minimise the need to heat and cool the house; closing gaps around doors and windows; planting a west-facing grapevine or deciduous tree that shades the house with its foliage in summer, keeping it cool, but lets the sun hit the house in winter by dropping its leaves; installing thick curtains to keep heat in (or out) as needed; and other equally mundane but useful things of this nature.

A range of small and more significant changes can add up to surprisingly large demand-side energy reductions. To explore the extent of possibility here, in recent years Samuel Alexander (present co-author) has been conducting 'action research' into suburban practices of energy descent in Melbourne. By experimenting with the variety of practices and retrofitting activities reviewed in this chapter, his household now draws approximately 75–80% less electricity from the grid per annum, compared to Australian households of the same size (which is also approximately 75-80% less compared to the Australian average). In concrete terms, this means drawing a little over 1 kWh per day, per person, from the grid. This also takes into account the fact they have completely disconnected from fossil gas. (Note, those figures are based on nine months of data to 1 July 2018, so adjustments have been made to include estimated additional energy from winter heating to more accurately reflect yearly consumption). Over this period of data collection, Alexander's household produced six times more electricity from their solar panels than they drew from the grid, making them a significant net producer of renewable electricity with no gas bills and net-zero cost electricity bills over the year. By cycling to work and taking public transport to school, the household reduces fuel costs to a minimum. They have also decarbonised their food consumption by variously adopting a very low or no meat diet. Every household and every context is different, of course, so generalisations should not be made. Obstacles to societal 'powerdown' remain. But the results of these energy descent practices are promising: none of this has required wearing hairshirts or living in a cave without lights. Perhaps Ivan Illich (1973, 1974) was right: low-energy living based on an ethos of sufficiency can be good living.

While there is obviously a privilege implied by owning a house—roughly 65% of Australians own their home—to some extent frugal financial practices and minimising superfluous consumption can free up income to invest in a solar array, a biogas digester, heat pump hot water system—all reviewed below—amongst other retrofitting investments. More and more households have been taking these types of action and practising energy descent here and now, while governments have been sitting on their hands. In 2012, Alexander and Ussher conducted what remains the most extensive empirical examination of the downshifting movement, and conservatively concluded that as many as 200 million people in Western nations are practising voluntary simplicity, although this subculture entails a wide range of practices, from light green consumerism to more radical expressions of simple living. Could this constituency yet radicalise, mobilise, and organise to become a social movement of transformative import? Journalist George Monbiot (2007: 42) famously declared that people never 'riot for austerity', but rioting for a new vision of frugal abundance no longer seems quite so implausible, even if this broad movement remains in its infancy as a political project.

While the systemic and structural challenges will be examined in due course, this research suggests that, in some suburban contexts, much can be done within existing structures to decarbonise the suburban household. Similar suburban cases studies are reviewed in David Holmgren's latest book, *Retrosuburbia* (2018), with similarly promising and inspiring results analysed in Anitra Nelson's recent book, *Small is Necessary* (2018). While the structural problem of carbon 'lock in' is very real for some households (Sanne 2002), it would be foolish to deny or obscure the fact that for many households, a significant portion of their carbon footprint is largely a *choice* or *habit*—a choice that could be made otherwise or a habit reformed. This highlights a cultural challenge, which can be resolved incrementally through ongoing grassroots activities and the evolution of new cultural practices and norms 'from below'. To talk of 'incremental change' and 'evolution', however, should not be interpreted as downplaying the urgency of change that is needed.

The behavioural practices are free but involve the challenge of changing habits, which humans are not very good at without nudging or other incentives (De Young 2014); the investments in efficiency or renewable energy production will cost money, and the challenge in that regard is about creating an ethos of sustainability that sees such investments as more important than other consumer commodities or experiences. That said, the economics of solar are becoming more attractive, such that household solar is becoming less of a 'cost' and more of an 'investment', even though the upfront expense can still be a barrier. Expensive housing and rent will also make such investments difficult for many, although financial space can open up for some households if more frugal and mindful spending practices were adopted, a point to which we will return.

While we certainly do not hold up such personal and household demand-side action as the complete solution to energy problems, and recognise that different households have different needs and capabilities, experience suggests that massive reductions in grid demand in the 75–80% range can be achieved in some household contexts without causing hardship. Making these changes, however, requires the *desire* or *incentive* to take energy demand seriously, which is lacking in many affluent cultures today, primarily because the dominant paradigm of techno-optimism pushes the message that we can just 'green' supply rather than go to the trouble of reducing demand. Our counter-message is that significant demand reduction is achievable in many suburban households, and it is important that decarbonisation in the city begins with these changes wherever they are available. As more households take these small but cumulatively transformative steps, we contend new cultural norms would arise in relation to which current political and macroeconomic goals would be re-evaluated and in time potentially revised. Without dedicated demand-side action, any transition to sustainable energy systems will fail.

Some hard-nosed political economists will be quick to dismiss such 'lifestyle' changes as being of little consequence, not recognising that the structural changes that are certainly needed will never arrive until there is culture that demands them. Practising energy descent at the household level is an indispensable part of that cultural r/evolution, representing a prefigurative politics that is necessary to any post-carbon or post-growth transition. The rest of the household actions reviewed in this chapter should be judged in that light also—not as direct, consumption-based 'solutions' to the problems of overproduction, but as necessary groundwork for creating the new culture of sufficiency that will need to precede any new politics or macroeconomics of sufficiency.

Solar

On the path of household decarbonisation, the second-best thing to do—after significantly reducing demand—is to invest in solar PV, a strategy most suitable for suburbanites with their typically low-density, stand alone houses and private roof space. Since the Australian Federal government is doing almost nothing positive with regards a clean energy transition, and is arguably doing more harm than good, there is an increased burden on households and communities to invest in their own renewable energy, even if this may not always be the most efficient way to do it. Household solar energy production is certainly more efficient than governments doing nothing! In any case, it is likely that a renewable energy future will be one that moves towards greater decentralisation of energy generation, especially if battery technology continues to advance. The tide of household solar installations is strengthening this current, and grid architecture will need to evolve to adapt to changing patterns of generation and use.

Using the sun more directly through solar ovens is another practice highlighting the elegance of simplicity (Alexander and Yacoumis 2018). While unable to completely replace an inside oven, solar ovens can reduce electricity for cooking several days a week, especially in the warmer months, while also teaching households important lessons about the art of living in accordance with solar energy flows.

An Electric 'Heat Pump' Hot Water System

One of the key features of deep decarbonisation involves electrifying energy services previously provided by fossil energy (provided electric appliances are powered by renewable electricity, since electric appliances running on coal-generated electricity can be more carbon-intensive than fossil gas appliances). Electric hot water systems used to cost much more than gas systems to operate, but developments in heat pump technology mean that electric systems are now up to 80% more efficient than they used to be. Without going into the technicalities, a heat pump absorbs heat from the air and transfers it to the water, minimising the need for further heating with electricity. This is a form of solar heating since the sun heats the air and that heat gets transferred to the water, effective even in winter. Best of all, these heat pump units generally have a timer, which means that they can heat the water when the solar panels have maximum sun exposure. For this reason heat pumps can be conceived of as a battery of sorts, with the sun and solar panels 'charging' the water when the sun is up, storing the energy in an extremely well-insulated tank, and residents using the hot water in the mornings or in the evenings when the sun is down. This minimises grid demand in ways that make a 100% renewable energy transition more affordable and manageable.

Biogas in the Suburbs

Most suburban blocks would have space for a domestic biogas digester, although this highly promising alternative technology is all but unknown in developed regions of the world. In this regard the so-called developing nations have much to teach, with China having 27 million biogas digesters and India having 4 million (Bond and Templeton 2011). With irony, blindness, and paradox, the discourse of 'development' can barely conceive of the possibility that 'advanced' nations might have things to learn from the 'less developed' nations. It is a costly arrogance that must be brought down to Earth, for the sake of Earth and our shared inhabitation of it.

Biogas is produced when organic matter biodegrades under anaerobic conditions (i.e. in the absence of oxygen). The primary benefit of biogas is that it is a renewable energy source with net-zero emissions. Whereas the production of oil and other fossil fuels will eventually peak and decline, humans will always be able to make biogas so long as the sun is shining and plants can grow. Biogas has net-zero emissions because the carbon dioxide that is released into the atmosphere when the methane burns is no more than what was drawn down from the atmosphere when the organic matter was first grown.

There are other benefits too. The organic matter used in biogas digesters is typically a waste product. By producing biogas, households can reduce the amount of food waste and other organic materials being sent to landfill, which also means less methane in the atmosphere. Furthermore, biogas digesters produce a nutrient-rich sludge that can be watered down into a fertiliser for gardens, homesteads, or farms. All this helps develop increased energy independence, build resilience, and save money.

Given the alarming levels of food waste in Australia (like other affluent nations), it makes sense to be diverting that waste from landfill to produce clean energy in the suburbs. Research (Reynolds et al. 2014) indicates that there would easily be enough food waste in Australia for all suburban households to cook on biogas without exhausting food waste streams. This would remain true even if food waste was significantly reduced and some food waste was reserved for feeding animals (e.g. chickens). Samuel Alexander's home biogas research shows that putting roughly 1.5 kg per day into the digester generates approximately 38 mins cooking gas each day, on average, which is more than enough to allow households to disconnect from fossil gas for cooking and radically reduce electricity consumption.

Biogas has the potential to be a disruptive alternative technology that could contribute to the demise of the fossil fuel industry, and governments should support suburban households in exploiting this innovation on the path to a post-carbon society. Although it can seem like an energy miracle, biogas is really nothing other than an elegant example of permaculture: working with nature and natural processes, rather than fighting against them.

Post-carbon Transport

We saw in Chapter 3 that electric vehicles will inevitably play some role in the transformation of transport in coming years and decades, however we argued that it is a mistake to think they can solve the problem of the carbon and resource intensity of private automobiles. Any genuine transport solution will not involve electrifying the world's currently growing addiction private motor vehicles but by finding ways to avoid the need for private motor vehicles (Moriarty and Honnery 2016). The alternatives, of course, are walking, cycling, and electrifying public transport, which have many environmental and health benefits (Higgins and Higgins 2005).

Electric bikes—especially electric cargo bikes—are also likely to be of transformative significance, providing a kind of 'middle way' between electric cars and the human-powered bicycle. Electric bikes retain most of the benefits of the human-powered version, while extending ranges and load capacity to cope adaptively with settlements and economies structured to suit cars and trucks. By making cycling lower impact on the rider and much more accessible, electric bikes could be a lynchpin technology for any degrowth transition, at least as an enabler that gets many more people engaged with post-car transport and gives people their first taste of the personal benefits and freedoms available to the cyclist.

Walking or cycling will be non-viable in certain contexts, and even public transport is not always available. These structural problems are well known and not easily or swiftly resolvable, even if the solution is relatively clear: build more infrastructure to support these low-carbon or post-carbon alternatives. Nevertheless, there is also vast scope for replacing a great deal of car trips with alternative modes of transport that are less carbon-intensive here and now, especially through a cultural embrace of cycling.

Cycling and walking provide a particularly clear win-win situation, offering both mental and physical health benefits while also decarbonising urban transport. For complex reasons, modern life has induced an obesity epidemic in many affluent nations—one of the 'diseases of affluence'—primarily due to cultural norms that lead to lack of exercise and poor diets. Many people also find themselves disconnected from nature, too often inside a building or car.

In Australia it has been estimated that three quarters of all personal car journeys are less than 10 km, with half being less than 5 km, and one third less than 3 km. It is reasonable to assume that a significant proportion of those trips could be replaced with cycling without hardship, while acknowledging also that disability, heavy freight, or other complexities would mean a full substitution would be difficult or impossible. Nevertheless, a study in the US (Higgins and Higgins 2005) has shown that substituting walking and cycling for short car trips, based on recommended daily exercise, could reduce US domestic oil consumption by up to 34.9% while also having huge health benefits and leading to reduced health care costs. No doubt other oil-dependent nations, like Australia, could also procure significant savings through this 'simple' strategy.

Ivan Illich (1973, 1974) was right to consider the bicycle one of the most convivial of all technologies, indisputably the most energy efficient means of land transit, and it must undergo a renaissance if there is to be any chance of approaching a post-carbon society. 'Participatory democracy', Illich (1974: 12) argued, 'demands low-energy technology, and free people must travel the road to productive social relations at the speed of a bicycle'. He was also right to argue that the need for such limits as an alternative to disaster is the strongest argument in favour of the bicycle.

Cycling is a good example of the potential of low-tech alternatives (Alexander and Yacoumis 2018)—vastly more promising than waiting for or paying for Teslas. It also highlights how transitioning to a post-carbon way of life is going to imply replacing energy services currently provided by fossil energy with human muscle power (the other key example being post-carbon or organic farming which would require less fossil fuel-dependent machinery, pesticides, and fertilisers, but more labour investment).

Car sharing—especially peer-to-peer sharing—is another promising innovation in terms of transport. By participating in the sharing economy, households can provide 'access without ownership' of a car to a wide range of people and thereby minimise the need for so many cars to clutter the streets. Still, this should be conceived of as a transitional strategy, given that ultimately, a post-carbon city will need to be essentially a car-free city (Moriarty and Honnery 2008). The recent research by Laskovsky and Taylor (2017), discussed in Chapter 3, bears reemphasis: the vast amount of urban and suburban space dedicated to cars, roads, and parking is deeply wasteful, especially when it is understood how inefficiently that space is used in terms of irregular occupation. Reclaiming this land for other purposes is an exciting urban prospect, as it would open up vast tracts of land for an array of retrofitting activities limited only by our imaginations.

As for carbon-intensive plane flight, the solution is not biofuels but avoidance and reduction. Video conferencing, localising holidays, and embracing 'slow travel' provide pathways to escape many if not most flights. (The challenge of re-localising the economy more generally will be taken up further in the next chapter).

Low-Meat Diets and the Other Great Taboo

We close this section on energy with a comment on decarbonising diets. The production of animal products is hugely energy (and carbon) intensive and there is absolutely no way that average Western levels of meat consumption could possibly be globalised in a sustainable way (Poore and Nemecek 2018). While there are some prospects for efficiency improvements in the production of animal products (which unfortunately might come at the expense of animal welfare), the necessary but rarely acknowledged part of the equation is drastically reducing (or, for some, eliminating) meat and dairy consumption in diets (Hadjikakou 2017; Hadjikakou and Wiedmann 2017).

Nevertheless, this issue ought to be approached with the subtlety it deserves. Global averages can mislead, and a localised economy necessarily means shortening to chain between production and consumption in ways that demand context-dependent analysis (Holmgren 2018). To provide an extreme example, it is no good asking the Inuit people to reduce meat consumption given that eating sea mammals is their primary means of sustenance, and there are communities around the world similarly dependent on animal agriculture to survive. Much land is not suitable for cropping, in which case the distinction between grain fed and pasture fed animals is important. Reducing the former could certainly open up more land for lower-carbon, non-meat food production, which would be far more energy efficient on account of feeding food to humans instead of feeding animals and then eating the animals. The role of grazing animals in landscape restoration and regeneration is also an important consideration (Massy 2017), too often overlooked by those ignorant of land management and the practical realities of food production.

None of this changes the fact, however, that in many affluent societies, including Australia, significantly reducing meat and diary consumption is one of the most significant things people can do to decarbonise their lives. Having small families is the other great taboo, yet both these strategies scarcely get a mention in mainstream environmental discourse. This willing blindness is a major cultural obstacle to any post-carbon transition and one that is not easily overcome, other than showing by example that low or no meat diets can be healthy, cheap, and delicious, and that having a small family accrues many benefits aside from the environmental ones (e.g. financial, increased free time, more sleep). Climate activist Bill McKibben (1999) suggested a good starting question for the next generation of parents-to-be: 'Maybe one?' As for diets, it is hard to improve upon the simple advice offered by food guru, Michael Pollan (2007): 'Eat [real] food. Not too much. Mostly plants'.

Towards a Post-carbon Suburban Homestead: Reimagining the Good Life

Beyond direct and indirect energy considerations, the emergence of a contracting degrowth economy 'from below' would obviously require a revaluation of values and practices in other domains of life too. Any consumerist culture is going to require a growth economy to meet its demands for ever-rising material living standards. The flip side of that coin is that a degrowth economy will depend on and require a material culture of sufficiency that embraces a post-consumerist existence of relative energy and resource scarcity. The dual value of embracing this strategy is that it both moves the culture of consumption in a more sustainable direction, but it also prepares the household for disruptive and unstable economic times in which reduced consumption is enforced rather than voluntarily chosen. That is, downshifting prepares the household for times of crisis or unplanned economic contraction, and thus increases resilience, even if the primary or initial motivating goal is sustainability.

By voluntary simplicity we are certainly not just talking about shorter showers, turning the lights off, and recycling. A degrowth culture of consumption must assume a far more radical form of downshifting. According to the ecological footprint analysis, humanity would need four or five planets if the Australian way of life were globalised. If the growing global population by 2050 had attained Australian living standards then humanity would need 10 planets—even more if Australians expect rising material living standards (Trainer 2010).

Few analysts of the global predicament seem to appreciate the magnitude of this challenge: it requires a 75–90% reduction in ecological impacts compared to living standards in the wealthiest regions of the world, even if sustainable living will always be a context-dependent practice. Given that efficiency, technology and the decoupling strategy are failing to bring the global economy within sustainable bounds, it follows by force of logic and evidence that globalising Western-style material living standards is a recipe for catastrophe—both ecological and humanitarian. A just and sustainable world necessarily involves some radically transfigured practices of consumption and production compared to the ecocidal forms which have emerged in the West, and that means, amongst other things, embracing the all but forgotten wisdom of frugality, moderation, and sufficiency (Princen 2005; Westacott 2016).

The reader is justified in being sceptical here, but it is no good critics dismissing this call for simpler living in the suburbs as 'wishful thinking'. We are neither oblivious to the obstacles nor so deluded as to think the revolution in consciousness this cultural transformation implies will be easily achieved. But when the full magnitude of ecological overshoot is recognised on a full to overflowing planet, there is absolutely no alternative but to abandon high-impact suburban affluence as we know it today and radically downshift average energy and resource demands in wealthy nations (Fleming 2016). This is both an ecological and a social justice imperative. Thus, it is not 'wishful thinking' but 'clear thinking' that informs our suburban economics of sufficiency, and any theorists who dismiss the logic of sufficiency are themselves fantasising by ignoring this necessary dimension of any coherent sustainability transition. As the slogan from Paris '68 goes: 'Be realistic—demand the impossible!'

Enlightened Material Restraint: The Practice of Sufficiency and Self-Limitation

What, then, might this alternative way of life look like in practice? As always, context is everything, but some broad comments may offer some general insight. We've already addressed energy, with the simple (but complex) formula being: radically reduce demand and invest in renewable energy. In affluent societies like Australia, some of the funds for such investment can be found simply by reducing expenditure elsewhere. Voluntary simplicity implies being extremely mindful with one's money and being aware that numerous small expenses (magazines, clothes, takeout food, that extra beer, etc.) over months and years can add up to considerable sums.

But this should not be presumed to imply hardship. Once sufficiency in material living standards is achieved, voluntary simplicity implies resisting the dominant cultural current that pushes people to seek ever-higher incomes and ever-more 'nice possessions', and instead seeking the good life in a range of non-materialistic sources of meaning and fulfilment. As the ancient Chinese philosopher Lao-Tzu stated: 'He who knows he has enough is rich'. This essential insight is supported by a vast body of social and psychological research showing that money and possessions have diminishing marginal returns—that is, the richer people get, the less money contributes to quality of life (Lane 2000; Kasser 2002, 2017). Acknowledging again that we live in a world increasingly spilt into 'haves' and 'have nots', the challenge is to work towards a form of societal organisation that provides enough for everyone, and which supports the middle way between overconsumption and under-consumption.

One could also invert Lao-Tzu's maxim and say, with an eye on affluent sectors of society, that those who have enough, but who do not know it, are poor. Some cultural theorists even talk of a condition called 'affluenza', which points to a deep malaise suffered by those who have discovered that consumerism does not satisfy the human craving for meaning (Hamilton and Denniss 2005). It follows, especially in an age of ecological limits, that there is an inescapable need for enlightened material restraint.

Buying second-hand clothes; avoiding the lure of fancy possessions; growing a portion of household food; capturing water in tanks; making or mending rather than purchasing; developing cheap and low-impact leisure activities; sharing and borrowing; brewing one's own beer or cider; minimising waste and avoiding packaging; etc. Households might find that these practices can reduce impact while also saving thousands of dollars every year—creating a surplus that can be directed into the clean energy revolution, or allow for reduced working hours which can open up more time to dedicate to community action, home-based production, or simply more time for family, friends, and private passions. Larger immediate financial savings can sometimes be found by living in modest accommodation, resisting cosmetic house renovations, avoiding that expensive car, or holidaying locally instead of at some overseas resort. Practising voluntary simplicity, therefore, isn't just about knowing how much is enough; it is also about knowing how much is too much. As Henry Thoreau (1984: 568) put it: 'Superfluous wealth can buy superfluities only'.

Of course, the usual proviso applies: many households even in affluent societies are living from pay cheque to pay cheque with little room for voluntary downshifting. But in consumer cultures there are many households that have normalised abundance with no conception of 'enough'. Such a normalisation of abundance must be unlearned. The less people need to purchase to maintain their way of life, the less they are obliged to work to pay for that market consumption. By thus reimagining the good life beyond consumer culture, voluntary simplicity offers a path to maximising freedom and advancing genuine wellbeing, a trade which some writers call 'alternative hedonism' (Soper 2008) or 'frugal hedonism' (Raser-Rowland and Grubb 2016). This rightly implies that self-interest is an incentive beyond environmentalism or concern for the world's destitute, and empirical research verifies that voluntary simplicity offers this hedonic reward (Alexander and Ussher 2012; Kasser 2017).

Even the most radically downshifted suburban households, however, are probably still overconsuming on a global scale, so the practice of sufficiency is an ongoing creative process, not a static destination to arrive at or achieve once and for all. This also points to the systemic crisis, since it can be very hard, and at times, impossible, to consume less within societal structures that have been created to promote limitless growth and unbounded consumerism. Nevertheless, as we have argued, the structural transformation will never transpire until there is a post-consumerist culture that is prepared to embrace material sufficiency, so the individuals and households exploring radical forms of downshifting are pioneering a more mindful and pared-back culture of consumption than the mainstream sustainability movement seems prepared to acknowledge as necessary. Again, that blindness is largely a result of techno-optimism, which assumes technology can solve the problem of overconsumption by decarbonising and dematerialising production.

The main weakness of the voluntary simplicity movement to date has been a tendency to be apolitical, in the sense of advocating individual lifestyle change *within* capitalism, rather than thinking through how downshifting practices can be leveraged to *transcend* and *transform* capitalism through collective and collaborative action and bring about the range of structural changes that will be necessary for both justice and sustainability.

The political significance of the voluntary simplicity movement is most apparent in how it can carve out *more time for people to create the new (suburban) economy*. The politics of voluntary simplicity is typically conceived of in terms of 'political consumers' who express their values through what they buy and where they spend. That is fine so far as it goes, but it misses the more significant matter of freedom and time. Building a new economy from the grassroots up will take time, and currently most households are 'time poor', locked into the work-and-spend cycle. By rethinking consumption levels, embracing frugality, and exchanging superfluous stuff for more free time, voluntary simplicity provides a pathway that can enable grassroots activism, while also being directly in line with the values of degrowth. Indeed, degrowth could be defined as the politics (and macroeconomics) of voluntary simplicity.

Eating the Suburbs

In terms of increased self-sufficiency, the obvious starting point is home-based food production (Gaynor 2006). There is a flourishing 'local food movement' in many cities today, even if its full potential has not yet been fully realised. Digging up backyards and front yards and planting fruit and vegetables, keeping chickens, and composting, are important practices, reconnecting people with the seasons, the soil, and the food on their plates. In the words of permaculture activist and educator, Adam Grubb, we should 'eat the suburbs'.

Furthermore, in an age of widespread 'nature deficit disorder' (Louv 2008) the rewards of home gardening go well beyond the environmental and health benefits of eating local, fresh food. Human beings are biophysical creatures, and spending too many hours indoors or in cars, under artificial lights, eating highly processed food from supermarkets, seems to be slowly eating away at our vitality and spirit. Getting into the garden and out of our cars offers existential rewards, although this is something that can probably only be experienced, not explained.

In terms of what can be produced in suburban plots, quantitative research is slowly emerging. For example, Kat Lavers, a prominent permaculture teacher and practitioner in Melbourne, produces more than 350 kg of fruit, vegetables and eggs, per year on 1/14th of an acre block in suburbia, indicating what can be achieved even on small plots. Scholarly analyses support this potential. Ted Trainer, long time advocate of 'the simpler way', has undertaken a detailed quantitative analysis of East Hills, an outer suburb of Sydney, Australia, where he lives. Trainer (2016) demonstrates that critics who dismiss the productive capacity of urban and suburban agriculture are wrong. Similarly promising analyses have been published by the Victorian Eco-Innovation Lab (VEIL 2018), at the University of Melbourne.

Nevertheless, few suburban households, if any, could be fully self-sufficient in fruit and vegetables, let alone in other foodstuffs like wheat, oats, and rice, as well as any number of other foodstuffs like salt, sugar, nuts, and milk. But producing as much as possible saves money, increases self-sufficiency, builds resilience, and as noted, reconnects people with the land and soil. Trainer's analysis, just noted, also highlights the importance of moving beyond merely 'self-sufficiency' and working towards a 'collective sufficiency' wherever possible. This would involve reclaiming under-utilised public land, especially roads and car parks (Laskovsky and Taylor 2017), and increased sharing of private land for food production.

In terms of creating soil, the suburban composting toilet may also have a place in a sustainable future, as households stop exporting nutrient-rich waste in potable water and instead treat their own waste onsite, as Sydney's Michael Mobbs, author of *Sustainable House* (2010), is already doing, as are other early adopters. This helps close the nutrient cycle; it creates fertiliser for fruit trees; and minimises or avoids the need to import fertilisers for the garden, saving money. Human waste needs to be respected for safety reasons but it need not be feared, as explained and scientifically justified in *The Humanure Handbook*, by Joseph Jenkins (2005).

Home-based food production also offers a means of escaping the market, to some extent, thereby undermining the industrial food industry by withdrawing financial support for it, and redirecting that support, when necessary, towards local farmers markets. Over time we can imagine food production crossing beyond household boundaries too, re-commoning public space, and this is in fact already underway as people reclaim nature strips for food production, plant fruit trees in the neighbourhood, establish community gardens, and cultivate unused land through 'guerrilla gardening'. Decarbonising food production generally means re-localising production—shortening the space between production and consumption—and urban agriculturalists are not waiting for governments to lead this transition.

Escaping the Market: Sharing, Gift, and the Urban Peasantry

We will close this incomplete survey by highlighting the importance of sharing, gift, and home-based production, all of which have untapped prospects for decarbonisation, dematerialisation, and relocalisation, and which will receive more detailed treatment in the next chapter. These are topics that also highlight how degrowth involves an upscaling of 'informal', 'non-monetary', and 'post-capitalist' modes of economy, as well as increased economic localisation (Albert 2004; De Young and Princen 2012; Gibson-Graham et al. 2013).

By sharing more between households—facilitated by the internet or by traditional community engagement—less energy and resource-intensive production needs to occur to meet society's needs. Indeed, even in a contracting economy (whether contraction is by design or by crisis), households can still secure access to the tools and other things they need, provided a culture of sharing emerges. This is the revolutionary reinterpretation of 'efficiency' implicit in the degrowth paradigm: produce less; share more. Beyond goods and services, Anitra Nelson's book *Small Is Necessary* (2018) explores the potential of sharing land and housing as a promising means of overcoming some of the access barriers to this fundamental need.

On a similar note, degrowth also implies an incremental re-emergence of the gift economy—to some extent, at least (Eisenstein 2011). If living standards are forever expected to rise, long working hours required to support that ongoing material advance will generally leave people 'time poor', making it difficult for people to gift their skills and resources in the spirit of community and neighbourly support. By consuming less and carving out more time for practices outside the formal economy, downshifting also can also enliven the informal 'gift' economy.

As this culture of decommodification emerges it becomes increasingly self-supporting: one household is liberated from the market economy to some extent by practising voluntary simplicity, allowing more time to gift skills and resources outside the market; but as other households do that too, the benefits and rewards of the gift economy return, reducing reliance on the market economy and making voluntary simplicity increasingly viable, which further supports the gift economy in a symbiotic loop of mutual support. Paradoxically, then, financial frugality enables generosity, solidarity, sharing and redistribution (Gibson-Graham et al. 2013).

Finally, degrowth in the suburbs implies turning the household into a place of production, not merely consumption. On this point, some inspiration can be found in the past. Patrick Mullins and Chris Kynaston (2000) assess what they call the 'urban peasant thesis', and their review of the evidence shows that up until the middle of the twentieth century, Australian urban households had operated a highly developed subsistence-based, domestic economy. This included the production of foodstuffs in suburban backyards, but extended to the manufacture of other household goods, including clothes, furniture and even owner-built housing. Thus the dwelling and the yard were seen primarily in utilitarian, rather than aesthetic, terms. This 'urban peasantry' declined however in the post-War boom, as the rise of mass consumer capitalism enabled households to purchase goods previously produced within the household. We contend that any degrowth or post-capitalist transition may well see the remergence of an 'urban peasantry' in this sense, albeit one shaped by different times and concerns.

Escaping the formal economy and reducing working hours are not strategies designed to create more time to watch television, although voluntary simplicity is the most direct path to increased leisure. But in a degrowth economy the distinction between work and leisure has the prospect of blurring in interesting ways, owing to the fact that the creative process of home-based production can offer genuine rewards of satisfaction and even pleasure. If there is one trait that presents itself as universal in an otherwise highly malleable 'human nature', it is arguably the joys of creative activity. Increasingly capitalism has alienated the worker from these joys through an extreme division of labour, but home-based production offers the prospect of reclaiming those joys while also undermining the mode of production upon which capitalism depends. Whether it is sewing, brewing beer, baking bread, gardening, craft, art, or producing other socially useful goods and services, home-based production can be a satisfying way to spend time, as the artisan knows, in ways that also helps the local economy meets its own needs.

Retrofitting the Suburbs: Prospects and Obstacles

Many of the practices, attitudes, and approaches reviewed in this chapter are not new, merely bringing together modes of living that homesteaders, eco-villagers, permaculturalists, hippies, and other counter-culturists have been doing for decades or more. These practices are eminently sensible—necessary but not sufficient—even if still often marginalised by the dominant culture. There are also a few new and emerging features like domestic biogas and sharing facilitated by the internet, whose cultural potential is highly promising but remains largely untapped. In all cases, the question is how to make these energy descent practices the 'new normal'. Most of the practices are also enabled by the suburban context, such as solar PV, biogas, food production, solar oven use, water collection, etc., which would be impossible, difficult, impractical, or at least significantly different in higher density inner-city contexts.

Again, these household practices are not a panacea to today's problems but it is likely that any successful transition to a sustainable society is going to require more suburbanites embracing them, albeit in context and household-dependent ways. Granted, things like second-hand clothes, biogas, composting toilets, home-based production and sharing offer a humbler vision of a sustainable future than the eco-modernist vision typically presented in glossy environmental magazines, but when the extent of ecological overshoot and the limits of techno-optimism are understood, this vision is much more coherent. We can't just 'green' supply of energy and resources; high-impact societies also need to radically reduce demand.

Promising and necessary though these practices of suburban downshifting are, things are not always or often as rosy or free from contradiction as they might first seem. We opened this chapter by acknowledging the deep structural obstacles of class, privilege and property ownership that lie in the way of any degrowth transition and which we consider further in the next two chapters. We are also disconcertingly aware of how many of the efforts to transition beyond fossil fuels depend, to date at least, on the very fuels those efforts are trying to transcend, as well as the globally integrated supply chains that are enabled by fossil fuels. Solar panels, biogas digesters, heat pumps, and bicycles are currently a product of fossil fuels, and the same goes for nails, screws, steel sheet, and windows, as well as all the commodities that make households function, from pots and cutlery, to furniture and musical instruments. Indeed, even households with vast net surpluses of renewable energy production will, in the absence of expensive battery storage, still draw from and depend on the fossil energy grid at night to keep the fridge running and the lights on after dark.

These critical reflections should not be interpreted as undermining the strategy or importance of retrofitting suburban households in the manner and spirit outlined in this chapter. It only points to the complexity of the predicament. Certainly, access to housing and land can be expensive, sometimes prohibitively so, but there are many suburban houses owned by their inhabitants. In Australia, as noted, approximately 65% of people own their own houses. While relatively marginal social movements for structural change are endeavouring to broaden such access, existing owners can get to work building new forms of life within existing structures, and, as this chapter suggests, there is a huge amount that could be done in that space. The household may not be the world economy, but changing the world will require changing the household economy.

Even though retrofitting can be expensive and that work-life balance can be difficult or elusive in insecure economic circumstances, committed practices of voluntary simplicity can create degrees of financial power. Tightening the belt may not open much financial space for those households already living on the breadline, but with the average Australian household earning around $107,000 p.a., this suggests that in consumer cultures there are many avenues for reducing outgoings through creative acts of self-provision and frugality, or by redirecting superfluous spending on luxuries towards funding the clean energy revolution. Achieving systemic change will no doubt eventually require deep 'top down' structural changes to capitalist economies, but according to the political strategy we have been defending, that systemic change may have to be driven 'from below', at the grassroots level.

Aim for Sustainability but Settle for Resilience?

If the radical downshifting of lifestyles became more widespread across culture, while home-based production increased, this could lead to a process of macroeconomic contraction, as conventionally measured by GDP. But if this contraction was well managed it could increase social wellbeing while also enhancing ecological conditions. We begin to see, then, how a culture of material and energy sufficiency underpins any coherent macroeconomics of degrowth. A prosperous descent no longer sounds so absurd or paradoxical, even if a great many questions remain unanswered. We consider this more closely in the next two chapters.

In any case, even if retrofitting the suburbs, as outlined, proves to be unable to dissolve the perfect storm of crises looming on the horizon, almost everything reviewed in this chapter would increase the resilience of households should unstable economic times return or intensify in the form of a Second Great Depression. Movements for change should aim for sustainability, of course, but in more pessimistic moods we are tempted to suggest the world may have to settle, at best, for resilience—the ability to withstand forthcoming shocks. After all, if a descent lies ahead, it is better to fall out of a ground floor window than a second or third story window. Or, as John Michael Greer (2015) advised in the epigraph to this chapter, perhaps we should 'collapse now and avoid the rush'.

References

Albert, Michael. 2004. *Parecon: Life after Capitalism.* London: Verso.

Alexander, Samuel (ed.). 2009. *Voluntary Simplicity: The Poetic Alternative to Consumer Culture.* Stead and Daughters: Whanganui.

Alexander, Samuel, and Amanda McLeod (eds.). 2014. *Simple Living in History: Pioneers of the Deep Future.* Melbourne: Simplicity Institute.

Alexander, Samuel, and Simon Ussher. 2012. The Voluntary Simplicity Movement: A Multi-national Survey in Theoretical Context. *Journal of Consumer Culture* 12 (1): 66–88.

Alexander, Samuel, and Paul Yacoumis. 2018. Degrowth, Energy Descent, and 'Low-Tech' Living: Potential Pathways for Increased Resilience in Times of Crisis. *Journal of Cleaner Production* 197 (2): 1840–1848. https://doi.org/10.1016/j.jclepro.2016.09.100.

Bauman, Zygmunt. 2004. *Wasted Lives: Modernity and Its Outcasts.* Cambridge: Polity.

Bond, Tom, and Michael Templeton. 2011. History and Future of Domestic Biogas Plants in the Developing World. *Energy for Sustainable Development* 15 (4): 347–354.

De Young, Raymond. 2014. Some Behavioural Aspects of Energy Descent: How a Biophysical Psychology Might Help People Transition Through the Lean Times Ahead. *Frontiers in Psychology* 5: 1255. https://doi.org/10.3389/fpsyg.2014.01255.

De Young, Raymond, and Thomas Princen (eds.). 2012. *The Localization Reader: Adapting to the Coming Downshift*. Cambridge, MA: MIT Press.

Eisenstein, Charles. 2011. *Sacred Economics: Money, Gift, and Society in the Age of Transition*. Berkeley: North Atlantic Books.

Fleming, David. 2016. *Lean Logic: A Dictionary for the Future and How to Survive It*. White River Junction, VT: Chelsea Green.

Gaynor, Andrea. 2006. *Harvest of the Suburbs: An Environmental History of Growing Food in Australian Cities*. Perth: University of Western Australia Publishing.

Gibson-Graham, J.K., Jenny Cameron, and Stephen Healy. 2013. *Take Back the Economy: An Ethical Guide for Transforming Our Communities*. Minneapolis: University of Minnesota Press.

Greer, John Michael. 2015. *Collapse Now and Avoid the Rush*. Danville: Founders House Publishing.

Hadjikakou, Michalis. 2017. Trimming the Excess: Environmental Impacts of Discretionary Food Consumption in Australia. *Ecological Economics* 131: 119–128.

Hadjikakou, Michalis, and Thomas Wiedmann. 2017. Shortcomings of a Growth-Driven Food System. In *Handbook on Growth and Sustainability*, ed. P.A. Victor and B. Dolter, 256–276. Cheltenham: Edward Elgar.

Hamilton, Clive, and Richard Denniss. 2005. *Affluenza: When Too Much Is Never Enough*. Crows Nest: Allen & Unwin.

Higgins, Paul, and Millicent Higgins. 2005. A Healthy Reduction in Oil Consumption and Carbon Emissions. *Energy Policy* 33 (1): 1–4.

Holmgren, David. 2018. *Retrosuburbia: The Downshifter's Guide to a Resilient Future*. Hepburn: Melliodora Publishing.

Illich, Ivan. 1973. *Tools for Conviviality*. London: Marion Boyars.

———. 1974. *Energy and Equity*. London: Marion Boyars.

Jackson, Tim, Wanger Jager, and Sigrid Stagl. 2004. Beyond Insatiability— Needs Theory, Consumption, and Sustainability. In *The Ecological Economics of Consumption*, ed. Lucia Reisch and Inge Ropke, 79–110. Cheltenham: Edward Elgar.

Jenkins, Joseph. 2005. *The Humanure Handbook: A Guide to Composting Human Manure*, 3rd ed. White River Junction, VT: Chelsea Green.

Kallis, Giorgos. 2017. Radical Dematerialization and Degrowth. *Philosophical Transactions of the Royal Society A* 375 (20160383): 1–13.

Kasser, Tim. 2002. *The High Price of Materialism*. Cambridge: MIT Press.

————. 2017. Living Both Well and Sustainably: A Review of the Literature, With Some Reflections on Future Research, Interventions, and Policy. *Philosophical Transactions of the Royal Society A* 375: 20160369.

Lane, Robert. 2000. *The Loss of Happiness in Market Democracies*. New Haven: Yale University Press.

Laskovsky, Jonathan, and Elizabeth Taylor. 2017. A Lot of Thought: The Space of Car Parks and Shopping Centres in Australian Cities. In *Proceedings of Automotive Historians Australia Automotive Histories: Driving Futures*, ed. Harriet Edquist, Mark Richardson, and Simon Lockrey, 1–18, Sept 1–2, 2016, Melbourne, Australia.

Louv, Richard. 2008. *Last Child in the Woods: Saving Our Children From Nature Deficit Disorder*. New York: Workman Publishing.

Massy, Charles. 2017. *Call of the Reed Warbler: A New Agriculture—A New Earth*. Brisbane: University of Queensland Press.

McKibben, Bill. 1999. *Maybe One? A Case for Smaller Families*. New York: Plume.

Mobbs, Michael. 2010. *Sustainable House*, 2nd ed. Sydney: New South Wales Press.

Monbiot, George. 2007. *Heat: How to Stop the Planet from Burning*. London: Allen Lane.

Moriarty, Patrick, and Damon Honnery. 2008. Low-Mobility: The Future of Transport. *Futures* 40: 865–872.

————. 2016. Global Transport Energy Consumption. In *Alternative Energy and Shale Gas Encyclopedia*, ed. Jay Lehr, Jack Keely, and Thomas Kingery. Hoboken, NJ: Wiley.

Mullins, Patrick, and Chris Kynaston. 2000. The Household Production of Subsistence Goods: The Urban Peasant Thesis Reassessed. In *A History of European Housing in Australia*, 9th ed., ed. Patrick Troy, 142–163. Cambridge: Cambridge University Press.

Nelson, Anitra. 2018. *Small Is Necessary: Shared Living on a Shared Planet*. London: Pluto Press.

Pollan, Michael. 2007. Unhappy Meals. *New York Times Magazine,* January 28. https://www.nytimes.com/2007/01/28/magazine/28nutritionism.t.html. Accessed 20 June 2018.

Poore, Joseph, and Thomas Nemecek. 2018. Reducing Food's Environmental Impacts Through Producers and Consumers. *Science* 360 (6392): 987–992.

Princen, Thomas. 2005. *The Logic of Sufficiency*. Cambridge: MIT Press.

Raser-Rowland, Annie, and Adam Grubb. 2016. *The Art of Frugal Hedonism: A Guide to Spending Less While Enjoying Everything More*. Hepburn: Melliodora Publishing.

Read, Rupert, Samuel Alexander, and Jacob Garrett. 2018. Voluntary Simplicity: Strongly Back by All Three Main Ethical-Normative Traditions. *Ethical Perspectives* 25: 87–116.

Reynolds, Christian, Vicki Mavrakis, Stine Hoj, et al. 2014. Estimating Informal Food Waste in Developed Countries: The Case of Australia. *Waste Management and Research* 32 (12): 1245–1258.

Roszak, Theodore. 1972. *Where the Wasteland Ends: Politics and Transcendence in Postindustrial Society*. Berkeley: Celestial Arts Press.

Sanne, Christer. 2002. Willing Consumers—Or Locked in? Policies for a Sustainable Consumption. *Ecological Economics* 42 (1): 273–287.

Soper, Kate. 2008. Alternative Hedonism, Cultural Theory and the Role of Aesthetic Revisioning. *Cultural Studies* 22 (5): 567–587.

Sorrell, Stephen. 2015. Reducing Energy Demand: A Review of Issues, Challenges and Approaches. *Renewable and Sustainable Energy Reviews* 47: 74–82.

Thoreau, Henry. 1984. Walden. In *The Portable Thoreau*, ed. Carl Bode. New York: Penguin.

Trainer, Ted. 2010. *The Transition to a Sustainable and Just World*. Sydney: Envirobook.

———. 2016. Remaking Settlements: The Potential Cost Reductions Enabled by the Simpler Way. http://www.thesimplerway.info/RemakingSettlements.htm. Accessed 20 June 2018.

VEIL. 2018. Publications. https://veil.msd.unimelb.edu.au/#publications. Accessed 20 June 2018.

Westacott, Emrys. 2016. *The Wisdom of Frugality: Why Less Is More—More or Less*. Princeton: Princeton University Press.

6

Degrowth in the Suburbs: Envisioning a Prosperous Descent

Humans are story-telling creatures—in part born of our own stories and myths—and a fundamental task today is to escape the ecocidal narrative of progress that currently constrains the urban imagination. One transgressive path beyond the dominant narrative is to tell new stories of human settlement on Earth, stories that seek to expand the conditions of possibility and open up space for new imaginaries to lay down roots. Visioning exercises are especially important in an era when it is commonly remarked that it is easier to imagine the end of the world than the end of capitalism. 'Where there is no vision', it is said, 'the people perish'.

This chapter envisions an alternative future—based on a radically curved yet possible trajectory—in which urban grassroots movements with politico-economic ambitions have managed to reinhabit the suburbs in the spirit of degrowth and thereby disrupt the current trajectory of history's momentum. We do so by way of a back-casting narrative in which we position ourselves in the year 2038, twenty years from now, and reflect on the changes that have transpired in the preceding two decades, focussing primarily on Australia albeit it in global context.

© The Author(s) 2019
S. Alexander and B. Gleeson, *Degrowth in the Suburbs*,
https://doi.org/10.1007/978-981-13-2131-3_6

Far from being a utopian fantasy, however, it will be seen that what ignited the sparks of change in the following narrative was not global enlightenment but global crisis, which we deem to be by far and away the most likely flint for revolutionary change, even if its exact form is unknowable in detail. Crisis, of course, is as much a question as it is an answer, but rather than answering that question by envisioning a descent into barbarism—which disconcertingly remains a possible future—in what follows we offer an alternative future scenario informed by the prospect of managing crisis prosperously in the spirit of degrowth. Our goal is to give more content to our title theme of 'degrowth in the suburbs' by sharing reflections on a future in which such a transformation has come to pass.

Reflections on the Future: Looking Backward from the Year 2038

Writing in this year of 2038 we are vaguely aware that this is a moment in history that will be remembered—the year our species, for the first time, witnessed the last fragments of summer ice melt away from the Arctic, stamping our age with a new image of Earth. It was in 1968 when the Apollo spaceship first captured those iconic pictures of our fragile planet floating mysteriously through the dark heavens of space. Within a century, human beings had altered that cosmological scene. We now possess the definitive yet haunting image of the Anthropocene: Earth without an icecap.

Of course, we knew this spectre lay in our collective future; we just underestimated the climatic feedback loops—especially the melting permafrosts—that would fast track its ghostly emergence. And yet, as we reflect on the science that was available decades ago, the wisdom of retrospection now strikes us with disarming clarity. How did we not see that our violent modes of economy were causing perilous geological disruptions to the functioning of fundamental ecosystems? Or more precisely, why did we not act, if only in our self-interest, to avert the disruptions so clearly written in the cards? With godly power, we have acted like Promethean children, lacking the maturity to wield such awesome industrial and technological power.

Nature eventually fights back, however, which is to say, the inevitable always occurs, despite those who prophesised with groundless hope about technological salvation. As the globalisation of carbon civilisation took hold in the early decades of the twenty-first century, a perfect storm of ecological, economic, political and cultural clouds began to gather on the horizon, threatening to engulf humanity in a concert of chaos. Lack of technology was never our problem. Our problems always flowed from what we were doing with the technology we had.

Today we would like to be writing an ode to human rationality and compassion, in which humans responded to these overlapping threats by shaping the future with sensible, evidence-based decisions and building a just and sustainable world through intelligent planning and bold democratic leadership. We would like to be able to say that people did not suffer and that the leatherback turtle, the orange-bellied parrot, and the Sumatran rhinoceros were not made extinct.

But who really thought the transition beyond global capitalism was going to be smooth, rational, and painless? Who really thought that the psychopathic transnational elite was going to give up its power and privilege voluntarily in the name of such abstractions as 'nature' or 'justice'? No, any transition beyond capitalism was always going to be a muddy transition, punctuated with crises of capital and ecology and moulded with conflict, blood, and the screams of unnecessary suffering.

Indeed, when looking back over the last few decades one must acknowledge that the global economy resembled, not an obedient servant, but a snake aggressively eating its own tail—a snake seemingly unaware that it was consuming its own life-support system. When capitalism finally choked on its own growth fetish, what was surprising was not how quickly it transformed into something else, but rather why so few people had foreseen its inevitable demise. Sadly, the lessons of history so often seem infantile when seen through the lens of hindsight.

As this era of great disruption draws to a hesitant close, not with a bang but with a sigh of relief, there may be some value in looking back on our long, uncertain, and painful recovery over the last two decades, if only so that we may better understand the present as we look to the future. It is a recovery—a transformative recovery—that we must attribute primarily to all those in the environmental and justice movements who, despite repeated, harrowing disappointments, kept fighting tirelessly and with unshakeable conviction for the causes they knew to be just.

Oil, Financial Crisis, and the Second Great Depression

The causes of capitalism's demise were many and interconnected; the variables at play, so diverse that the unfolding of descent could never have been anticipated with any precision. Nevertheless, as we reflect on the disruptions which ushered in the post-capitalist era, we can see that there were various dynamics at play which, though not predictable as such, were at the same time quite foreseeable in a general sense to the discerning analyst.

Amongst the predictable surprises was the role oil shocks played in disrupting a globalised petro-capitalism that was so chronically, indeed fatally, addicted to cheap fossil fuels. This price volatility was primarily attributable to the fading shale boom in the United States, whose demise was as swift as its rise. Given the global economy's deep dependence on a ready supply of cheap fossil energy inputs, sharp increases in the price of oil inevitably drew discretionary expenditure away from the non-energy economy. Almost like clockwork, this tightening of oil markets had the recessionary effect of economic contraction, ultimately inducing what is now known as the Second Great Depression.

High oil prices had particularly destabilising effects on heavily indebted societies and oil-dependent urban landscapes. Households and producers alike found their energy (especially transport) bills going up; the price of other energy-dependent commodities increasing; their prospects for employment going down; and yet the interest obligations on their debts staying the same or rising. This inevitably led to a litany of debt defaults, which induced economic instability and financial crisis. Consumers lost confidence, and for financial security had an incentive to stop spending and save any discretionary income, further compounding economic troubles in ways John Maynard Keynes described a century ago.

Even as the price of oil rose sharply, investors generally lacked confidence to reinvest in shale production given the extent of losses when the first bubble burst, and thus the industry never re-emerged in any significant way. The oil industry more generally was also burdened by the slow but relentless rise of the climate movement, a variable that too often was analysed independently of geological constraints on oil production. As the real-world effects of climate change became clearer year by year, growing public concern meant that a political response to fossil fuels became unstoppable, but this was occurring just as the oil industry was finding itself unable to meet increasing demand.

On the one hand, the divestment movement continued to undercut the prospects of financing new fossil energy production. This was especially so with regards the most carbon intensive shale and tar sand reserves, which were utterly incompatible with tightening carbon budgets but necessary for meeting increasing oil demand in a world addicted to liquid fuels. This meant less capital was being invested in new oil projects for fear that they would become 'stranded assets', further exacerbating the effects of reduced production due to the shale bust. On the other hand, the climate movement more broadly was pressuring governments around the world to introduce carbon taxes as a decarbonisation strategy, but naturally this made fossil fuels, including oil, more expensive, at a time when geological constraints were also putting upward pressure on prices.

To cut a far longer story short, the concerns first voiced by the peak oil school decades earlier re-emerged as if from the dead, even if the unfolding of the phenomenon took hold almost two decades later than the more pessimistic analysts first expected. Regrettably, during those two decades little was done by way of preparing societies for a post-petroleum future, especially given that the shale boom deflated prices for many years, deepening the global addiction to oil and slowing the transition to renewable energy. Since the shale bust, however, the price of oil, though volatile, has been firmly on an upward trend, putting contractionary pressure on an oil-dependent global economy that had kept afloat since 2008 only by going ever deeper into debt. Something had to give.

There were further causes of economic instability. The first of these was a relatively small but radical downshifting movement that emerged, seemingly out of nowhere, in the early-to-mid 2020s. While social theorists had long lamented the vapidity of consumer culture, especially its post-War form, this had failed to induce the broad anti-consumerist social reaction for which advocates of voluntary simplicity had always hoped. The environment movement more broadly had similar hopes disappointed. Nevertheless, a new urban movement, born of disillusionment with consumerism and a desire for deeper living, did emerge in the early 2020s. One contributing factor was an underground effort by groups alarmed by the spiralling mental health epidemic amongst young people which had links to social media and digital addiction more generally. This raised awareness of how people were being manipulated by marketers wielding the most powerful psychological tools and by Silicon Valley engineers charged with 'weaponising' this knowledge. By becoming aware of how these tools and knowledge were being used to undermine people's freedom, agency and ultimately happiness, people actually became more aware of how to seek fulfilment beyond screens and consumerism.

The fact that this 'movement' so-called was not widely foreseen can be attributed primarily to the fact that it was constituted by a wide range of movements that were not always aware—at least not at first—that they were working in unison. People gathered under various banners, including permaculture, voluntary simplicity, degrowth, transition, climate justice, collaborative consumption, localisation, eco-socialism, and more, each contributing to what some commentators have called 'the quiet revolution'. If there was a thread that united them, it was through the practice of what participants often called 'a simpler way'.

Portions of affluent societies began seriously to reject consumer culture and seek meaning and purpose in life via non-materialistic sources of wellbeing, including social activism, community engagement, art, and creative practices of self-sufficiency within the urban boundary. Mainstream media first dismissed this subculture as an 'urban peasantry' or as being comprised of 'frugal hedonists'—pejorative epithets that the movement quickly embraced. This new urban peasantry declared that participatory self-governance was a right and a duty, a mood that began to shape democratic culture more broadly. Less affluent sectors of society were equally committed to increased self-governance and collective sufficiency, creatively developing informal and salvage economies as the formal economy continued its catabolic deterioration.

For immediate purposes it was the direct economic effects on the old system that deserve note. Although the core movement, at most, would have included merely 10% of the populations of the affluent nations, the frugal and self-reliant economic practices of the participants were sufficiently radical that they were able to reduce their dependency on the market economy by 50% or more. The result came to be described dryly by commentators as the world's first 'voluntary recession', for reasons that should be clear: 10% of the population deliberately reducing their formal market activity by 50% implies a 5% contraction of overall economy, which was a Great Recession that in time became a Great Depression. This class of radical downshifters, relatively small though it was, played a defining role in transforming the nature of global capitalism that needed growth for stability.

Such a social movement had been anticipated or at least theorised two decades ago by David Holmgren, who described it in an essay called 'Crash on Demand'. The simple but profound insight was this: in an age of growing economic instability, a small social movement that radically reduced consumption in a growth-dependent economy could be enough to crash the system, forcing a system change. Most participants in the movement, however, were neither familiar with that essay nor motivated by the goal of deliberately inducing an economic crisis. Their motivations were primarily personal and environmental, even if they were also driven by a deep antipathy to the capitalist mode of production that was doing such violence to people and planet.

Nevertheless, in retrospect we see that this movement was in fact a significant contributor to our global economic turning point, highlighting the disruptive potential of even small social movements when they are sufficiently bold. All this was occurring at precisely the same time as the global economy was suffering the burden of increasingly expensive oil, making it extremely fragile and causing even mainstream commentators to begin speaking of the prospects of an imminent civilisational collapse. Certainly, an era of descent was widely acknowledged. Social discontent and economic insecurity were beginning to mobilise the disaffected and disenfranchised more broadly, suggesting that the social conditions for global revolution were emerging in unprecedented ways and to an unprecedented extent.

A final nail in capitalism's coffin was, perhaps fittingly, geopolitical in nature: war and its discontents. It is often said that modern war is nothing but the handmaiden of capitalism, increasingly necessary according to its own logic, especially in an era of increasing resource scarcity. As resource hungry governments engaged in a new era of violence for resources, and as the oil-rich Middle East nations became increasingly unstable and marked by deeper conflict, this had a very predictable inflationary effect on oil prices, as key supply chains were threatened and regularly disrupted. This further undermined the economies of the world, but at a cultural level it also sparked a new era of anti-war and anti-austerity sentiment, civil disobedience, and resistance—in forms both violent and non-violent. We need not rehash the details, which today are known all too well. Suffice to say that the citizenries of a dying world order had been reignited, like embers in a gust of wind. All these phenomena, in a swirling morass of intensifying disruption, contributed to the end of the world as we knew it—but it was not the end of the world.

Life After Growth: Crisis as Opportunity in Australia

The era of resource abundance and cheap energy was over, and this was to change everything. It was the 'new normal' that forced the citizens of carbon civilisation to become something else, whether we wanted to or not. This was especially so given the highly interconnected, globalised economy, burdened by excessive debt and painfully addicted to oil. One way or another, for better or for worse, the future was not much going to resemble the past. The march of history had been radically disrupted.

Every crisis, they say, is an opportunity—from which the optimist infers that the more crises there are, the more opportunities there are. While the Apocalypse never arrived, this was certainly an era of great instability, uncertainty, and hardship. Humanity did not so much embrace a new way of life voluntarily so much as a new way of life forcefully embraced us, with the global financial crisis of 2008 merely signifying the beginning of a long emergency that has only recently, albeit tentatively, abated. When the crises eventually hit Australia, it was only then that our nation was provoked into action. Only then, in the high-impact chambers of consumer culture, were we shaken awake from our long, dogmatic slumber. The hour was darkest just before dawn.

Recession in Australia soon deepened into a depression, marked by the bursting of the property bubble. As the comfortable years of consumer affluence were taken from us, this challenged our economy—indeed, the very civilisation of which we were a part—to refashion itself and find or create a new identity, a new narrative of progress. No matter how unsettling it might have been, this cultural identity crisis came with a surprisingly large silver lining, one that was to spark all the positive changes that were to come later.

We discovered, for example, that we could thrive at a far lower material living standard than we had thought, adapting to the absence of most luxuries and superfluities with a shock but often without genuine hardship. We also discovered that we were both much hardier than we had thought—dealing with really tough economic times with surprising resilience—and we discovered we were much more creative and resourceful than we had given ourselves credit for. We also came to see that our community spirit, which had seemingly faded in the years of consumer culture, was still intact, desperately waiting beneath the surface of culture for a time when we could reengage each other as human beings and re-establish ourselves as neighbours, and not merely interact as atomistic consumers acting only in the void of self-interest.

Even the bursting property bubbles offered some respite in the cities, a break from the ravages of development capital. This allowed suburbanites to regain control over their localities, with community groups moving from reactionary defence against conventional development to a bolder assertion of a new urban imaginary. House prices fell sharply, leaving many households with negative equity but also opening up access to housing to new segments of society.

Although there were, of course, those people and communities who, in search of security, became increasingly self-centred as economic crises deepened, overall most people showed the wisdom to live with an ethos of solidarity, through which members of communities found true security, and often fulfilment, in keeping each other afloat. It was a cultural consciousness that ensured the weakest and most vulnerable were cared for and supported. Graffiti art sprayed all over Melbourne captured the spirit best: 'I have a little; you have nothing; therefore, we have a little'.

It had become clear, however, that we could no longer solve the problems we faced with the same kinds of thinking that caused them. It was time to think, act, and live differently. And if our national and state politicians, who seemed unable to think beyond austerity politics, were not going to act decisively in the face of crisis, then we would have to act decisively ourselves, at the community level. A significant wake-up call to the environmental movement came when the recycling industry collapsed in Australia, a consequence of China in 2018 refusing to continue importing our waste and thereby exposing how even small steps towards a green economy had been unsuccessful under the capitalist growth model. We did not even know how to recycle! A renaissance of participatory democracy took hold in Australian political culture along with a deepening ecological consciousness—which over time, in the face of much resistance, filtered upwards through the various levels of political governance. This decentralised power in the process, while re-localising the economy and transforming the urban and suburban landscape in ways we will soon outline.

And thus the Great Resettlement, as we now call it, began amongst the grassroots of diverse urban communities in the wake of capitalism's demise. There was hardly going to be a radical politics until there was a culture that demanded it. Agitated but inspired social movements and community groups emerged and networked throughout the cities of Australia, in a vast biodiversity of guises and forms, representing a growing sense of dissatisfaction and disillusionment with the old ways of doing things.

Already bubbling under the surface of culture in the early decades of the twenty-first century, these urban movements—the workers, the disenfranchised, the environmentalists, social justice activists, and others—only came into their own and scaled up when crisis in the regime intensified and provoked local activism in a way that stable and comfortable (albeit deeply unsustainable) times did not. But rather than leave the city to create the new world, as the ecovillage movement in previous decades had tended to do, these urban transition movements sought to transform life *within* the urban boundary, and as we will now describe they met with considerable success. They helped prepare societies for economic disruption—disruption that in turn provoked deeper social activism and engagement. Labels like 'Save our Suburbs' and 'Transition Initiatives' began to fade into the fabric of ordinary life in urban contexts. People had had enough of the same old story, so they began writing a new story, not with words, but with deeds.

Degrowth in the Suburbs: Embracing the Sufficiency Imperative

When the notion of 'degrowth' first received attention it was typically discussed in terms of *planned* economic contraction. That gave the impression that the vision of transition would be entirely voluntarily and orderly. It turns out, of course, that economic contraction was not induced pre-emptively in order to avoid crisis; rather, as we have just explained, the economic contraction was forced upon us, and thus the practice of degrowth involved planning for this involuntary contraction, while it was taking place. As the overinflated financial system finally burst as it collided with ecological realities, the challenge was to make the best of an economic depression that was already underway. The range of urban social movements that defined the Great Resettlement were key to turning this crisis into an opportunity.

To better understand the changes that this wrought, it might be instructive to reflect on the deepest transformations that occurred in the Australian suburbs, given that this urban landscape was a representative bastion of heavily indebted, energy-intensive, high-consumption house-holds that both drove and depended upon the globalised growth economy. It was here in the heartlands of suburbia that an economics of collective sufficiency took surprisingly radical forms, which commentators today refer to as suburbia's 'prosperous descent'. Although each suburban household or community collective obviously dealt with its crises in context-dependent ways, some general remarks can invoke a relatively clear image of the changes that have occurred. We start by describing the altered provision of basic material needs in a degrowth economy, specifically water and food, before discussing other essential elements including new modes of production, transport, energy and housing.

Water

We begin this suburban exposition with the issue of water security, this being one of the most essential biophysical needs for any form of life. It is an issue of increasing concern in Australia as our summers become hotter and more intense, and the years of drought more frequent. Conditions worse than the Millennium drought (1996–2009) have come to represent the new normal, with urban populations putting constant pressure on depleting water catchments and reservoirs, with many dams often threatening to be at record lows. Of necessity, unprecedented water regulations have been instituted in most urban centres, but just like during the Millennium drought, households and businesses adapted quickly, recognising along the way how casually wasteful they had been in prior circumstances of apparent resource abundance. Suburban communities self-organised to educate themselves about frugal water practices and DIY installation of water tanks.

Hard economic times mean that, from a governmental perspective, desalination plants have come to be seen as a techno-solution that is unaffordable (both financially and energetically), which rightly implies that the primary response to the problem of increasing water scarcity has been demand reduction. This has been incentivised by the upward creep in the price of water services. Given that these price increases

came in concert with declining incomes and reduced employment prospects, further regulations were required to ensure that water services
were never cut off, even from households unable to pay their water bills.

In some contexts this led to nationalisation of water services, but
more often, private service providers have been constrained by laws that
essentially guarantee basic water services for all people, irrespective of
ability to pay. We see here how socialistic governance can achieve equitable and efficient outcomes by significantly constraining markets but
without necessarily abolishing them, in ways laissez-faire neoliberalism refused to accept. In our Western culture, steeped in traditions of
private property, the more appropriate path to societal transformation
was through the radical transformation of inherently malleable property institutions, rather than their abolishment. Property entails both
rights and responsibilities, and how those are shaped is a social decision;
which is to say, property is and ought to be a social construction, not
something that has a pre-ordained neoliberal essence. In recent years
urban social movements have contributed to the reinstatement of the
right to water, providing increased security of basic human needs.

Although the water grid remains a necessity in most urban and suburban centres—with roof space being insufficient to capture essential
water supply for most households—the 'Water is Life' campaign for
household water capture proved extraordinarily successful. This campaign was prompted by the catastrophe in Cape Town in 2020, which
was the first large city to have its water mains turned off due to chronically depleted storage. Today it is rare to see an Australian house in
the suburbs that is not surrounded by water tanks, large or small, and
grey-water systems have become the norm. This has put far less pressure on water catchments, with dam levels rising over the last two years
to healthy levels for the first time in a decade, despite limited rainfall.
While few households are fully off-grid, demand from the water mains
has reduced from around 230 litres per person, per day, in the first decade of the twenty-first century, to around 70 litres today. This is more
than enough for a dignified existence, without leaving much room for
waste. Such is life in a degrowth economy.

One of the most significant ways of reducing water consumption
has come from most suburban households transitioning away from

flush-toilets and towards composting toilets. As well as saving water, this transition is already promising to minimise the need for energy and water-intensive infrastructure in the future. As old attitudes die, it is now broadly accepted that a civilised society in an era of water scarcity should not defecate into potable water and should instead close the nutrient cycle by turning human and animal waste into nutrient-rich soil for the expanding suburban gardens and orchards.

Urban Agriculture

The most notable features in the provision of food over the last two decades have been, first, the fundamental shift towards localisation and organic (or post-carbon) methods of production, and second, reduced consumption of meat and dairy products by almost half. In part this transition was voluntary, as household gardening and urban agriculture movements successfully highlighted the value of reducing the suburban dependency on global and carbon intensive agri-business. But ultimately the more compelling incentive was sheer economic hardship. When finances are tight and paid employment is precarious, why have a lawn or a concrete backyard when you can have vegetable gardens, an orchard, beehives, and a chicken coop? Increased 'heat stress' events have also led to growing concerns about food insecurity in a changing climate, providing a further incentive to self-provide low-carbon food whenever possible and thereby increase resilience.

Backyards and front yards throughout suburbia have turned into productive spaces of increased household sufficiency, with an emerging trend to remove some fences between houses, increasing sun exposure for gardens while also fostering a new sense of community. Just as the 'Dig for Victory' movement helped increase food security in Britain during the Second World War through the multitude of 'victory gardens' and 'relief gardens', in recent years similar campaigns and grassroots activities have helped adapt to the financial pressures of the Second Great Depression.

An even more illustrative analogy perhaps is the Cuban response to energy descent during the so-called 'special period' after the collapse of the Soviet Union in 1989. Almost overnight the Cubans found themselves with greatly reduced oil supplies from their Soviet benefactors, meaning that their old methods of oil-dependent food production were simply non-viable. In other words, Cubans had to adapt to a *geopolitically* induced 'peak oil' in a way that Australians—who were accustomed to importing most of their oil—have had to adapt to reduced oil supplies enforced through a confluence of geology, climate politics, and the Second Great Depression. But the response has been remarkably similar, in the sense that Australian cities and their peri-urban landscapes have turned into green spaces of organic food production in a remarkably short time—a matter of months. It seems that nothing incentivises quite like necessity, and when people are threatened with hunger, they do not wait for government permission to grow food.

Not only has household food production increased many times over, the more interesting part of the transition took place as private citizens reclaimed public space for local self-provision. In other words, the commons have been reclaimed and expanded, and there has also been significant growth in sharing private land, as keen gardeners are connected via the internet with under-utilised land for mutual benefit. This expansion of urban agriculture has had the added benefit of reducing the 'heat island effect', as concrete is increasingly replaced with edible landscapes. Almost all unused land has come under cultivation by the new urban peasantry, whether that is fruit trees in nature strips, goat or chicken farms on the large areas on the edge of train tracks, aquaculture enterprises on underused car parks, or raised garden beds on edges of wide roads. Given that the property bubble has burst, there is no longer much pressure from developers to sub-divide suburban plots and turn backyards into apartments, which is another silver lining to an otherwise challenging economic depression.

Due to social pressure from engaged citizenries, municipal councils have come on board as facilitators of the localisation movement, planting fruit trees throughout suburban neighbourhoods, thereby socialising food production to some extent. Organised 'working bees' of volunteers have become regular social events in suburbia. Even some sports fields have been turned into urban community farms, which naturally caused instances of social conflict, but it turns out food is even more important to Australians than sport. Households have become urban farmers not because they chose to, as such, but generally because they had to.

Nevertheless, this enforced experience of re-localising food production often led to a range of unforeseen personal and social benefits. Due to the ongoing economic depression, working hours in the formal economy have been in decline for the first time in half a century, but this means people have had more time to self-provide in the informal economy, and first and foremost this means less time in the office or factory and more time in the backyard or community gardens. Unsurprisingly, the increased physical activity reversed the obesity trends, increasing health and thereby lessening the burden on the health system that is underfunded. Just as the Cubans, at the turn of the century, were in better health than citizens of the US at one tenth of the cost, so too is Australia heading in that direction, freeing up more of the public purse for the energy transition.

Furthermore, the act of gardening or farming inevitably connects people with their land base, seasons, and local ecology in ways that subtly creates an ecologically sensitive consciousness and brings various other mental health benefits. For example, we no longer suffer from nature deficit disorder. Because people eat mostly what is available in their immediate bioregion, societal health has been greatly increased as low-meat, seasonal and fresh food diets have become the norm, working in conjunction with more active lifestyles. The urban landscape is reshaping the human form as it is being shaped by it. Vast tracts of land once dedicated to growing food for livestock have been made available for carbon sequestration and, in appropriate contexts, rewilding.

Increasing self-provision obviously reduces dependency on the global market economy, and since households are generally unable to meet all their own food needs, every suburb these days has their own local farmers market, usually twice a week, where people either purchase or barter for necessary supplies or services, as well as enjoy the vibrancy and social interaction of the community gathering. The farmers markets are efficiently organised through open-source software called 'The Open Food Network', which makes it easy to connect local producers with urban and suburban markets, and this minimises 'food miles' for those food stuffs not producible within the urban boundary. This shows the extraordinary value of the internet when put to noble social purposes, reminding us that technologies, like knives or fire, are neither good nor bad in themselves, but depend on the ends towards which they are put.

This thriving suburban food movement has led to the collapse of the big supermarket chains, which were dependent on industrial agriculture and which could not survive expensive oil or the cultural shift towards localisation and increased self-sufficiency. As these institutions broke up, their assets were often acquired by farmer-owned cooperatives, fundamentally changing the power relations that had previously governed food production and provision in Australia. We see here how a social movement that withdraws financial support from mega-corporations while also increasing self-sufficiency can lead to structural shifts in the macro-economy in ways that were unanticipated by those who could not see the transformative potential of 'mere lifestyle changes' implied by urban and suburban agriculture. But withdrawing financial support from corporate power was only half the task; building the alternative economy was the other half.

Work, Production, and Self-Employment in the Informal Economy

One of the most significant implications of the transition away from the globalised industrial food production has been the increased labour needed for organic modes of production. In the past, environmentalists too often overlooked this issue. While it is widely accepted that organic production can be more productive *per acre* than industrial food production, organic production is generally more *labour-intensive*. The increased labour requirements arise primarily from the less frequent use of mechanised (oil-dependent) farm machinery, but organic fertiliser production and pest control are also typically more time-intensive than industrialised techniques (although permaculture practices can reduce this disparity through things like companion planting, chop and drop fertilising, self-watering wicking beds, etc.).

The corollary is that organic food production is entirely capable of feeding the world—indeed, it is the only means of doing so sustainably—but to do so it required a huge increase in the provision of agricultural labour compared to the petroleum era. This simply had to be accepted as an implication of the transition to a post-carbon degrowth economy; however as implied above, it is one with a range of personal, social, economic and ecological benefits. Most importantly, perhaps, it created a significant demand for farmers, both urban and rural, which has kept unemployment levels manageable even in a (conventionally) depressed economy. Robots, it turns out, did not leave us all without work. Of course, not everyone is expected or required to be involved in food production, but these days the vast majority of people are to some extent, even if that means contributing to a working bee at the local community garden.

Wages for farmers are generally low compared with previous eras but they are sufficient for households to meet their modest needs, and in insecure economic times most people see that a reliable job, doing socially valued work, with decent hours, is better than no job at all. Others have leapt at the opportunity to get out from behind a desk and into urban or peri-urban farms. In unexpected ways this demand for farmers also reduced pressure on the housing markets in dense urban centres, as significant flows of people left the capital cities of Australia to find reliable work and cheap housing in rural towns, leading to the revitalisation of those towns and reduced population pressures on the big cities. This demographic shift away from the main urban centres was also supported by the huge labour force required as the renewable energy infrastructure started seriously being built.

Nevertheless, many people lost their jobs in the Second Great Depression. Households that once had two incomes, now must get by on one, or even one part-time income. A social ethic of frugal self-sufficiency is now widely accepted and practised, driven by these hard economic times. A post-consumerist attitude to waste has emerged, drawing on the previous Depression-era slogan: 'use it up, wear it out, make it do, or do without'. To deal with this challenging economic contraction, people have been essentially forced to contribute to the 'informal' economy through practices of home-based production, often salvaging from household and industrial waste streams to creatively reuse materials and give them a second (or third, etc.) life. In this sense a form of circular economy is emerging, where products at the end of their lives are used to create the next generation of goods.

Many garages that used to house cars have been converted into workshops, where people now produce furniture, clothes, alcohol, tools, and other useful products—for themselves or for trade—as well as provide services like bike, shoe, and tool repairs. Practical 'reskilling' workshops in the arts of self-sufficiency are regularly organised by groups resembling Transition Town Initiatives, even if that terminology is rarely used today. Small artisan producers, cooperatives, and not-for-profit enterprises have returned to local centres, organised and given security by unions and guilds; others simply trade or barter their goods and services at the local markets.

For many people, less work or reduced working hours in the formal economy also means more time to self-provide in other ways too, whether that is fixing the gutter, painting the house, producing food or clothes, or looking after the children—all of which makes reduced income less challenging. Given that this degrowth economy emerged out of a liberal society, it is notable that gender roles have become relaxed and fairer, including in the household economy of care.

The days of consumer affluence are gone for most Australians today, but as people say, there has been 'an upside to down'. When communities take on more of these essential productive functions they become more resilient, interconnected and cohesive, and the work is generally more fulfilling because it is often creative and necessary to meet important social needs. The huge increase in the sharing economy, facilitated online via the 'Good Karma Networks', has also made communities more resilient in the face of economic contraction. Even though there are far fewer things being produced, people do not feel the bite because generally what they need can be borrowed, bartered, or shared. Most suburbs have also developed their own local currencies that are helping stabilise and support localised economic transactions beneath the surface of the dying markets of global capitalism.

The rise of the sharing and gift economies have also brought with it large social benefits, as neighbours have come to see each other as interconnected parts of highly localised self-provision. After all, which community is richer: the one where everybody owns their own cheap drill in affluent isolation? Or the one where the community is connected via a communally owned tool shed where a few high-quality tools are shared amongst the neighbourhood? The abundance of these informal sharing and gift transactions in the non-market economy are totally missed by the formal accounting of Gross Domestic Product, which helps explain why life seems better today despite GDP contracting as the old economy continues to deteriorate. The promise of degrowth is being fulfilled.

Given that most households are poorer in monetary and material terms than previous eras, there is far less discretionary income for paid entertainment, so people now spend their leisure time engaging in low-impact creative activity like music or art, home-based production, or sport. In particular, the new forms of local economy that have arisen provide many avenues for meaningful and fulfilling self-employment as an artisan, often blurring the boundary between work and leisure in ways that would have been incomprehensible to most in the old economy.

Transport in a Local Economy

As well as reducing dependence on the formal economy, the thriving local economies throughout suburbia also minimise the need for carbon-based travel to places of work. Many people now work from home, or only work three or four days in the formal economy, or work only a short bike ride away from work. Even longer commutes are now generally undertaken by bike. Throughout city landscapes are 'bike repair kitchens', run by social networks of volunteers or worker cooperatives, which make bike transport essentially free, again making meagre incomes more manageable.

Many people cycle 10 kilometres to work, or more, no matter the weather. With the right wet weather gear and good lights this proves to be little to no hardship, and has the added benefit of keeping people fit and healthy. The elderly or less able are often found riding electric bikes, as are those travelling longer distances, and many households and most neighbourhoods have electric cargo bikes, available for those times when heavy loads need to be transported, including dropping multiple children at school. Electric cars are still on the rise, but progress is slow as few households can afford them, and their ecological credentials remain dubious in many respects.

Electrified public transport systems are also developing as a necessary part of the post-carbon transition, but unfortunately the new infrastructure is lagging behind culture, meaning that the trams, trains and buses are often overburdened as the shift away from car culture continues. It is a great shame this infrastructure transition did not begin in earnest when the formal economy was in better shape. The millennial shift away from privately owning a car has continued, which is made very easy today due to peer-to-peer car sharing and car-pooling networks, again facilitated by the internet that essentially eliminates transactions costs. The economics of privately owning a car are now clearly unattractive to most people, given that access without ownership is so readily available, although there are some households (without public transport access) and some professions (e.g. builders and brick layers) who remain locked into driving.

Nevertheless, with petrol becoming ever-more expensive, in recent years councils have been put under tremendous social pressure to maximise space available for bike lanes, and this has helped strengthen the shift away from fossil fuel-dependent cars and even lightens the burden on public transport. Increasingly sections of suburbia are being declared 'car free'—one extra block per year without cars is the goal of several progressive councils today. This is causing congestion elsewhere, but on the plus side, this just provides a further disincentive to drive and makes cycling and walking increasingly safe and attractive. The roads and car parks on some cul-de-sacs have been overtaken with gardens or food forests, a trend destined to continue, leaving only a single lane for cars and often no car parking. The suburbs are not car free yet, but the technological balance has shifted dramatically. Urban and suburban planning now privileges the cyclist and the pedestrian over the driver, and this has greatly reduced noise and air pollution, making cities far more attractive and convivial places to live and be.

The emergence of the local economy also means that during the day the suburbs are vibrant, densely populated, and safe centres of economic and cultural activity—not emptied from 8 a.m. to 6 p.m. as they were in the recent past. As noted, the internet remains a useful social tool—keeping global cultural and knowledge transfer alive, facilitating sharing, and widely used for video conferencing to avoid air travel—but it is no longer the centre of social life. Eco-cities are emerging, but not in the form of infill densification and vertical sprawl, but in the form of highly interconnected and localised economic hubs of suburban sufficiency, retrofitted for the transition beyond carbon capitalism.

Even the culture of holidaying has evolved as the degrowth economy emerged, with international trips to homogenous luxury resorts being a thing of the past for most households. Holidays today are usually taken in one's bioregion, generally enforced by economic hardship but ultimately offering hidden delights to those with the curiosity to explore the wonders of their own locality by train, bus, bike, or perhaps a borrowed electric car. The old culture of regular flying is well and truly dead—again, primarily due to the sheer unaffordability of plane travel in an era of oil scarcity, rising carbon taxes, more video conferencing, and greater ecological awareness.

Managing Energy Descent

Perhaps the most important feature of the new suburban economy is that we do not (and cannot) use anywhere near as much energy as we did in earlier decades, motivated again by high prices and made viable through the range of energy descent practices outlined above. In practical terms this means less transport and transformation of materials, less heating and cooling, and less data transfer and manipulation. But minimal but sufficient electricity supplies are provided by our shift to highly distributed renewable energy technologies, primarily wind and solar, now providing more than 85% of our electricity. Technology continues to develop, contributing to the incremental decline in the price of batteries and smart metres that help manage peak demand, but ultimately reduced demand has been our greatest achievement on the path to a post-carbon society. It has proved far cheaper and easier to reduce energy demand than to 'green' the extravagant supply of an energy-intensive consumer society.

Given that our levels of production and consumption have been radically downscaled, meeting our limited electricity needs with solar, wind and hydro has not been technologically or economically prohibitive. Along with household and neighbourhood solar arrays, most suburban homes and many communities now also have their own biogas digesters. As well as providing a renewable source of energy generation, these digesters greatly reduce food waste going to landfill and provide a constant stream of nutrient-rich fertiliser for the expanding edible landscapes. By walking, cycling, using public transport, producing food organically, retrofitting houses, and re-localising much of our economy, we have also been able to reduce our use of energy—including oil—to less than half of what it once was, and consumption continues to fall.

This energy transition has also been quite disruptive. As it took hold, the profits of the fossil energy industry were decimated, an industry already destabilised by the divestment movement. Even electricity grid operators and retailers have been undercut by the uptick in household solar production, which massively reduced grid demand as noted, prompting services providers to increase their fees to stay afloat, which only incentivised more people to get solar. Thus the 'death spiral' took hold, leading to a necessary and fundamental reconfiguration of the grid to accommodate distributed generation.

These dynamics have led to several large fossil energy companies and service providers being nationalised to manage the descent in a relatively stable way. Last year the final coal power plant in Australia was closed, but all fossil energy workers have been given a job guarantee in the many renewable energy factories that are obviously required to replace the old fossil infrastructure. It is not quite 'war time mobilisation' but an extraordinary transformation of energy infrastructure is, at last, underway.

Carefully managed woodlots beyond the urban boundary also provide some fuel for heating, and a relatively small amount of bio-ethanol made from sugarcane is produced to provide some liquid fuel for the most necessary industrial tasks. But the key point is this: high energy prices have incentivised greatly reduced energy demand, which reduced the amount of renewable energy infrastructure that was required to meet that demand, making the transition more affordable. The post-carbon transition is not complete, but it is well on its way, transforming society as it takes form.

Reimagining the Built Environment

The issue of housing is particularly complex and in many respects unresolved. Sometimes well-meaning environmentalists liked to imagine that eco-cities in the future were going to look like some techno-utopia, where everyone was living in expensive high-rise apartments such as those glorified in glossy architecture magazines, or else like some agrarian village, where everyone was living in mud houses they built themselves. The fact is, however, that the built environment has a very slow replacement rate—less than 5% per year in Australia. This means that people are, and for the foreseeable future people will be, living within the housing infrastructure that is already with us. Just as people make lemonade when life hands them lemons, we have made the best of the infrastructure we have inherited, which in most regards, of course, was terribly designed from an environmental perspective.

Poorly designed though it is, Australians have come to reinhabit the built environment of suburbia with remarkable creativity. Most houses have been fundamentally retrofitted for energy efficiency, water capture, and onsite treatment of grey and black water; and we have already reviewed how households have maximised their food growing potential and how houses (especially garages and spare rooms) have turned into places of production, not merely consumption. Another key shift has been the densification of suburbia, not by building up or out, but simply by opening spare rooms to boarders, students, or friends and family in need. Furthermore, as many superfluous industries have closed as the depression hit home, their business premises have provided new space for creative housing.

Furthermore, a culture of co-housing and land sharing has emerged in response to housing challenges. This assisted household finances, while also making better use of existing infrastructure, given that many houses during the consumer years were built significantly larger than many families needed them to be. It is not uncommon today to see 'tiny houses' on wheels in suburban driveways where cars used to be, again providing a cheap and creative housing solution for difficult times. At first councils resisted, but soon enough the tide of culture saw the value in this innovation.

Over time the existing housing stock will need to be replaced and built with materials sourced as locally as possible, and designed for long-term durability and to the highest standards of energy efficiency. More people and communities are taking part in the construction of their own homes to reduce costs and to liberate people from oppressive mortgages, especially given that paid employment has reduced for many households. To reduce the resources required, as well as limit the spaces needed for heating and cooling, new houses are modest in size, and across the housing sector dwelling occupancy rates have increased to sensibly optimise the use of available space.

As well as suburban transformation, many people have also been incentivised to leave dense, high-rise urban centres by the prospect of far cheaper land and housing in small towns in rural Australia. As noted above, small town Australia is undergoing a revitalisation in ways that resemble the suburban sustainability transformations. In fact, the scale of small towns makes the transformations outlined above easier to implement and maintain. The ecovillage movement has also been given new flexibility by the 'Low-Impact Development' laws, which provide regulatory space for communities to establish ecovillages on rural land with far few planning limitations or conditions.

Given that these self-transformed suburban, small town, and rural landscapes have proven so successful over the last decade, *new* urban and suburban developments have come to be shaped in their image, with presumptions of distributed energy systems, urban farms, bike lanes, and local economies now being supported, rather than inhibited, by planning decisions. In this way we can come to understand how bold grassroots social movements can, over time, filter upwards and shape top-down politics.

A Prosperous Descent

It was the twentieth-century philosopher Jean-Paul Sartre who once said that the French were never as free as when the Germans occupied their country during the Second World War. His point was that their lives, in the midst of crisis, were suddenly infused with meaning and purpose, in contrast with the humdrum unfreedom they had been living as comfortable middle-class consumers, with their blinding overemphasis on social status and materialistic concerns.

The same could be said of Australia, and indeed affluent society more generally, during the last decade of deep economic contraction. Amid crisis, torn from our televisions and shopping malls, we were freer perhaps than we had ever been before, despite the hardships and constraints we faced. In the process of creating a new way of life and new modes of collaborative economy, our lives were unexpectedly infused with new meaning, and that was the invisible force that drove the creative process of adapting to a new era. As Friedrich Nietzsche once said: 'He who has *why* to live, can bear almost any *how*'.

The economic depression we have lived through meant that most people had very little discretionary income, so we found ourselves sharing more (because we had to); growing more of our food (because we had to); biking more and leaving our cars in the driveway (because we had to); travelling less, mending our clothes, reusing waste (because we had to)—all of which reduced our ecological footprint by almost three-quarters of what it had been. But somehow, at the same time, we were living more. Consumer culture was forcefully taken from us, so we had to create a new culture of consumption as the old modes of production broke down. We embraced a simpler way of living—and, to the surprise of many, we found it to be good. If it was not always comfortable, especially on a planet still locked into ravages of climate change, it was for the most part, at least, fulfilling. This is the paradox of simplicity, the wisdom of which had been lost in the consumer age: less can be more.

The degrowth society that we have today is a product of these cultural forces eventually finding political and macroeconomic expression. By reordering our priorities, and re-conceptualising what progress meant for our communities and our nation, we found that investment in renewables was not financially prohibitive, even in hard economic times, but merely a matter of social and political commitment. But do not misunderstand us. Of course we had to make some sacrifices elsewhere; of course people suffered at times, and still suffer. Certainly, we could not afford to sustain a growth-orientated, consumer society on renewable energy. Far from it! Huge structural and lifestyle changes were required to manage economic contraction, adapt to climate change, and support our transition to a low-carbon society. We have become a nation of radical recyclers, menders, makers, salvagers, gardeners, and retrofitters. But do not pity us either! We may live simply, modestly and creatively, but we live well. We have reimagined the good life and resettled the suburbs, and this is reflected in our emerging economics of collective sufficiency.

7

Regoverning the City: Policies for a New Economy

Structures for Sufficiency

This penultimate chapter provides an opportunity to step back and reorientate ourselves in relation to the global predicament that has both framed the analysis and shaped the alternative urban imaginary we are developing in response. Let us recall that we are living in the urban age, an epoch in which *homo urbanis* is being challenged to undertake a Great Resettlement on Earth, in this perilous Anthropocene. As noted in the introduction, if this 'big picture' is lost sight of then our recommended modes of response might seem too drastic or radical. However, if the overlapping crises are seen without rose-tinted glasses, it should be clear that the conservatives who defend or merely tinker with the status quo are, in fact, the radicals—and dangerous ones at that. Unfortunately, that category of conservative politics today would include many in the mainstream environmental movement, who seem content to strive in futility to give capitalism a 'green face'.

In the previous chapter we unpacked our view that ever-deepening crisis in the existing system of global capitalism is the most likely spark for a paradigm shift both in the political economy of growth and its

© The Author(s) 2019
S. Alexander and B. Gleeson, *Degrowth in the Suburbs*,
https://doi.org/10.1007/978-981-13-2131-3_7

reflection in urban praxis and planning. Indeed, the back-casting narrative we presented was designed to invite reflection on how such a crisis could be our best hope for providing the great disruption needed to shake *homo urbanis* awake. But we must not be seen to be romanticising or desiring crisis like some dreamy-eyed optimists. In fact, the theory of change that is underlying our urban imaginary is clearly based on a deep pessimism about the prospects of smoother and less disruptive modes of societal transformation. When the crisis of capitalism deepens—perhaps in the form of a new financial crisis or a Second Great Depression—the task will be to ensure that such destabilised conditions are used to advance progressive humanitarian and ecological ends rather than exploited to further entrench the austerity politics of neoliberalism. We recognise, of course, that the latter remains a real possibility, as did the arch-capitalist Milton Friedman (2002: xiv) who expressed the point in these terms:

> Only a crisis – actual or perceived – produces real change. When that crisis occurs, the actions that are taken depend on the ideas that are lying around. That, I believe, is our basic function: to develop alternatives to existing policies, to keep them alive and available until the politically impossible becomes the politically inevitable.

After restating the essential contours of the global predicament, this chapter charts bold directions for structural change that could facilitate the emergence of a new suburban economy of degrowth. These constitute a program of wholesale eco-socialist transition that is underpinned by the principles of justice, self-limitation, and ecological democracy. In short, the transition is to the convivial, low energy, low speed society advocated nearly half a century ago by Ivan Illich. The program measures range in scale from planetary to local, as radical change must come through reinforcing shifts at all levels. Although stated as general transformations, they will, in an urban age, be largely applied and realised in cities and closer human settlements. They provide the underlying structural supports for transition to the post-growth suburbia that our book has flagged for human aspiration.

Our position is that these policies are unlikely to *initiate* the degrowth transition but instead will be the *outcome* of urban social movements— social forces that emerge out of crisis or a series of crises and which actively create the cultural consciousness that sees policies for degrowth as both necessary and desirable. It is through crisis that we see comfortable suburban middle classes becoming sufficiently perturbed such that the sedative and depoliticising effects of affluence might be overcome. In our view, it is better that citizens are *not* in fact protected from every disruptive situation, given that the encounter with crisis can play an essential consciousness raising role, if it triggers a desire for and motivation towards learning about the structural underpinnings of the situation itself. Social movements should be preparing themselves to play that educational role.

Only through this dialectical interaction between crisis, culture, and political economy can there be any hope for a prosperous descent in the form of 'degrowth in the suburbs'. Through this process can we imagine the emergence of new, post-carbon suburban forms, powered by limited but sufficient renewable energy; defined by relocalisation of economy and a collective re-inhabitation of the built environment; facilitated by redistribution of access to housing and land; and grounded upon a new material ethics in which the provision of basic needs for all take privilege over superfluous affluence for a few.

In the absence of such a response to crisis, we fear that suburbanites (and affluent society more generally) might well sleepwalk into an ever-deepening ecological and/or financial catastrophe, at which point it would be too late to avoid a brutal and unprosperous societal decay. At that stage we might have much to learn from picking up the books of urban catastrophists like James Kunstler (2005). Until then, of course, we should be focussing all our energies on ensuring that such urban futures are avoided.

New Economics for a Full Planet

If once our species lived on a planet relatively empty of human beings, today we live on a planet that is evidently full to overflowing. The human population has grown exponentially to reach seven-and-a-half billion people, increasing by more than 200,000 people every day, and trending to exceed eleven billion by the end of the century. As this expanding population continues to urbanise and seek ever-rising material living standards by way of sustained economic growth, the global economy is being driven into gross ecological overshoot, dangerously crossing or threatening to cross a range of planetary boundaries with dire consequences that are already unfolding. Indeed, the metaphor of 'Earth as a Petri dish' has become worryingly apt, given that the dominant colony seems to be consuming all the available resources and is at risk of poisoning itself from its own wastes, raising questions about whether *homo urbanis* can muster the intelligence to avoid the fate of common bacteria. Techno-optimists and free marketeers promise ecological salvation via continuous 'green growth', all the while capitalism expands ravenously to every corner of the globe, leaving an increasingly brutalised planet in capital's wake.

Lifting the poorest billions out of destitution is likely to place further burdens on global and local ecosystems. This confluence of ecological and social justice imperatives further delegitimises ongoing economic expansion in the already high-impact, consumerist societies of the world, and the prospect of an energy descent future makes such ongoing growth increasingly non-viable as well as unjust. What is most troubling of all, perhaps, is that even those sectors of society that have achieved the so-called consumerist ideal—the house in the right suburb, the nice car, the latest gadgets, the stylish clothes, the exotic travel, etc.—all too often find themselves discontented, overworked, and alienated despite their unprecedented material abundance.

In recent decades this cultural malaise has been established consistently and independently by a litany of sociological and psychological studies (see Lane 2000; Kasser 2002; Hamilton and Denniss 2005), indicating that growth capitalism's defining goal is deeply misconceived. This is arguably the strongest case for degrowth: that present structural arrangements fail on their own terms. There seems to be an emptiness to consumer affluence that is never acknowledged in slick advertisements, let alone discussed in schools or around the dinner table. It is perhaps the dominant culture's final, unspeakable taboo. For whom, then, do we destroy the planet? Or for what?

Unthinkable in mainstream economic and political discourse, the only coherent response to this context of ecological overshoot, inequality, and cultural malaise is planned economic contraction of the energy and resource demands of the most 'developed' regions of the world, as well as a reconceptualisation of sustainable development in the Global South, beyond the conventional path of growth-dependent industrialisation. This 'limits to growth' position signifies an extremely complex, challenging, but ultimately necessary paradigm shift in the dominant conception of human progress, one that we have been developing in this book in the context of suburban theory and praxis.

Although the degrowth movement is diverse and defies singular definition, we have argued that it will involve initiating a transition beyond the existing order of globalised growth capitalism and in its place building a constellation of highly localised economies of sufficiency, based on (limited) renewable energy supply, convivial technology, participatory democracy, increased social control of the economy, and non-affluent but sufficient material cultures of voluntary simplicity. Once more, we contend that this new suburban degrowth economy will need to be driven into existence from the grassroots up, with top down change being more of an outcome than a driving force of this transformation.

Counter-intuitively, perhaps, we also contend that a degrowth transition can maintain or even increase quality of life, by reshaping cultures and societal structures to promote non-materialistic forms of meaning and wellbeing beyond consumerist conceptions of 'the good life'. We do not argue that degrowth is likely, only that it is the most coherent response to the global predicament, and thus deserves critical attention. And even if, as is likely, the degrowth movement fails to create the just and sustainable society which is its goal, we argue that the attempt to prefigure a new self-limiting economy within the decaying shell of capitalism remains the most promising strategy for preparing individuals, households and communities for increased energy and resource scarcity, thus increasing societal resilience in the face of destabilised climatic conditions and forthcoming economic, financial, and/or environmental crises.

Degrowth, Austerity Urbanism, and the Politics of Culture

We acknowledge that most people do not recognise the need for a degrowth economy and therefore would reject the following policy proposals as unacceptable or unnecessary. But as the limits to growth tighten their grip on economies in coming years and decades, we believe the debate will inevitably evolve, and the question will not be *whether* a degrowth economy is required, but rather *how* to create one—by design rather than disaster. Indeed, already we sense an emerging deep-seated, gut-level recognition that humanity needs to develop something *other* than the economy we have today, one that nurtures and feeds the human thirsts for meaning; for awe and ecstasy; for belonging and contributing; for connection and creativity.

In fact, it could be that the social conditions are ripe for something like the radical position we are developing in this book. Research by interdisciplinary scholars Richard Eckersley (2018a) and Melanie Randle and Eckersley (2015) show that only a small majority in the developed world think quality of life is improving (in Australia in 2015, 16% said it was getting better and 49% said it was getting worse). Furthermore, a majority of people in the West (based on a 2013 survey of the US, UK, Australia and Canada) believe that there is a high probability (greater than 50%) of our way of life collapsing in the next 100 years. A larger majority still (78% in the survey) believed we need a new worldview and way of life if we are to create a better future for the world. Eckersley (2018b) reflects:

> These perceptions find no expression in politics, which is tightly bound by social inertia and vested interests, and functions in an out-dated paradigm of progress. Our political leaders (even the 'good ones') do not yet believe we face problems that conventional policy responses can't solve. Maybe they can't believe it, so they continue to be preoccupied with lower-order issues and causes.

In Europe, cultures seem more receptive to post-growth futures and even mainstream political institutions are being challenged to consider alternative economic paradigms. One reason for this greater openness to post-growth futures could arise from the fact that many parts of Europe (e.g. Greece, Spain, and Italy), are still enmeshed in economic crises that germinated in the Global Financial Crisis. In such contexts where the conventional growth trajectory is looking unlikely to recover, the search for alternative models is greatly incentivised, far more so than in places like Australia where the global financial crisis (2007–2008), by and large, was evaded—or perhaps merely deferred (Keen 2017).

We must also acknowledge that many economies today are having to deal with an 'austerity' politics which is far cry from the notion of planned and equitable contraction envisioned by degrowth scholars and activists. Such austerity politics inevitably manifests in urban and suburban contexts, as disenfranchised city-dwellers suffer the brunt of economic hardship through things like mortgage foreclosures, low or no employment prospects, and deteriorating urban infrastructure and services. Unplanned recession in a growth-dependent economy is not degrowth, even though degrowth may need to involve planning for recession.

Even within economies that seem to fare better—like the United States—the benefits of GDP growth remain grossly unequal in their distribution, with many American cities mouldering in austerity urbanism despite national GDP appearing relatively healthy (Peck 2012). Detroit is the oft-cited example of urban decay, the economy of which collapsed with the car manufacturing industry, leading to an exodus of over half its population in recent decades and the swift deterioration of much of its built environment (Galster 2012).

Nevertheless, Detroit also offers some examples of how creative and proactive communities can turn even the hardships of austerity urbanism into opportunities for urban renewal. Recession tends to deflate house and land prices, and lead to capital and population flight. In Detroit all of those things have happened, and certainly there has been and remains significant hardship and economic insecurity. But access to cheap housing and land has opened up new, albeit precarious, opportunities. For instance, there is a promising urban agriculture movement laying down roots and rising out of the ashes of industrial capitalism. Self-organised by communities and with enterprises often structured as worker cooperatives, this new economic movement is emerging from the grassroots up and moving towards increased collective sufficiency that reflects an ethos of degrowth (if not the vocabulary). Here we see positive fragments of a degrowth urbanism emerging 'from below' in response to urban recession. In spite of this, of course, the city continues to live with the terrible and wasteful legacy of failed industrialism (Galster 2012).

Despite still being marginalised, the cultural reception of post-growth futures more broadly does seem to be warming. A survey in Spain, for example, indicates that one third of people think that growth should either be ignored as a policy goal or should be actively resisted (Drews and van den Bergh 2016). The UK government commissioned a report from Tim Jackson (author of *Prosperity without Growth*) and Robin Webster (2016) which updated the 'Limits to Growth' report, with similar approaches being taken in France (Stiglitz et al. 2010) and Germany. Pope Francis (2015, para.: 193) called for degrowth in the rich world, even if he didn't use that word. '[T]ime has come', he declared, 'to accept decreased growth in some parts of the world, in order to provide resources for other places to experience healthy growth'.

More directly, degrowth has been explicitly debated in the Parliament of Catalonia in Spain and by members of the European Union (Demaria 2017). The Australian Greens political Party has begun to recognise the need for a post-growth economy, even though it treads very carefully knowing that it must not alienate a voting constituency that is still developing a post-growth consciousness. But again, given the contradictions inherent in pursuing limitless growth on a finite planet, we are confident that the consciousness needed for a post-growth or degrowth economy is destined to increase in coming years and decades as the ecocidal engine of growth collides ever-more violently with fundamental ecological realities. When deeper crisis in the existing system makes the case for degrowth undeniable, progressive movements must be prepared with a policy platform to present (Cosme et al. 2017).

Policies for a New Economy

The following proposals are not intended to be comprehensive, and they are not presented as a blueprint that could be applied independent of context. Instead, the review outlines a range of key issues that would need to be addressed in any 'top down' restructuring for degrowth (see also, Frankel 2018). This is self-consciously a work of political imagination, not of politics, as such. It responds to the evident need for radical narratives, signifiers, and 'stories' that can reanimate discussion of human social futures. The contribution is to what political theorist John Barry (2012: 274) calls 'dissident thinking in turbulent times'.

While we keep an eye on the suburban context, most of the policies are macroeconomic and therefore apply across the urban landscape and indeed across society more broadly. Nevertheless, these proposals are intended to dissolve some of the obstacles that lie in the way of urban grassroots movements scaling up. We see here, once more, the dialectical relationship between culture and political economy: culture must radicalise in order to create the social conditions for political and macroeconomic change beyond growth; and when (or if) that policy change arrives or begins, it can open further space for grassroots movements to regovern the city for justice, sustainability, and resilience; which can lead to further and more progressive policy; and so forth.

All this implies a broader political shift in which urban grassroots movement work to restore democratic control to cities and even urban and suburban councils, winding back the neoliberal legacy and extinguishing the corporate shadow state which functions to legislate and shape urban policy in the service of capital, not the common good. As argued in Chapter 4, our position is that democracy must be accomplished again, for the conditions of today, and this means the emergence of a social renewal movement in which people take power back from the corporate elite, and through participatory practices of self-governance democratically steer the nature of their urban and suburban localities, including what infrastructure projects are undertaken and how urban services are provided. This is not (just) the old top down state model. Some centralised action will be required, including some of the ideas discussed below, however our vision of the 'good city' or the 'good suburb' is ultimately one governed by a highly decentralised politics, in which democratic planning and the use and deployment of key urban resources, including land and the built environment, are explicitly organised by the people and for the people.

Explicit Adoption of Post-growth Measures of Progress

In order to transcend the paradigm of growth economics as well as the modes of urban development that the growth paradigm engenders, the first thing needed is to adopt better and more nuanced measures of progress than GDP. What we measure, and how we measure it, matters. It is now widely recognised that GDP is a deeply flawed measure of societal progress (Stiglitz et al. 2010; Ward et al. 2016), yet it remains the dominant way to assess politico-economic success. GDP is an aggregate of market transactions—useful so far as it goes—but it makes no distinction between economic activities that contribute positively to sustainable wellbeing and those that diminish it.

For example, GDP can be growing while at the same time our environment is being degraded, inequality is worsening, and social wellbeing is stagnant. Accordingly, an urban politics and economics 'beyond growth' must begin by explicitly adopting some post-growth measure of progress, such as the Genuine Progress Indicator (GPI), the Index for Sustainable Economic Welfare (ISEW), or in Australia, the Australian National Development Index (ANDI). These alternative metrics take into account a wide range of social, economic, and environmental factors that GDP ignores, thus representing a far more comprehensive picture than GDP alone (Lawn 2005). If we do not measure progress accurately, we cannot expect to progress (Diener and Seligman 2004).

Public understanding of and support for such post-growth accounting systems would open up political space for political parties and council representatives to defend policy and institutional changes—such as those outlined below—which would genuinely improve social wellbeing and enhance ecological conditions, even if these would not maximise growth in GDP. In particular, it would allow for a new era of urban and suburban planning, designed to advance the interests of people and planet, not the narrow interests of capital. In particular, a post-growth orientation could facilitate the rolling back of neoliberal privatisation and corporatisation of urban infrastructure, services, and planning. We envisage a re-democratisation of the entire urban process, including a commitment to democratic metropolitan governance that ensures solidarity between richer and poorer and which engages rather than 'manages' urban social movements seeking suburban renewal.

Reduce Impacts via Diminishing 'Resource Caps'

One of the defining problems with the growth paradigm is that the wealthiest nations now have resource and energy demands that could not possibly be universalised to all nations. The quantitative 'scale' of our economies is overblown in ways that neoliberal capitalism is proving wholly unable to resolve. It follows that any transition to a just and sustainable world requires the wealthiest nations to stop overconsuming the world's scarce resources and reduce resource and energy demands significantly.

This contraction is necessary if there is to be any 'ecological room' for the Global South to meet basic needs, to say nothing of the ecological room required to maintain or regenerate a flourishing biodiversity. The need for degrowth in the Global North is especially clear when it is recognised that the realisation of new urban or suburban models in the Global South—which are required to lift great multitudes out of existing horrid slums (both sprawling and high rise forms)—would almost certainly involve an increase in material and energy demands. Clearly the 'limits to growth' predicament is as much a distributive justice issue as an ecological one (Lawn and Clarke 2010).

Although in theory efficiency gains in production provide one pathway to reduced demand, the reality is that within a growth economy, efficiency gains tend to be reinvested in more growth and consumption, rather than reducing impact. After all, efficiency gains can reduce the costs of production, making a commodity cheaper, thus incentivising increased consumption of the commodity.

In order to contain this well documented phenomenon, a degrowth economy would need to introduce diminishing resource caps—that is, enforce well defined limits to resource use—to ensure that efficiency gains are directed into reducing overall resource consumption, not directed into more growth. In fact, diminishing resource caps would actually incentivise efficiency improvements, because producers would know that there would be increasing competition over key resources and so would be driven to eliminate waste and create a 'circular economy' where products at the end of their life are reused, as far as possible, in the next phase of production. In an age of ecological overshoot, the overconsuming rich nations need to achieve significant absolute reductions in resource demand (absolute decoupling) not just productivity or efficiency gains (relative decoupling).

Determining where to set the resource caps, how quickly they should be reduced (e.g. 3% per year to allow markets to adjust), and where they should be aiming to stabilise, are open questions that can be debated. Such voluntary limits are necessary to achieve sustainability, and as Illich (1974: 47) advised: 'The magnitude of voluntary limits is a matter of politics'. Formulating a workable policy in this domain would require, amongst other things, a highly sophisticated and detailed scientific accounting of resource stocks and flows of the economy, and some rationing of key resources may be required to ensure distributive equity. David Fleming and Shaun Chamberlin (2011) argue cogently that a policy based on 'Tradable Energy Quotas' is the best way forward, the aim of which is to achieve steep, but managed reduction in the use of fossil fuels while forestalling fuel poverty by guaranteeing fair entitlements to the energy that is available. We see promise in this general approach, and it deserves wider attention and debate. But the first step is simply to recognise that, in the overdeveloped nations, policies that cap and reduce emissions and overall resource consumption are a necessary part of achieving the contraction in resource use that is required for justice and sustainability. Suburban affluence, as we have known it, is not a viable conception of good living. We need social, economic and political structures that support alternative forms of flourishing, and that means moving towards increased social control of the economy, in ways that could be defined as 'market (eco)socialism'.

Working Hour Reductions

One obvious implication of diminishing resource caps is that a lot less resource-intensive producing and consuming will take place in a degrowth economy. That will almost certainly mean reduced GDP, although there is still great scope for qualitative growth (including technological innovation and efficiency improvements).

But what implications will a contracting (suburban) economy have for employment? Growth in GDP is often defended on the grounds that it is required to keep unemployment at manageable levels. If a nation gives up the pursuit of GDP, therefore, it must maintain employment via some other means. Restructuring the labour market is essential for the stability of any post-growth economy (Victor 2008). Today, Australians work some of the longest hours in the OECD, but, as the evidence clearly shows, such long hours do not improve our health and wellbeing (Hamilton and Denniss 2005). Could we work less but live more?

By reducing the average working week to, say, 28 hours, a degrowth economy would share the available work amongst the working population, thereby minimising or eliminating unemployment even in a non-growing or contracting economy, while at the same time increasing social wellbeing by reducing overwork (Coote and Franklin 2013). The aim would be to systematically exchange superfluous consumption for increased free time (from commitment to the formal economy), which could also bring environmental benefits.

While some of the increased free time could be spent enjoying local, low-impact leisure activities, some of it would also be spent engaging in the informal economy, such as activities of self-sufficiency (e.g. various forms of household production, growing food, house maintenance, sharing, volunteering, etc.) and local barter. This increased self-sufficiency and community engagement would also mitigate the impacts of reduced income in a degrowth economy by easing household expenditure on basic needs. In this way a degrowth economy would not induce spiralling unemployment or hardship as is often feared. Once more, a deliberately created degrowth economy is very different to unplanned recession. Indeed, planned contraction of the formal economy has the potential to liberate people from the work-to-spend cycle and provide people with more autonomy, meaning, and variety in their working lives. Such policies could stimulate thriving local economies and create eco-cities that resemble networks of collective suburban sufficiency.

Rethink Budget Spending for a Degrowth Transition

Governments are the most significant entity in any economy and have the most spending power. Accordingly, if governments decide to take the limits to growth seriously this will require a fundamental rethink of how public funds are procured, invested, and spent. Public spending in the transition we envisage would not aim to facilitate sustained GDP growth but instead support the projects and infrastructure needed to support a swift transition to a degrowth economy, including degrowth in the suburbs. As far a possible this would be decentralised via participatory budgeting at the local, suburban level, where ordinary citizens demand a more active role in the allocation and distribution of public funds.

Initial moves in any rethink of public spending might include huge divestment from the fossil fuel economy and a co-relative reinvestment in renewable energy systems (see next section). But it would also require huge investment in other forms of 'green' infrastructure and social safety nets. Due to higher taxes, there would be less income for private consumption but more social wealth spent on public goods including key urban services. The importance of creating new infrastructure highlights the fact that consumption practices in a society do not take place in a vacuum. Instead, consumption takes place within structures of constraint, and those structures make some lifestyle options easy or necessary, and other lifestyle options difficult or impossible. Currently, many people find themselves 'locked in to' or 'lock out of' high-impact lifestyles due to the structures within which they live their lives. A new suburbia requires new structures of support.

To provide one example: it is very difficult to stop driving a private motor vehicle if there is poor public transport, insufficient bike lanes, or a lack of understanding about how to safely navigate road networks dominated by cars. Change the infrastructure, however, and new, low-impact lifestyles implied by a degrowth economy would be more easily embraced. Greening infrastructure will therefore require a significant revision of government expenditure, both local and national. Recognising climate change as a national 'security threat', for example, and on that basis redirecting a significant portion of military spending towards renewable energy and efficient systems of public transport, is one path to funding the infrastructure (and other post-growth policies) needed for a stable and flourishing degrowth economy.

Government spending on healthcare (especially prevention and promotion) is particularly important. People need a social safety net otherwise there will be an incentive to earn as much as possible just in case future health bills are large. However, if health care is deemed a basic right in a society, provided for by a public health care system, then this provides more security to embrace a modest income without fear and anxiety. As with some of our prescriptions, this imperative is already well tried and tested in countries, such as the UK and Australia, that have constructed national health systems, and which enjoy superior population health and equity conditions to those that have not, such as the USA. There is also room to spend limited public funds more effectively. For example, Cubans enjoy better health than citizens of the USA, despite spending ten times less on healthcare. Strong publicly maintained health and human service frameworks generally reduce economic waste, social inequity, and human anxiety, and must be integral to a post-growth dispensation.

Renewable Energy

In anticipation of the foreseeable stagnation and eventual decline of fossil fuel supplies, and recognising the grave dangers presented by climate change, a degrowth economy would need to transition swiftly to renewable energy and more efficient energy systems and practices.

This provides a hugely promising space to meaningfully employ large segments of the population as the fossil fuel economy enters terminal decline.

But just as important as 'greening' the supply of energy is the challenge (too often neglected) of reducing energy demand, which has been a key theme in this book. It will be much easier to transition to 100% renewable energy if energy use is significantly reduced through behavioural changes, reduced production and consumption, and more efficient appliances. Indeed, the extremely tight and fast diminishing carbon budget for a safe climate now makes this 'demand-side' response a necessity, yet the significantly reduced energy demand required for a safe climate is incompatible with the growth model, because energy is a fundamental driver of economic growth.

Accordingly, a degrowth politics would initiate a transition to 100% renewable energy financed in part by accurately pricing carbon, and undertake a public education campaign to facilitate reduced energy demand. Given how hard it will be to fully replace the fossil fuel economy with renewable energy (especially the 96 million barrels of oil currently consumed everyday), it is also worth reemphasising that post-carbon economies will have to adapt to an energy descent context and are likely to be a far more localised economies than the globalised, fossil fuel-dependent economy we know today.

While there would still be some greatly reduced role for global trade in a degrowth economy, most production would seek, by default, to use local resources from the bioregion to meet mostly local needs, thereby shortening the links between production and consumption. As well as running the economy primarily on renewables, a degrowth strategy could also involve planting up huge tracts of land with trees to sequester carbon and placing a moratorium on the cutting down of old growth forests. Any coherent climate strategy must also address the huge carbon footprint of meat (especially red meat) and accordingly promote significantly reduced meat consumption (Poore and Nemecek 2018) and regenerative forms of agriculture (Massy 2017). New regulations and subsidies would fast track the uptake of appropriate technologies, like biogas in the suburbs, solar PV, and heat-hump hot water systems.

Governments could provide households with interest-free loans for such things, as a means of deconstructing financial barriers to the renewable energy transition.

Transformation in Banking and Finance Systems

Currently, Western-style systems of banking and finance essentially have a 'growth imperative' built into their structures. Money is loaned into existence by private banks as interest-bearing debt, and in order to pay back that debt plus the interest, this requires an expansion of the money supply. Banks are incentivised to offer credit to people or institutions that are most likely to generate stronger financial returns from their investments. Furthermore, there is so much public and private debt today that the only way it could be paid back is via decades of continued GDP growth. This type of banking system requires growth for stability and yet limitless economic growth, as we have argued, is the driving force behind the environmental crisis.

In order to move towards a stable, degrowth economy, part of the institutional restructuring required involves deep reform of banking, monetary, and finance systems. This is a complex transition that could take various forms, but at base it would require the state taking responsibility for creating banking, finance, and monetary systems that do not require growth for stability, and strictly regulating these systems to ensure equity. Policies that allowed for the creation of local currencies would help too, since local currency design is potentially a powerful tool in the restructuring of local and communitarian economic relations.

A post-growth transition might also require 'debt jubilees' in some circumstances, especially in developing nations that are unjustly being suffocated by interest payments to rich world lenders. Developing nations, for example, receive about $136 billion in aid from donor countries but pay about $600 billion servicing debt (Hickel 2017a). No fancy theorising or political sophistry can plausibly defend such a situation.

A New Paradigm for Housing and Land

Most of the policies being discussed in this chapter will be controversial, but perhaps none will be as controversial as the claim that any transition to just and sustainable degrowth economy will require a new paradigm for housing and land, especially in cities. The controversy arises primarily over the fact that deep reform of housing and land governance requires fundamental revision of property rights, and property sits at the conceptual core of capitalism. Accordingly, a degrowth economy would need to be post-capitalist in the further sense that access to housing and land would not simply be allocated according to market forces alone.

While it could be argued that ultimately a degrowth economy should aim to socialise land and housing, leaving constrained markets to allocate other commodities, at this early stage we wish to highlight various transitional strategies that, while not socialising property as such, do involve significantly increased social control of housing and land. The aim would be to ensure a 'basic needs' guarantee for decent, affordable, and secure accommodation as well as a broader distribution of this important social resource. This could involve a general requirement for housing to be used for the primary purpose of providing homes, shelter, and security, rather than as investment vehicles. This broader distribution of property rights could involve an expanding ownership class, but it could also involve new policies to ensure that people renting are able to acquire secure, long-term leases. In terms of security of tenure for renters, some European nations are far ahead in this regard than nations like Australia, New Zealand, and the US.

One of the greatest scandals that shape urban development under contemporary capitalism is the fact that many people face housing insecurity or are homeless at a time when literally thousands upon thousands of investment properties and apartments lie empty. This makes a mockery of capitalism's claim to achieve allocative efficiency. Efficient for whom? Efficient in what sense? Various policy interventions could help broaden access to land and housing infrastructure, including the abolishment of negative gearing and various progressive property taxes that would curtail the socially pernicious accumulation of properties amongst a minority of the population. Why should some people own ten or twenty or fifty properties while a great proportion of the population owns none? It is a simple but revolutionary question about what it means to live in a decent society; what it means to live in a 'good city'.

In a section below we note various wealth and estate taxes that could serve to distribute society's wealth more broadly, and the proceeds of such taxes could be used to fund a guaranteed right to decent shelter through public housing. A reconceived banking system could also make governments or community-owned banks, not private banks, the issuer of most mortgages, which could provide a means of reinvesting the profits from interest payments into more public housing. Within ecological bounds, a society is limited only by its imagination. The past does not exhaust the range of property systems available to humanity, and it is flawed thinking to believe that one must choose between capitalism as we know it and Soviet-style state communism. Ours is a post-capitalist vision of decentralised eco-socialism, which recognises a role for markets, but markets that are always constrained by baseline regulations that operate to protect and advance the common good.

And let us not for a moment forget that we currently live in an age of highly regulated markets—only it is regulation informed by a neoliberal political ideology that functions to concentrate wealth and serve corporate interests. What the neoliberal laissez-faire theory fails to appreciate is that governments do not interfere in markets but constitute markets. 'Hands off' is not an option. As legal theorist Karl Klare (1991: 81) points out: 'The state can withdraw from central planning but it cannot withdraw from its role in defining market structures and property entitlements'. Thus citizens have a democratic right to constitute or reconstitute markets and property entitlements as they see fit, in ways that serve the many rather than the few.

Without trying to provide a comprehensive statement, we would also emphasise the role progressive new policies and regulations could play supporting ecological resettlement beyond the urban boundary. A particularly promising innovation is the 'Low-Impact Development' policy in Wales, which explicitly seeks to support ecovillage living in rural or semi-rural areas (see Nelson 2018: 133–38). Not only does this open up access to land for people unable to afford property in urban centres, by encouraging people to leave the densest urban centres, it also reduces pressure on real estate markets in those urban centres. Further policies could be developed which could support new economic enterprises in dying towns, where there is cheap and under-utilised housing infrastructure but insufficient employment opportunities to attract households. With the right incentives and support, we can see those dying towns becoming vibrant hubs of collective sufficiency and economic security.

Population Policies

While policies for property reform would be controversial, there is also the population challenge, often referred to as the 'elephant in the room' that few are talking about. As the (ever urbanising) population grows, more resources are required to provide for the basic material needs of humanity (food, clothing, shelter, etc.), increasing our demands on an already overburdened planet. It is absolutely imperative that nations around the world unite to confront the population challenge directly (Alcott 2012), rather than just assuming that the problem will be solved when the developing world gets rich.

Population policies will inevitably be controversial but the world needs bold and equitable leadership on this issue. As we've noted, research suggests that the world is facing a population of around 9.8 billion by mid-century and 11 billion by the end of this century, which would be utterly catastrophic from both a social and environmental perspective. To re-quote Paul Ehrlich: 'whatever problem you're interested in, you're not going to solve it unless you also solve the population problem'.

The first thing needed is a global fund that focuses on providing the education, empowerment, and contraception required to minimise the millions of unintended pregnancies that occur every year. If these unplanned pregnancies were avoided, this would be a great step in the right direction. Furthermore, all financial incentives that encourage population growth should be abolished and the benefits of small families should be highlighted. Importantly, national population policies should not be shaped with the goal of maximising economic growth, which could well imply significantly reducing immigration flows. But given that wealthy nations have been most responsible for climate change and other ecological harm, immigration policies should also recognise the moral imperative to accommodate increasing numbers of climate refugees in coming years and decades.

Distributive Justice

Last but not least, environmental concerns cannot be isolated from social justice concerns. The conventional path to poverty alleviation is via the strategy of GDP growth, on the assumption that 'a rising tide will lift all boats'. Given that a degrowth economy deliberately seeks a non-growing economy—on the assumption that a rising tide will sink all boats—poverty alleviation must be achieved more directly, via redistribution, both nationally and internationally. In other words (and to change the metaphor), a degrowth economy would eliminate poverty and achieve distributive equity not by baking an ever-larger economic pie but by slicing it differently. Government support for the sharing economy would also mean that more value can be acquired from the same 'slice' of economy.

Any attempt to systemically redistribute wealth via taxation or property reform will be highly controversial, especially in our neoliberal age, but present concentrations of wealth demand a political response. Capitalism is failing most of humanity. Research from Oxfam published in 2018 shows that the richest 6 people on the planet now own more than the poorest half of humanity. Dwell on that for a moment.

This highlights the point that growth itself will not resolve poverty. Policies are needed that directly redistribute wealth; that ensure a dignified material baseline for all people; and that structure the economy in ways that ensure corrosive and undemocratic inequalities of wealth do not arise in the first place. There is no single best policy for eliminating poverty or achieving a just distribution of wealth. Bold, creative, and considered experimentation is required. Key policy options include:

(i) a basic income for all, which guarantees every permanent resident with a minimal, living wage; (ii) a 'negative income tax', which guarantees a minimum income for those who earn below a certain threshold, or a 'job guarantee', where the state is the employer of last resort; (iii) progressive income or consumption tax policies (i.e. the more you earn or consume, the higher the tax rate) which could culminate in a top tax rate of 90% or more; (iv) wealth taxes, that systematically transfer 3% of private wealth from the richest to the poorest recognising the large social component in wealth production; and (v) estate taxes of 90% or more to ensure the laws of inheritance and bequest do not create a class system of entrenched wealth and entrenched poverty. These and other tax-and-transfer policies should be explored to eliminate poverty and ensure distributive equity. Obviously, arguments that such policies would inhibit growth do not hold water within a degrowth framework.

From a global perspective, it must be acknowledged that the market forces of capitalism too often results in rich nations of the Global North siphoning away resources from poorer nations in the South, leaving only environmental destruction in its wake (Hickel 2017b). Australia and other rich nations must renew their depleted aid programs, which can and should take various forms, including increasing financial support; abolishing the suffocating debts that keep the poorest nations down; freely transferring technological and medical knowledge and equipment; and ensuring that corporate and institutional power does not unduly influence economic development in the Global South. These should be considered first steps in a transformation in global relations towards increased solidarity, whereby degrowth amongst the rich nations provides some ecological room for the poorest nations to improve their economic capacities according to a new vision of global 'post-development'. These are obviously bold and ambitious ideas, but anything less will be insufficient. It is no good being what critics might call 'realistic' if being realistic only leads to ecological and/or humanitarian catastrophe.

Other Policies?

Beyond these policy proposals, it should go without saying that any degrowth transition would require an array of other revolutionary reforms, including policies to create (or recreate) a 'free press'; policies to ensure that campaign financing rules do not permit undue economic influence on the democratic process; and policies to promote alternative corporate forms, such as worker cooperatives. Furthermore, governments must not unduly interfere with or inhibit the emergence and development of informal and non-monetary economies. We do not pretend to have provided a complete political agenda for a degrowth economy. The proposals above are merely key aspects of such a transition and a good place to begin thinking about how to structure a just, sustainable, and flourishing economy (see also, Frankel 2018).

Regoverning the City: Suburban Implications

We contend that these policy proposals—all in need of detailed elaboration and discussion—should be the opening moves in a 'top down' transition to a new economic dispensation. To be employed in concert, they clearly challenge the dominant macroeconomics of growth and would require far more social control over the economy than neoliberal capitalism permits today. Markets work well in some circumstances, no doubt, but leaving everything to the market and thinking this will magically advance the common good has been proven dangerously false. It follows that a degrowth economy must be a post-capitalist or eco-socialist economy, with vastly increased democratic planning and perhaps even some rationing of key resources to ensure distributive equity. The policies above also depend upon a society that sees the necessity and desirability of a degrowth economy, hence the special importance of grassroots education campaigns and story tellers who are able to weave new narratives that show in emotionally convincing ways that the emergence of new, post-consumerist cultures of consumption are not just necessary but desirable.

Although the policies outlined are macroeconomic and would thus impact on all sectors of society and all manifestations of the built environment, this book has been focussing on the suburban landscape. In Chapters 5 and 6 we reviewed a range of practices of material sufficiency, energy descent, sharing, and home-based production that we argued will need to shape the suburban economy if a degrowth transition is to lay down roots and scale up. But we also emphasised that many suburbanites were either 'locked in' to high-impact lifestyles or 'locked out' of household sufficiency due to the societal structures that produced distributive inequity, including unaffordable and grossly unequal access to housing and land, as well as other forms of economic insecurity. The politics of degrowth reviewed above sought to outline a new structural context that would support rather than inhibit the practices of sufficiency in the suburbs. As stated earlier, our prescription for suburbia includes commitment to metropolitan governance, which remains weak in many contemporary new world cities. We acknowledge that more needs to be said about the design of metropolitan governance that would ensure solidarity and service provision at the regional scale, without extinguishing the local self-determination that must be pivotal to the Great Resettlement of suburbia.

One must never forget that there is no such thing as a *neutral* politics or economics. All political and economic structures—including so-called free markets—function to make some ways of life easy or necessary and other ways of life difficult or impossible. Shaping structures therefore is inevitably a value-laden exercise demanding an answer to the questions: what sort of society do we want to create? What do we want our cities to look like? Currently, the out-dated politics of growth are designed to require and encourage lifestyles of ever-increasing consumption, and this has produced a particular suburban mode of existence, one that is disastrous from an environmental perspective and often socially corrosive, both in terms of wellbeing and justice.

A new suburban form will require the emergence of an alternative political economy, and we have put forward degrowth as the most coherent alternative. The new structures proposed would make it difficult to consume and produce unsustainably at the expense of people and planet, and instead support and encourage lifestyles of sufficiency, moderation, sharing, and frugality. This is a very different conception of prosperity to what we hear about from most economists and even most environmentalists, who still seem convinced that technology and markets are going to 'green' the capitalist economics of growth in some magical way. The alternative goal of a politics of degrowth is to create an economy that provides enough, for everyone, forever. The good news is that we can create this new economy with today's technology—if only we show the wisdom and courage to live, think, and act beyond the economics of growth.

This book has not sought to end the conversation on this incredibly complex new direction. Our goal has been to draw more people into the discussion, so that together we can navigate our way towards a form of life that is ecologically viable, socially just, and yet consistent with a diversity of pursuits of human happiness. Our argument has been that a new paradigm of degrowth should inform a new urban imaginary if we are to achieve these bold but necessary goals. We believe that this is possible, but we also see that the window of opportunity is closing.

We are at the crossroads and are in the process of choosing our fate.

References

Alcott, Blake. 2012. Population Matters in Ecological Economics. *Ecological Economics* 80: 109–120.

Barry, John. 2012. *The Politics of Actually Existing Unsustainability*. Oxford: Oxford University Press.

Coote, Anna, and Jane Franklin. 2013. *Time on Our Side: Why We All Need a Shorter Working Week*. London: New Economics Foundation.

Cosme, Ines, Rui Santos, and Daniel O'Neill. 2017. Assessing the Degrowth Discourse: A Review and Analysis of Academic Degrowth Policy Proposals. *Journal of Cleaner Production* 149: 321–334.

Demaria, Federico. 2017. When Degrowth Enters the Parliament. *The Ecologist*, January 16.

Diener, Ed., and Martin Seligman. 2004. Beyond Money: Toward an Economy of Wellbeing. *Psychological Science in the Public Interest* 5 (1): 1–31.

Drews, Stefan, and Jeroen van den Bergh. 2016. Public Views on Economic Growth, the Environment, and Prosperity: Results of a Questionnaire Survey. *Global Environmental Change* 39: 1–14.

Eckersley, Richard. 2018a. Closing the Gap Between the Science and Politics of Progress: Science's Greatest Challenge. *Social Indicators Research*. https://doi.org/10.1007/s11205-018-1843-1. Accessed 20 June 2018.

————. 2018b. Personal Communication. 21 May 2018.

Fleming, David, and Shaun Chamberlin. 2011. TEQs (Tradable Energy Quotas): A Policy Framework for Peak Oil and Climate Change. *All-Party Parliamentary Group on Peak Oil and Climate Change*. London: Calverts. https://www.teqs.net/APPGOPO_TEQs.pdf. Accessed 20 June 2018.

Francis, Pope. 2015. *Laudato Si: On Care for Our Common Home*. https://w2.vatican.va/content/francesco/en/encyclicals/documents/papa-francesco_20150524_enciclica-laudato-si.html. Accessed 20 June 2018.

Frankel, Boris. 2018. *Fictions of Sustainability: The Politics of Growth and Post-Capitalist Futures*. Melbourne: Greenmeadows.

Friedman, Milton. 2002. *Capitalism and Freedom*. Chicago: University of Chicago Press.

Galster, George. 2012. *Driving Detroit: The Quest for Respect in the Motor City*. Philadelphia: University of Pennsylvania Press.

Hamilton, Clive, and Richard Denniss. 2005. *Affluenza: When Too Much Is Never Enough*. Crows Nest: Allen & Unwin.

Hickel, Jason. 2017a. Aid in Reverse: How Poor Countries Develop Rich Countries. *The Guardian*, January 14.

————. 2017b. *The Divide: A Brief Guide to Global Inequality and Its Solutions*. Cornerstone: William Heinemann.

Illich, Ivan. 1974. *Energy and Equity*. New York: Harper and Row.

Jackson, Tim, and Robin Webster. 2016. Revisited: A Review of the Limits to Growth Debate. http://limits2growth.org.uk/wp-content/uploads/2016/04/Jackson-and-Webster-2016-Limits-Revisited.pdf. Accessed 20 June 2018.

Kasser, Tim. 2002. *The High Price of Materialism*. Cambridge: MIT Press.

Keen, Steve. 2017. *Can We Avoid Another Financial Crisis?* Cambridge: Polity.

Klare, Karl. 1991. Legal Theory and Democratic Reconstruction: Reflections on 1989. *University of British Columbia Law Review* 25: 69–103.

Kunstler, James. 2005. *The Long Emergency: Surviving the Converging Catastrophes of the Twenty-First Century*. New York: Grove/Atlantic.

Lane, Robert. 2000. *The Loss of Happiness in Market Democracies*. New Haven: Yale University Press.

Lawn, Philip. 2005. An Assessment of the Valuation Methods Used to Calculate the Index for Sustainable Economic Welfare (ISEW), Genuine Progress Indicator (GPI), and Sustainable Net Benefit Index (SNBI). *Environment, Development and Sustainability* 2: 185–208.

Lawn, Philip, and Michael Clarke. 2010. The End of Economic Growth? A Contracting Threshold Hypothesis. *Ecological Economics* 69: 2213–2223.

Massy, Charles. 2017. *Call of the Reed Warbler: A New Agriculture—A New Earth*. Brisbane: University of Queensland Press.

Nelson, Anitra. 2018. *Small is Necessary: Shared Living on a Shared Planet*. London: Pluto Press.

Peck, Jamie. 2012. Austerity Urbanism. *City* 16 (6): 626–655.

Poore, Joseph, and Thomas Nemecek. 2018. Reducing Food's Environmental Impacts Through Producers and Consumers. *Science* 360 (6392): 987–992.

Randle, Melanie, and Richard Eckersley. 2015. Public Perceptions of Future Threats to Humanity and Different Societal Responses: A Cross-National Study. *Future* 72: 4–16.

Stiglitz, Joseph, Amartya Sen, and Jean-Paul Fitoussi. 2010. *Mis-measuring Our Lives: Why GDP Doesn't Add Up*. New York: The New Press.

Victor, Peter. 2008. *Managing Without Growth: Slower by Design, Not Disaster*. Cheltenham: Edward Elgar.

Ward, James, Paul Sutton, Adrian Werner, Robert Costanza, Steve Mohr, and Craig Simmons. 2016. Is Decoupling GDP Growth from Environmental Impact Possible? *PLoS ONE* 11 (10): e0164733. https://doi.org/10.1371/journal.pone.0164733.

8

A New Suburban Condition Dawns

The inner crisis of our civilisation must be resolved if the outer crisis is to be effectively met.
—Lewis Mumford

Sisyphus in the Suburbs

According to Greek mythology, Sisyphus was condemned by the gods to roll a rock up a mountain, only to watch it roll down the other side, and to repeat this futile labour, over and over again, for eternity. In 1942 the philosopher and novelist Albert Camus wrote a philosophical treatise on this myth, using it as a metaphor to describe the absurdity of the human condition, declaring that the labours of human existence, just like the efforts of Sisyphus, were meaningless by any external or cosmological standard (Camus 2000). But rather than advocating suicide or nihilism as the solution to this human predicament, Camus defiantly embraced humanity's absurd fate and formed a philosophy of living in which the human subject was required to *create* meaning rather than pretend to find meaning in some unfounded metaphysical dogma.

© The Author(s) 2019
S. Alexander and B. Gleeson, *Degrowth in the Suburbs*,
https://doi.org/10.1007/978-981-13-2131-3_8

Thus, the objective meaninglessness of the human condition was not a cause for despair. Indeed, Camus (2000: 111) closed his essay, rather obscurely, declaring that despite everything, the 'struggle itself is enough to fill a man's [sic] heart. One must imagine Sisyphus happy'.

As the manuscript of the present book was being completed, we found ourselves blowing dust off this old Greek myth, strangely drawn to its story and themes, prompting us to reflect: might the myth of Sisyphus still hold some relevance for urban life in the twenty-first century? Just as Camus was trying to understand the existential void left by an absent God, we find ourselves living in an age—an urban age—where the old dogmas of growth, material affluence, and technology are increasingly exposed as false idols. Like a fleet of ships that have been unmoored in a storm, *homo urbanis* is drifting in dangerous seas without a clear sense of direction. Where are the new sources of meaning and guidance that all societies need to fight off the ennui? Pioneering socialist Emile Durkheim used the term 'anomie' to refer to a condition in which a culture's traditional norms have broken down without new norms arising which are able to give sense to a changing world. Perhaps that is the condition which best explains our existential situation today. We are coming to realise that we have lost our way, as the conditions that are supposed to represent 'progress' according to dominant cultural myths are increasingly experienced as breakdown.

The myth of Sisyphus resonates especially in light of our book's central themes of degrowth and energy descent. Since industrialisation humanity has been pushing the rock of economic growth up a vast energy mountain of fossil fuels, but the same rock which still absorbs and defines humanity's labours today has obscured the view of what lies ahead. People look backwards and assume that the future must look more or less like the recent past—a constant rise in energy supply and productive capacity—and so our species continues to march ever-upward, not seeing that beyond the rock we approach the peak of energy availability. Like all mountains, this one, too, will have a bumpy downslope, but as Camus (2000: 110) wrote: 'There is no sun without shadow, and it is essential to know the night'.

Many deny this prospect of descent and say that our existing form of life is non-negotiable; that human ingenuity will constantly push back or transcend any environmental limits. But in fact the laws of physics are non-negotiable, and our forms of life must and will abide—whether by design or disaster, that remains to be seen. From the perspective of deep time, the extraordinary upslope of the industrial era will prove to be but a brief anomaly in the ongoing story of our species. The non-renewable nature of fossil fuels means that what goes up, must come down. Today we look forth from atop this dark mountain.

The early chapters of this book argued that the overlapping challenges of fossil energy depletion, deep decarbonisation, and distributive equity, mean that the age of energy abundance is coming to an end and that an energy descent future lies ahead. In doing so we sought to expose the green illusions that seduce so many into thinking that technology and 'green growth' can escape biophysical limits. Add to this the delinquent idealism that imagines green cities in a reformed sustainable growth economy. As the downslope approaches—in one form or another—we have argued that humanity must learn to embrace its energetic fate, and our focus herein has been on what this might mean in terms of resettling the suburbs of a carbon civilisation in decay. In offering the radical imaginary of 'degrowth in the suburbs', we have dared to imagine Sisyphus happy, with all the complexities and uncertainties that implies.

The bravura with which we have tried to present our arguments was meant to convey a sense of hope in the face of grave and mounting epochal threats. As our opening chapters made clear, these are indeed perilous times that have unmasked the soothing, stupefying buoyancy of growth capitalism. We must acknowledge Terry Eagleton's (2017) injunction for 'hope without optimism'; truly a Sisyphean ideal for the times. Let us be conscious of our chains and burdens, but also, especially, of our power.

Journalist Rebecca Solnit (2016: 5) notes, 'the future is dark, with a darkness as much of the womb as the grave'. Nobody can know for sure how the future will unfold. Black swans might lie around every bend in the river. How, then, is one to live? What is to be done? More fundamentally, perhaps, how is one to *be*? Carbon civilisation has evolved over the last two centuries and produced a particular suburban form. This concrete jungle has atomised our cultures, decimated communities, all but abolished the necessary human connection with nature, and seemingly deadened the human spirit by fetishising technology and consumption.

Might this time of crisis actually shake us awake and provide an opportunity for some unexpected existential rejuvenation? We leave the reader to digest the inner dimension of these themes, noting only that the next and dangerous stage of our species' journey may require a reappraisal, not dismissal, of what we might loosely call 'spiritual' engagement with the world. This is not a call for any resort to dogma, of course. Camus would have none of that. Rather, it is an invitation—even an incitation—for humanity to anticipate and confront this energetic turning pointing in the human story with all the creativity, wisdom, and compassion it can muster. In doing so, let us declare with Camus (1951: 36): 'I revolt, therefore we are'.

What Is to Be Done? Raise Hell!

In that spirit of revolt, we close by calling attention to the violence that is now every day enacted by a system that will not relax its destructive hold on human fortunes. This is starkly apparent in contemporary Western cities, the foreground for this book, where intensification— what we termed hypertrophic urbanism—is revealed in the vertical sprawl that takes the growth paradigm to newly absurd and ruinous heights. Here we recognise violence to be something much more than the infraction of law (increasingly, by a troubled and desperate precariat), extending to include an economy, and its urban machine, that mindlessly maims ecology, solidarity, and hope. Half a century ago, Illich accused the growth machine of 'mutilating' and 'industrially deforming' human society and natural integrity. This violence has increased in scope and intensity during the long neoliberal dispensation that has followed his censure. What is perhaps most remarkable about the devastation of contemporary urbanisation is not its destructive vehemence but the silence that attends it. We wish this to end and urge radicals and progressives—indeed all who experience a sense of care and responsibility for viable human futures—to loudly indict a dying but still lethal capitalism for its crimes against human and natural prospects.

Despite the intellectual confoundments and social deteriorations of the last thirty years, we still exist in a post-enlightenment world. To be sure, in an age of populist reaction, the term and its formal corollaries, especially disenchantment, have assumed a new irony and significance. Nonetheless, surely none of us propose to reinstate magic or mindless tradition as guiding stars. Recognising this, and the implausibility, indeed dangers, of idealisation as a social logic, Sigmund Freud (2010: 604) found the modern scientific task captured in Virgil's refrain:

If I Cannot Bend the Higher Powers, I Will Move the Infernal Regions

And we agree. The work of radical scholarship and praxis, as never before, is *to raise hell*. In two ways. First, to expose the reality of hellish violence that attends urban daily life for an increasing multitude of the poor and precarious. This is necessarily a double act: to expose both this denied reality and the cruel legitimising work of neoliberal fallacies like the 'liveable city'. Second, to raise hell about this through critical interpretation, counter proposition and counter practice. This is the reason we have offered a new urban imaginary—of suburban degrowth—in radical opposition to the conventional wisdom that frames and strangles debates about cities. We hope our book has offered reinvigorated propositions and practices that reach regeneratively for futures unimaginable from within those neoliberal confines.

If, as it seems inevitable, humanity must endure a distressing retrenchment of globalised capitalism, let us commit to the heartening work of fashioning a more careful dispensation in its wake. Let us work together in free association and in the spirit of defiant positivity, knowing that while the future will not be easy, there is scope, at least, for the inevitable suffering and hidden joys that will flow from urban resistance and renewal to be meaningful—and in that sense, for the descent ahead to be prosperous. There is, of course, no underestimating the difficulty of this task and the terrible things that a dying system will put in its way. The times call for courage and outrage, as much as they beckon new ideals. We should raise an infernal racket about the narcosis that has settled in the dying hours of capitalism. Sleepers awake! We have the right to imagine and create a more enlightened world. To work…in the suburbs, now.

References

Camus, Albert. 1951. *L'homme Revolte*. Paris: Gallimard.

———. 2000. *The Myth of Sisyphus*. London: Penguin.

Eagleton, Terry. 2017. *Hope Without Optimism*. New Haven: Yale University Press.

Freud, Sigmund. 2010. *The Interpretation of Dreams*. New York: Basic Books.

Solnit. Rebecca. 2016. *Hope in the Dark: Untold Histories, Wild Possibilities*, 3rd ed. Chicago: Haymarket Books.

Index

Made in the USA
Middletown, DE
30 September 2021